Prison I tance

This book explores prisoners' experiences of prison education and investigates whether participation in prison education contributes to an offender's ability to desist from crime and increases social capital levels.

While the link between prison education and reduced rates of recidivism is well established through research, far less is known about the relationship between prison education and desistance. The book demonstrates how prisoners experience many benefits from participating in prison education, including increased confidence, self-control and agency, along with various other cognitive changes. In addition, the book examines prisoners' accounts that provide evidence of strong connections between prison education and the formation of pro-social bonds which have been shown to play a role in the desistance process. It also highlights the links between prison education and social capital and the existence of a form of prison-based social capital arising from the prison culture.

Written in a clear and direct style, this book will appeal to those engaged in criminology, sociology, penology, desistance, rehabilitation and the sociology of education and all those interested in learning more about the positive impact of prison education on prisoners.

Geraldine Cleere is a lecturer in law and criminology at Waterford Institute of Technology. She is an active member of various research groups and networks related to her research interests that include prison education, desistance, prison officer education and role development, social and prison-based capital and prison law.

International Series on Desistance and Rehabilitation

The *International Series on Desistance and Rehabilitation* aims to provide a forum for critical debate and discussion surrounding the topics of why people stop offending and how they can be more effectively reintegrated into the communities and societies from which they came. The books published in the series will be international in outlook, but tightly focused on the unique, specific contexts and processes associated with desistance, rehabilitation and reform. Each book in the series will stand as an attempt to advance knowledge or theorising about the topics at hand, rather than being merely an extended report of specific a research project. As such, it is anticipated that some of the books included in the series will be primarily theoretical, whilst others will be more tightly focused on the sorts of initiatives which could be employed to encourage desistance. It is not our intention that books published in the series be limited to the contemporary period, as good studies of desistance, rehabilitation and reform undertaken by historians of crime are also welcome. In terms of authorship, we would welcome excellent PhD work, as well as contributions from more established academics and research teams. Most books are expected to be monographs, but edited collections are also encouraged.

Desistance and Societies in Comparative Perspective
Dana Segev

Governing Delinquency Through Freedom
Control, Rehabilitation and Desistance
Géraldine Bugnon

Prison Education and Desistance
Changing Perspectives
Geraldine Cleere

For more information about this series, please visit: www.routledge.com/criminology/series/ISODR

Prison Education and Desistance

Changing Perspectives

Geraldine Cleere

Routledge
Taylor & Francis Group
LONDON AND NEW YORK

First published 2021
by Routledge
2 Park Square, Milton Park, Abingdon, Oxon OX14 4RN

and by Routledge
605 Third Avenue, New York, NY 10017

First issued in paperback 2022

Routledge is an imprint of the Taylor & Francis Group, an informa business

Publisher's Note
The publisher has gone to great lengths to ensure the quality of this reprint but points out that some imperfections in the original copies may be apparent.

British Library Cataloguing-in-Publication Data
A catalogue record for this book is available from the British Library

Library of Congress Cataloging-in-Publication Data
A catalog record for this book has been requested

ISBN 13: 978-0-367-69410-4 (pbk)
ISBN 13: 978-0-367-43386-4 (hbk)
ISBN 13: 978-1-003-00283-3 (ebk)

DOI: 10.4324/9781003002833

Typeset in Bembo
by Apex CoVantage, LLC

To Mam and Dad.

Contents

Series editor introduction

The *International Series on Desistance and Rehabilitation* aims to provide a forum for critical debate and discussion surrounding the topics of why people stop offending and how they can be more effectively reintegrated into the communities and societies from which they came. The books published in the series will be international in outlook, but tightly focused on the unique, specific contexts and processes associated with desistance, rehabilitation and reform. Each book in the series will stand as an attempt to advance knowledge or theorising about the topics at hand, rather than being merely an extended report of specific a research project. As such, it is anticipated that some of the books included in the series will be primarily theoretical, whilst others will be more tightly focused on the sorts of initiatives which could be employed to encourage desistance. It is not our intention that books published in the series be limited to the contemporary period, as good studies of desistance, rehabilitation and reform undertaken by historians of crime are also welcome. In terms of authorship, we would welcome excellent PhD work, as well as contributions from more established academics and research teams. Most books are expected to be monographs, but edited collections are also encouraged.

Studies of desistance in the Republic of Ireland are still rare beasts (with Deidre Healy's study – published in this series – being one of the very few). It is therefore a pleasure to see Geraldine Cleere's study of desistance and prison education programmes published in this series. Geraldine studied the programmes and individual inmates undertaking them in two Irish prisons, namely Mountjoy and Shelton Abbey prisons, and analyses the resulting data through the lens of social capital. Geraldine found that, when compared with a group of those who were not engaged in prion education, participants in prison education programmes experienced many benefits. These included increased confidence, self-control and agency. Additionally, the accounts derived from the inmates Geraldine spoke to provides evidence of the strong connections between prison education and the formation of pro-social bonds – which, ever since Sue Rex's study some 20 years ago, have been shown to play a role in the desistance process. I welcome Geraldine's study to the series and am sure that it will provide much thinking for both academics and practitioners.

Stephen Farrall,
Sheffield,
August 2020.

Acknowledgements

A special word of thanks must be extended, first and foremost, to all of the men who willingly gave of their time to be interviewed in Mountjoy Prison, Shelton Abbey and the Pathways Project. The honesty and passion of your words brought this research to life. I hope that this book does your experience justice. It could not have happened without you; I wish you all the very best on your journeys.

Thank you to the Irish Prison Service, the Prison Education Service and the Pathways Initiative for facilitating the research.

Thank you to my former research supervisor Dr. Niamh Maguire, who was an incredible source of support on my PhD journey.

Thank you to my examiners Professor Fergus McNeill and Dr. Kevin Warner, who were wonderfully constructive in their examination. I hope some of the insightful feedback and recommendations you made are well reflected within this book. A special word of thanks to you, Kevin, for your kindness and guidance over the years; I am incredibly grateful for your enthusiasm for the research and the support you have always offered.

I am grateful to Waterford Institute of Technology, and in particular the School of Humanities and Department of Law and Criminal Justice, for supporting this project with a Research Connexions grant.

Thank you to the great people at Routledge, especially Thomas Sutton, Jessica Phillips and Stephen Farrall for your enthusiasm and support from the outset.

Thanks to my family and friends for understanding my silence and absence this year.

Finally, thank you to my husband Eoin. I think you may have secretly enjoyed having an absent wife at times, but I am grateful that you allowed me the time and space to undertake this book without complaint. You have been incredibly understanding of this process and have supported me in every way you could. I am very lucky to have had such wonderful support. Thank you.

Abbreviations

ABE	Adult Basic Education
AVP	Alternatives to Violence Programme
COE	Council of Europe
DES	Department of Education and Science
ETBI	Education and Training Board
ICT	Information and Communication Technology
IPS	Irish Prison Service
ISM	Integrated Sentence Management
PES	Prison Education Service
TR	Temporary Release
UNESCO	United Nations Educational, Scientific and Cultural Organisation
VET	Vocational Educational Training

Glossary

Da	Dad
'em	them
Garda	police officer in Irish police force
Gardaí	National Irish Police Force
Ma	Mum
me	my
meself	myself
missus	wife or girlfriend
munch	food
Non-participants	those who were not participating in prison education
Participants	those who were participating in prison education
tae	tea
The 'joy	Mountjoy Prison
ya	you
yap	chat
yer	your

Chapter 1

Introduction

"He who opens a school door, closes the prison", is the famous proclamation of Victor Hugo. On the face of it, it appears that Hugo is endorsing the value of education in reducing criminality. Yet there are those who argue that Hugo is referring instead to the role that education has to play in the liberation of the person from the prison of the mind. It matters little which interpretation is favoured; both have merit. Education undoubtedly has a role in developing skills and opportunities that provide the person with a legitimate source of income and ties to society and immerses them in pro-social norms that prevent them from offending. However, notwithstanding the development of skills and opportunities, education's true power often lies in its ability to open the human mind to the world, creating a taste for knowledge and a capacity to explore the self and training the mind to use its own resources. Education is considered a basic human right, not only because of an entitlement to the acquisition of knowledge but because it is inherently linked to our capacity to be human, to think critically and to behave humanely. Therefore, while education is often seen as a structural asset, it is a deeply personal resource that allows us to participate fully as citizens in society.

In terms of criminality and the closing of the prison, both interpretations of Hugo's statement apply. In order to "close the prison", a person must be provided with the skills and opportunities associated with traditional education in order to participate actively in society and circumvent the social disadvantages that lead to offending. Conversely, the impact of education on the mind of the person is liberating, allowing one to think independently and critically, broadening horizons and perspectives, enhancing self-awareness and morality and creating a sense of empowerment. Such facets ground the person, creating stability and supporting their role in society, in an indirect way keeping them from criminality. For those whom education eludes, destabilisation in society and consequent offending is a real risk due to either structural or cognitive weakness or both. It is true that the vast majority of prisoners are typically undereducated by comparison to the general population (O'Mahony, 1997; Morgan and Kett, 2003). While the links between prisoners' levels of education and offending are indirect, such a prevalent deficit among prisoners must surely play a role in their criminality. Education in prison is a means of addressing this issue. And consistent with the two possible interpretations of Victor Hugo's statement, the purposes of prison education include both the traditional aims of education to create skills and opportunities and also the power of education to liberate the human mind from the confines of both actual and metaphorical prison, enhancing the whole person and their ability to experience the world. Given its potential, it is little wonder that education is often used in prisons as a staple part of "rehabilitative" efforts.

Despite the significant potential of prison education, is a vastly under-researched discipline. However, this is gradually changing with a continuing desire to know "what works". While academic interest in the area is gathering pace, the output is still minimal by comparison to other areas of criminology. Prison education can be seen to be a valuable resource, having been shown to have an impact on recidivism rates (Steurer et al., 2001). Furthermore, taking a more subjective approach, other studies have shown that education increases self-confidence and the belief in one's ability to succeed (Tewksbury and Stengel, 2006), increases self-esteem and decreases behavioural problems (Callan and Gardner, 2005), can help repair broken ties with family (Porporino and Robinson, 1992) and mitigates the harms of imprisonment (Council of Europe, 1990; Warner, 2007). While this is only a brief synopsis of the benefits that can be attributed to prison education, it is clear that it has significant capacity to contribute to the lives of prisoners. The research that underpins this book seeks to ascertain education's true potential. This is achieved by exploring experiences of prison education from the perspective of Irish prisoners with a view to finding a unique way of conceptualising the impact of prison education and to begin connecting prison education to the wider criminological framework. The research seeks to step away from the traditional use of recidivism rates as a measure of education's value, instead seeking to understand the ways in which education can support the development of the mind, the individual's own personal growth and the process of escaping each conceptualisation of Hugo's prison.

Research framework

Prison populations have been increasing globally in recent decades, with a reported growth of 20% in the numbers incarcerated between 2000 and 2015 to the current estimate of 10.3 million people incarcerated worldwide (Penal Reform International, 2019). In the European context, the prison population has increased from 102.5 per 100,000 in 2018 to 106 per 100,000 in 2019 (Aebi and Tiago, 2020), representing a significant jump in a one-year period. Ireland compares favourably with these figures, with a total prison population of 4214 persons in custody (Irish Prison Service, 2020), though this rate of imprisonment is rising, increasing from 79.5 per 100,000 in 2018 to 81.2 per 100,000 in 2019 (Aebi and Tiago, 2020).

Recidivism contributes significantly to these statistics, posing a challenge for criminal justice systems in each state. In Ireland, O'Donnell et al. (2008) found that 27% of Irish prisoners return to prison within the first year of release, with this figure gradually rising to 49% after four years. This was confirmed in a more recent study where the Probation Service (2012) found an identical recidivism rate of 27% for the first year post-release. In the most recent study, the reconviction rate at two years was 58.3% and was 62.3% within three years (Irish Prison Service, 2013). The United Kingdom has a one-year recidivism rate of 29.2%, rising to 75% within nine years of release (Ministry of Justice, 2020). Australia reports a two-year reconviction rate of 53% (Fazel and Wolf, 2015). The United States federal rate stands at 60% within two years, jumping to 83% after nine years, though this is based on rearrest as opposed to reconviction (Alper and Durose, 2018). Norway reports a 20% reconviction rate at two years post-release (Fazel and Wolf, 2015). While this is merely a snapshot of the recidivism figures, it highlights the significant problem that reoffending poses. The average cost a prison bed in Ireland is €73,730 per annum (Aebi and Tiago, 2020). High reoffending rates therefore add a considerable financial burden to penal budgets. This is without even considering the high social costs of crime and imprisonment such as the emotional and financial impact on victims and the impact of reincarceration on the offender, their family, their friends and their community in terms of fractured relationships and decreased social capital. With such high financial and social costs, it is little wonder that there is such a focus placed on finding ways to reduce recidivism and discovering "what works" in rehabilitation.

Like in most jurisdictions, prisoners in Ireland mostly come from socially disadvantaged backgrounds. O'Mahony (1997) found that 56% of prisoners in Mountjoy Prison came from six communities in Dublin, all of which are characterised by high levels of socioeconomic deprivation. The typical offender experiences serious social and personal problems including drug or alcohol addiction, social exclusion, economic deprivation, ruptured family ties, poor mental and physical health and, of most relevance, low levels of educational attainment and skills (O'Donnell, 2002). Education levels among prisoners appears to be a serious issue, with the National Crime Council (2002) stating that low levels of education attainment is one of the leading causes of offending, due to the limitations it places on a person's life choices and opportunities. Studies have shown that education levels among prisoners are much lower than in the general population (Morgan and Kett, 2003; Hawley et al., 2013). O'Mahony (1997) found that 80% of the prisoners had left school before the age of 16, with no formal skills or qualifications. Furthermore, 29% had significant problems with literacy (O'Mahony, 1997). These results are echoed by Morgan and Kett (2003), who found significantly low levels of literacy among the prison population. These points highlight the problems that prisoners are facing. In an increasingly educated workforce, literacy and skills are prerequisites to many advancement opportunities in life. Therefore, being illiterate or having low levels of education are severely limiting factors. Furthermore, when offenders leave prison, often significantly depleted by the experience, they face further social exclusion and barriers to reintegration, such as broken family ties, limited access to social services, homelessness, addiction and limited healthcare, which perpetuate the cycle of reoffending outlined earlier (Martynowicz and Quigley, 2010). In order to break this cycle, repeated calls have been made to focus on measures that facilitate the reintegration of prisoners (National Economic and Social Forum, 2001; Irish Penal Reform Trust, 2019). One such measure is education (Irish Penal Reform Trust, 2019), which has been shown to have an impact on reoffending rates (see for example Steurer et al., 2001; Lochner and Moretti, 2004; Chavez and Dawe, 2007; Anders and Noblitt, 2011; Nally et al., 2012; IPSOS, 2018). However, as outlined earlier, prison education remains an under-researched discipline and, despite its reported role in reducing recidivism, the research tends to underrepresent other aspects of its potential in supporting reintegration.

What might be standing in the way of understanding the true value of prison education is the way in which it is researched. The "what works" movement seeks to ensure that rehabilitative efforts are evidence-based. The drive to discover "what works" to reduce recidivism underpins much of the research that has been carried out in relation to prison education, which tends to be quantitative in nature and focused only on recidivism as the measure of success or failure. Steurer et al. (2001) stated that the most likely reason for investigating correctional education is in order to decide whether funding will continue to be applied to a particular programme. Such an approach is limiting in several ways. First, it leads to a very narrow focus. Education by its nature is a broad concept, yet by focusing on a singular outcome the scope of education is reduced to being an instrument of rehabilitation and nothing more. Any programmes developed on foot of such narrow research will undoubtedly end up being rehabilitation-focused and limited in scope, aimed only at correcting a flaw rather than at developing the whole person. Moreover, with such an approach to researching prison education, its value is reduced to a sole outcome – that is, a lack of recidivism – and therefore ignores the many other benefits that education can have for the person. It also assumes that education was the catalyst for behaviour change. There is no scope to assume that a person may have wanted to settle down, have had a child, or have had to care for an aging parent or have won the lottery. It ignores the other factors that may be had an impact on the journey away from criminality. Finally, while the prison education research shows what can be achieved in terms of reduced recidivism, it tells us nothing of the process by which this occurs. Why does it have this impact? How does it help the person? What are the mechanisms by which prison education supports change? These are not new questions, yet they remain unaddressed. As far back as 1976, Robert Martinson, who is synonymous with the "what works" movement, asked "(b)ut what specifically is the method? . . . what is it? What is the actual process that takes place by which "recidivism is reduced?" (Martinson, 1976: 189). While these are complex questions and certainly outside of the scope of just one study, it is these questions that this research sets out to answer in order to find a road away from "what works" to "what helps" and "how and why it helps".

The desistance framework appeared to be the most logical and appropriate framework in which to situate this study. The correctional and desistance literature is already aligned in their respective findings. The benefits of prison education outlined briefly earlier such as increased confidence, self-awareness, employability and parenting skills, for example, are closely related to the composite elements of various theories of desistance such as theories of cognitive change, social bonds theory and the concept of social capital. Unpacking and exploring these links would be beneficial in reconceptualising the effects of prison education in the wider criminological framework. Furthermore, desistance relates to the *process* of change. While recidivism and desistance have generally been seen to be incompatible paradigms, they have much in common, including their focus on change. Desistance is best understood as a process and not just a singular event, which is contrary to the one-dimensional approach that has characterised prison education research to date. It explores the factors that support the transition to a life of conformity. Only by knowing why and/or how a person changes can we truly tailor supports that compliment that process. In the context of understanding the potential of prison education, it is important to move it beyond "what works" thinking and to connect the research to the wider body of criminological research. This research uses this philosophy as its foundation. The aim is to move away from the focus on recidivism and to begin exploring prison education from the perspective of those who have undertaken it and to connect any impacts or benefits to the wider desistance and criminological frameworks in order to illuminate the processes through which education may be supporting the desistance process.

This approach appears to satisfy both schools of thought reflected in Hugo's quote. On the one hand, the idea that prison education's goal is to minimise the harm to the person during the prison sentences is addressed through the subjective exploration of prison education's benefits. The measurement of social capital levels among those participating and not participating in prison education also demonstrates the benefits of education and the manner in which prison education can minimise the harm of the prison sentence. On the other hand, in terms of the idea that prison education is a means of reducing reoffending, the situation of the benefits of education within the wider desistance framework demonstrates how prison education can facilitate a reduction in reoffending. However, the advantage of using desistance as the focus, rather than recidivism, is the ability to explore the intervening processes of change that occur when a person engages in prison education. The recidivism figures reveal little information on how or why prison education is working; the desistance literature, however, is concerned with examining the processes involved in leaving criminality behind. It is proposed that much more can be learned about how and why prison education works by exploring it subjectively and qualitatively, particularly by contextualising it in the wider desistance framework.

Overview of the book

This book will take a comprehensive approach to examining prison education, relevant aspects of desistance, the concept of social capital theory and the links between each of these phenomena. Given the multidisciplinary nature of the study and the various concepts that are involved, this book is necessarily comprehensive. For ease of readability and accessibility, it is broken down into eight chapters. Each chapter will have a particular focus, exploring a particular aspect of the study and findings and each following the previous in a logical sequence. Throughout each chapter, there will be some analysis of the findings and an effort to begin to link the various aspects of the study together. However, in order to avoid repetition and to logically discuss the findings in their totality, the main part of the discussion will be included in the final chapter. Following is an outline of the structure of the remainder of the book and the general contents of each chapter.

Since this work is based on a piece of empirical research, it is important at the outset to provide a detailed account of the various research methods used throughout the study. The prison is a closed environment, and research within the walls of a prison raises unique and challenging considerations. Chapter 2 will outline the rationale for the key methods used in the study, including the selection of methods, choosing and accessing the research sites, selecting the sample, the development of the data collection instruments, data collection issues and data analysis procedure. A significant consideration in any piece of prison research is site access, and the issues and challenges that arose in relation to gaining access to the prison and those who participated in the study will be discussed here. Furthermore, the issues and procedures in relation to accessing a sample of ex-prisoners to give their retrospective accounts will also be examined in detail. The chapter will conclude by examining the ethical issues that arose in designing and undertaking the research and how these issues were dealt with at each stage of the research.

The primary thread running through the entire book is the concept of prison education. Chapter 3 will therefore serve as an introductory chapter for this concept, and its purpose is to give a very detailed overview of the issues and literature relevant to the topic. The chapter starts out with a general overview of prison education, including its historical development. At the core of the provision of prison education is the question of why? This chapter will undertake a detailed rationale for providing prison education, including theories such as opportunity theory, moral development theory and social psychological development theory. Much of the guiding literature on policy and good practice is to be taken from the various European and International policies and documents relating to prison education. These positions and policies will be considered, with a focus on drawing out the two competing approaches in prison education, namely the whole-person approach and the academic approach. The chapter will conclude by considering the adult education approach to teaching in prisons that underpins prison education provision in many jurisdictions. Therefore, key pieces of research from the mainstream adult education literature, particularly Mezirow's (1991) theory of transformational learning are explored, along with policy statements from various providers and researchers in the realm of prison education.

Chapter 4 begins to present the empirical findings from the study, particularly those relating to participation in prison education. This chapter will explore the motivations for accessing and continuing in prison education. While little is known about the reasons that prisoners participate in prison education, even less is known about the reasons that they do not. Chapter 4 will also present the findings of interviews with those prisoners who were not participating in prison education, examining the various reasons they gave for either not participating or for leaving education. A discussion of all of these issues will be undertaken, and this will ultimately facilitate the provision of evidence-based recommendations for improving participation rates in education in prisons. Finally, the chapter will conclude by exploring some ancillary findings in relation to prison education participation such as criticisms that were made of its provision and considering the school space as a rehabilitative environment in itself.

While the two preceding chapters are aimed at exploring the concept of prison education, Chapter 5 and Chapter 6 will examine the other major concept relevant to the theoretical framework of this book – desistance. These chapters will aim to give the reader an overview of desistance to the extent that it is relevant to the current study. Chapter 5 will give a very general introduction to desistance before focusing on narrative theories of desistance, examining the mechanisms for intrinsic change and then contextualising the findings of the current study within this framework. Chapter 5 will also outline the stages of desistance, namely primary desistance that occurs in the early stages when a person is often seen to be "betwixt and between" (Healy, 2010: 424) and secondary desistance that occurs later and is often characterised as being true desistance. Again this will lead to a discussion of the findings of the study in the context of the stages of desistance with a view to showing prison education as a potential form of pre-desistance. Chapter 6 will explore the structural theories of desistance and the relevant findings from the interviews to continue drawing out the links between the literature and prison education. This will involve exploring the key structures such as employment, marriage, parenthood and peer relations to examine how social bonds can impact desistance and will also consider how prison education can support the formation of pro-social bonds based on the findings of the current research.

Chapter 7 will explore the notion of social capital, beginning with a detailed overview of the concept, including the various definitions and debate surrounding the exact nature of social capital. It will then move on to explore the links that already exist within the literature in relation to social capital and its importance in the criminological context. The findings of the current study will be presented and then discussed. The final concept explored in this book is the idea of prison capital. Draine and Wolff (2009) speculated that social capital is depleted by the prison experience and replaced with a type of social capital unique to the prison setting. This study attempted to verify whether incarcerated persons were aware of or identify with the various aspects that might make up prison-based social capital. The analysis of this small and experimental element of the study will be discussed, in addition to drawing conclusions based on the totality of the data presented in the chapter.

The findings of the research that ground this proposed book are broad and wide reaching, given that the research design aimed to draw together several significant concepts to show their mutual relationships and interactions. A full discussion of the interplay between each would be overly burdensome and highly repetitious if undertaken in each chapter. Therefore, Chapter 8 will recap the main points from each chapter and draw together the main findings in order to discuss the full impact of prison education on the desistance process from both the prison education and criminological perspectives. This will be followed by a discussion of the implications of these finding for policy makers and practitioners and the final recommendations going forward.

References

Aebi, M.F. and Tiago, M.M. (2020) *Prisons and Prisoners in Europe 2019: Key Findings of the Space 1 Report*. Strasbourg: Council of Europe.

Alper, M. and Durose, M. (2018) *2018 Update on Prisoner Recidivism: A 9-Year Follow-Up Period (2005–2014)*. Washington, DC: U.S. Department of Justice, Bureau of Justice Statistics.

Anders, A.D. and Noblitt, G.W. (2011) Understanding Effective Higher Education Programs in Prisons: Considerations from the Incarcerated Individuals Program in North Carolina. *The Journal of Correctional Education* 62(2), pp. 7–23.

Callan, V. and Gardner, J. (2005) *Vocational Education and Training Provision and Recidivism in Queensland Correctional Institutions*. Adelaide: NCVER.

Chavez, R. and Dawe, S. (2007) International Research and Trends in Education and Training Provision in Correctional Settings. In Dawe, S. (ed) *Vocational Education and Training for Adult Prisoners and Offenders in Australia*. Adelaide, Australia: National Centre for Vocational Education Research.

Council of Europe (1990) *Education in Prison: Recommendation No. R (89) 12*. 13th October 1989. Strasbourg: Council of Europe.

Draine, J. and Wolff, N. (2009) *Social Capital and Reentry to the Community from Prison*. New Brunswick: Centre for Behavioural Health Services and Criminal Justice Research. Research Brief.

Fazel, S. and Wolf, A. (2015) A Systematic Review of Criminal Recidivism Rates Worldwide: Current Difficulties and Recommendations for Best Practice. *PLoS One* 10(6), e0130390. doi:10.1371/journal.pone.0130390.

Hawley, J., Murphy, I. and Souto-Otero, M. (2013) *Prison Education and Training in Europe: Current State-of-Play and Challenges*. London: GHK Consulting.

Healy, D. (2010) Betwixt and between: The Role of Psychosocial Factors in the Early Stages of Desistance. *Journal of Research in Crime and Delinquency* 47(4), pp. 419–438. doi:10.1177/0022427810375574.

IPSOS (2018) *Evaluation of Prisoner Learning: Initial Impacts and Delivery*. London: Ipsos MORI Social Research Institute.

Irish Penal Reform Trust (2019) *Progress in the Penal System (PIPS): A Framework for Penal Reform (2019)*. Dublin: Irish Penal Reform Trust.

Irish Prison Service (2013) *Irish Prison Service Recidivism Study 2013*. Longford: Irish Prison Service.

Irish Prison Service (2020) *Irish Prison Service Annual Report 2019*. Ballinalee, Co. Longford: Irish Prison Service.

Lochner, L. and Moretti, E. (2004) The Effect of Education on Crime: Evidence from Prison Inmates, Arrests, and Self Reports. *The American Economic Review* 94, pp. 155–189.

Martinson, R. (1976) California Research at the Crossroads. *Crime and Delinquency* 22, pp. 180–191.

Martynowicz, A. and Quigley, M. (2010) *'It's Like Stepping on a Landmine': Reintegration of Prisoners in Ireland*. Dublin: Irish Penal Reform Trust.

Mezirow, J. (1991) *Transformative Dimensions of Adult Learning*. San Francisco: Jossey-Bass.

Ministry of Justice (2020) *Proven Reoffending Statistics Quarterly Bulletin, England and Wales, January 2018 to March 2018*. London: Home Office.

Morgan, M. and Kett, M. (2003) *The Prison Adult Literacy Survey: Results and Implications*. Dublin: Irish Prison Service.

Nally, J., Lockwood, S., Knutson, K. and Ho, T. (2012) An Evaluation of the Effect of Correctional Education Programs on Post-Release Recidivism and Employment: An Empirical Study in Indiana. *The Journal of Correctional Education* 63(1), pp. 69–88.

National Crime Council (2002) *Tackling the Underlying Causes of Crime: A Partnership Approach*. Dublin: The Stationary Office.

National Economic and Social Forum (2001) *The Reintegration of Prisoners: Forum Report No. 22*. Dublin: National Economic and Social Forum.

O'Donnell, I. (2002) The Reintegration of Prisoners. *Administration* 50(2), pp. 80–97.

O'Donnell, I., Baumer, E. and Hughes, N. (2008) Recidivism in the Republic of Ireland. *Criminology and Criminal Justice* 8(2), pp. 123–146.

O'Mahony, P. (1997) *Mountjoy Prisoners: A Sociological and Criminological Profile*. Dublin: Stationary Office.

Penal Reform International (2019) *Prison Reform International: Annual Report 2018*. London: Penal Reform International.

Porporino, F.J. and Robinson, D. (1992) *Can Educating Adult Offenders Counteract Recidivism?* Ontario: Correctional Services of Canada.

Probation Service (2012) *Probation Service Recidivism Study 2007–2011*. Dublin: The Probation Service.

Steurer, S.J., Smith, L. and Tracy, A. (2001) *Three State Recidivism Study*. Washington: United States Department of Education.

Tewksbury, R. and Stengel, K.M. (2006) Assessing Correctional Education Programs: The Students' Perspective. *Journal of Correctional Education* 57(1), pp. 13–25.

Warner, K. (2007) Against the Narrowing of Perspectives: How Do We See Learning, Prisons and Prisoners? *Journal of Correctional Education* 58(2), pp. 170–183.

Chapter 2

Research methods

This chapter will explore the methods used to carry out the study upon which this book is based. This will involve outlining the research problem and the methods that were used throughout the study including the site and sample selections. Researching in a prison raises many methodological issues, particularly surrounding access, procedures and ethics. The methods used to address and overcome these issues will be outlined. The data collection and analysis procedures will be explained, and the chapter will conclude with a look at the methodological limitations of the study and the ethical safeguards that were put in place.

Given the potential impact that prison education can have on the lives of those who undertake it, it is widely under-researched. Most studies in the area use recidivism rates to quantify the success of prison education. Such an approach only demonstrates the impact of prison education on one sole outcome – reoffending. This may overestimate causality on the one hand by ignoring any intervening circumstances which might also result in reduced reoffending. Moreover, it does not provide any meaningful insight into the process through which prison education can impact an offender's ability to cease their offending behaviour. An objective of the current research is to add to the understanding of this intervening process and gain some insight into the process through which prison education can result in desistance from crime. There have also been calls for prison education to become more social capital than human capital focused (Costelloe, 2003). With this in mind, given that social capital is proposed as having a strong role in facilitating desistance, another objective of this research is to address these gaps by looking for links among prison education, social capital and the desistance process.

Research methodology

Given the exploratory nature of the current study, the interpretative approach was particularly appropriate. The use of qualitative methods to examine prison education, while relatively uncommon, can lead to much richer, deeper data than that which would be expected of a quantitative approach (Bryman, 2016).

The qualitative interview is a method of gaining rich insights into experiences, opinions and attitudes (Fontana and Frey, 1994; May, 2001; Denscombe, 2017). In the case of the semi-structured interview the interviewer can maintain more control through the use of a specified list of questions or conversational prompts. This style is much more conversational than with the structured interview, and the focus is on the interviewee elaborating on points of interest and giving open-ended answers (Denscombe, 2017). This approach fitted well with the current research that aimed to be exploratory, yet had a particular focus and specific objectives that required a degree of control over the topics covered by the interviews.

However, while the interpretative approach was suitable to the investigation of most of the research questions, achieving the objectives relating to social capital required the use of methods from the quantitative paradigm. The indicators of social capital can be observed qualitatively, a method used by Farrall (2004). However, they are usually measured by quantitative methods (Lin and Erickson, 2008). In the prison context, prison-based surveys must take account of literacy problems and a self-completion questionnaire is generally seen to be unsuitable (Davies et al., 2011). This requirement did not prove methodologically problematic in designing the research since the survey could be administered at the same time as the semi-structured interviews (Bryman, 2016). A simultaneous methodological triangulation approach was adopted (Morse, 1991). Simultaneous methodological triangulation is appropriate where the researcher wishes to compare both qualitative and quantitative data gathered concurrently to determine how the themes identified in the qualitative element compare with the statistical data (Creswell et al., 2003), such as in the current study. Another advantage to this method was that there was only one data collection phase (Creswell et al., 2003), which is desirable in the prison setting where follow-up access to prisoners who have participated in one phase of data collection may be impossible due to transfers, early release or temporary release measures.

Data collection

Once the research methods had been chosen, the next task was to identify and gain access to the research population. The study population comprised prisoners who were serving or who have served custodial sentences in Irish prisons. It was also decided to include a small number of ex-prisoners who had participated in prison education in order to gain a retrospective perspective of whether and how prison education had helped them in reintegration and desistance.

Selection of the research site

The mainstay of the Irish penal system is the closed, medium-security prison. The closed prison is used to incarcerate the typical prisoner – predominantly male, between the ages of 20 and 40, incarcerated for offences against the person, property offences, drug offences or firearm offences (Irish Prison Service, 2020). While there is little information available about the breakdown of the characteristics of prisoners committed to each prison, it appears that the populations in regional medium-security prisons such as Mountjoy, Limerick and Castlerea are representative of the typical prisoner in terms of age, background, sentence length and nature of offences (Irish Prison Service, 2020). Mountjoy Prison was chosen as a research site for these reasons. It is a large, medium-security closed prison in Dublin used to incarcerate prisoners serving sentences for a wide range of offences, and it appears that the population is typically representative of the general prison population. It contains four wings, a school, a separation unit for at-risk prisoners and a medical unit. The Irish Prison Service reports an operational capacity of 755 at present, with an average daily number in custody of 684 in 2019 (Irish Prison Service, 2020). In terms of activities, prisoners can access the school, a gym, several workshop options and also employment opportunities in the kitchen, bakery or reception, for instance. Those who do not wish to participate in these activities during their "out-of-cell" time can remain in their cells or on the landings or go to the prison yard (O'Reilly, 2009). The school in Mountjoy Prison employs at least 26 full- and part-time teachers. It has a wide and varied curriculum, and courses range from basic literacy to degree-level courses. However, Further Education and Training Awards Council courses and state examination preparation are the mainstay of the provision in the school. The latest figures available for education participation give an overall participation rate of 20.4% (Maslauskaite and Mooney, 2018). The school is accessible by way of a staircase located near to the main entrance hallway of the prison and is therefore equally accessible to prisoners on each wing. Another factor in the decision to use Mountjoy in the study, rather than one of the other closed, medium-security prisons, was that the researcher had already established links with key people within the prison and the prison school and this made it much easier to negotiate access to both the research site and population since a relationship with the "gatekeepers" was already established in Mountjoy Prison.

A second prison was chosen for the study for comparative purposes. In contrast to Mountjoy Prison, Shelton Abbey, located close to Arklow in County Wicklow, is an open, low-security prison often used for prisoners nearing the end of their sentences and those deemed as requiring lower levels of security (Irish Prison Service, 2020). The prison's capacity is 102, and admission is usually based on transfers from other prisons (Irish Prison Service, 2020). Prisoners have several options including work, education and extensive recreational activities. The prison farm provides work for many prisoners, involving livestock work, rearing bedding plants, working on welding in the farm workshop and valeting of machinery (Department of Justice, 2019). Prisoners can also work in the prison kitchen, training in catering, food service, record keeping and so on. The education participation figures show that 56.5% of prisoners were participating in education (Maslauskaite and Mooney, 2018). Education courses range from literacy provision right up to Open University courses, but Further Education and Training Awards Council (hereinafter FETAC) courses and state examination preparation are the courses most commonly undertaken by students (Irish Prison Service, 2009).

Access to research sites

The prison is a unique setting given the closed nature of the environment and the considerations involved such as security and order. In terms of negotiating access to Irish prisons, there were three criteria that needed to be satisfied. The first was to gain ethical approval from the Irish Prison Service Prisoner Based Research Ethics Committee (hereinafter "the Ethics Committee"). This involved a detailed application to the Ethics Committee outlining all of the foreseen ethical issues and the measures proposed to ensure the safety of everyone involved in the research. The process of gaining ethical clearance took over one year. Once the approval of the Ethics Committee had been granted and the sites chosen, the researcher began to make contact with the relevant people. First, the approval of the prison governors in each of the two prisons was needed. In both cases, this proved unproblematic and was gained by telephone. Once the governors' consent had been obtained, the researcher made contact with the head teachers in each of the prison schools. This was facilitated and aided by contacts that had been made with teachers and other personnel within the Prison Education Service. While the prison governor could grant access to the prison, it was the head teachers who were responsible for granting access to the school and the majority of the research population. Following face-to-face meetings with each of the head teachers, final procedures were approved and access was granted to the research sites.

Sample selection

Researchers typically engage in one of two broad categories of sampling, namely probability and purposive (non-probability) sampling (Ritchie et al., 2003). Probability sampling uses a random selection method and is the most likely method to yield a representative sample (Bryman, 2016; Denscombe, 2017). Purposive sampling is the non-random selection of units with direct relevance to the research questions being asked (Ritchie et al., 2003; Bryman, 2016). In the current study, a hybrid of the both probability and purposive sampling was used. An element of purposive sampling was required in order to determine those who were participating in education. Here a list of those who were participating in school classes on that particular day was obtained from the head teacher. A random sampling of those on the list was then performed. All other sampling was probability in nature. For the sample of prisoners who were not participating in education, the researcher was provided with a list of all those in custody in the prison and through random selection chose those prisoners who were to be approached for interviews. The names that were selected were compared against the list of those who were participating in education to ensure they were actually a non-participant. Finally, in relation to ex-prisoners, this was again a combination of probability and purposive sampling. The staff of the Pathways Centre, a post-release centre in Dublin city centre, obtained consent to share contact details with the researcher from a large number of the people who use the service and who had participated in prison education. The researcher then randomly selected the sample of ex-prisoners to be contacted about participating in the study until the sample quota was reached.

Since the surveys and interviews were conducted simultaneously, it was not feasible to have a very large sample size for the surveys, as is often considered optimal for generalisability of results. However, the aim of this research was to be exploratory, exploring the key concepts and looking for connections rather than definitive, causal relationships. Denscombe (2017) stated that while large samples are suited to studies which seek to meet the requirement for generalisability, in practice social research projects frequently use relatively small numbers (between 30 and 250) for sampling. The numbers of interviews and surveys conducted therefore meet the requirements of the small scale exploratory study.

Semi-structured interview design

The semi-structured interview was selected as the appropriate qualitative data collection method. While the semi-structured interview can be conversational and informal in nature, the preparation of an interview guide or research schedule remains important (May, 2001). To that end, an interview guide was drawn up with specific questions and generic questions for each of the three groups that were interviewed. The first part of the interview guide was designed to collect demographic and other important data necessary to supplement the interview and survey data. This included name, age, offences, previous offending and educational history among other things. The remainder of the interview guide contained questions and prompts designed to maintain a focus on the issues related to the research objectives (see Appendix 1). Despite the existence of a list of questions, the researcher took a flexible approach. While there were certain "compulsory" questions which were asked of each prisoner, if issues of relevance or interest arose, the interviewer was free to explore these to the exclusion of other questions. However, in practice, during the interviews, within the flow of conversation, many of the questions on the list were answered without requiring a prompt or question, which allowed for a relaxed and conversational tone.

Survey design

A key research objective was to explore the concept of social capital. The greatest weakness of social capital is the absence of any consensus on how to measure it (Fukuyama, 2001). Social capital is a concept that spans many disciplines and is utilised in various frameworks. Because of the difficulties in defining social capital, most researchers tend to consider the concept in light of their own discipline and adopt their own definition (Adam and Roncevic, 2003). However, for investigation or measurement of social capital, a set definition is not required; rather an operationalisation of the concept being examined is more important and the indicators used should be guided by the scope of the study (Collier, 2002). In light of these issues, it appears that the definition, operationalisation and measurement of social capital within each study is a matter for the researcher to establish in line with the aims of the particular study, the nature of the discipline and the approach being taken. In the current study, it was decided that some form of definition was required in order make the operationalisation of social capital and the adoption or development of a tool of measurement feasible. However, despite many theorists suggesting the composite elements of social capital, very few actually suggest definitions. Forrest and Kearns (2001) "definition" of social capital was adopted since it appears to be both comprehensive and the most closely aligned with the view of social capital taken in the desistance literature. They state that social capital "involves empowerment, participation, association, support and reciprocity, collective norms and values, trust, safety and belonging".

There is little guidance from the social capital literature on measurement tools or on the questions that ought to be asked in measuring social capital. In the current research, a tool was required that was flexible, offering the scope to be adapted and applied to the prison context and that was concise enough to be administered in a relatively short period of time. Time was a factor since the amount of time with each prisoner was constrained by the prison schedule and the requirement that interviews be conducted in the prisoners' out-of-cell time. There were two options available in deciding upon a measurement tool. Use or adapt a previous survey or design one specific to the prison setting. The former proved impossible with those various surveys used in previous community-based studies offering little flexibility or scope for adaptation or being prohibitively long and extensive for using within the constraints of the prison setting. It became apparent that choosing an existing measurement tool and adapting it to the prison setting would be impossible or methodologically problematic at the very least. For these reasons, it was decided to design the survey from scratch.

The "Social Capital Question Bank" (hereinafter referred to as "SCQB") (Ruston and Akinrodoye, 2002) was used in order to facilitate the development of the survey. The SCQB is a matrix of questions from the National Statistics Office in the United Kingdom that compiles the wording of questions included in 18 major government and non-governmental surveys and that is intended as a reference tool for people interested using social capital questions to measure the concept (Ruston and Akinrodoye, 2002). The questions in the SCQB are divided into five themes that represent the broad indicators of social capital. The five main themes were (1) participation, social engagement and commitment; (2) control and self-efficacy; (3) perceptions of community-level structures or characteristics; (4) social interaction, social networks and social support; and (5) trust, reciprocity and social cohesion. Indeed, a reason for choosing to use the SCQB as a resource in the development of the survey was that the five themes under which the questions were organised broadly reflected the main elements of the Forrest and Kearns (2001) definition outlined earlier. Each of these themes in the SCQB is divided into a number of subthemes and, within this framework, the questions used in the previous surveys are listed under the themes and subthemes to which they are relevant. Therefore, someone wishing to use political or voting activity as an indicator of social capital in their survey would go to the theme "participation, social engagement and commitment", which contains the subtheme "political or voting activity", and under this heading the researcher can find a list of questions asked in the previous studies which examine that particular aspect of social capital. In order to ensure transparency and consistency, each question lists the survey and the particular measurement techniques used in the study the question was taken from. The SCQB allowed the researcher the flexibility to design a survey that reflected the main aspects or "themes" of social capital, adapt it for the prison setting, have access to the methods of scoring the survey questions and tailor the survey to the time constraints of the closed setting.

In designing the survey, each of the themes was used and, where feasible, one question from each subheading was included. Since there was often more than one question under each subheading, the decision as to which one to use primarily came down to two things: first, the degree of adaptability to the prison setting and, second, suitability to the Likert-style approach. Once the questions had been chosen, the survey was compiled with questions under each of the five themes of social capital. They were scored with weightings from 4 for the most favourable response to 0 for the least favourable, which was in line with the weightings on several of the surveys in the SCQB. The same survey was administered to both prison education participants and non-participants and was modified slightly for the ex-prisoners to reflect the fact that they were in the community. The surveys were piloted two months prior to the full data collection phase and modified accordingly. The modifications were minimal and involved the adjustment of the wording of several questions and the removal of two questions that were repetitious.

Overview of data collection figures

Overall, 47 interviews and surveys were carried out in three different locations. The study was piloted in Mountjoy Prison with five prisoners in late February 2011. Once these interviews were analysed and amended, the researcher returned to Mountjoy for four weeks in May 2011 to conduct the remainder of the interviews and surveys. As mentioned earlier, the interview and survey were administered simultaneously: the qualitative interview first, followed directly by the survey. This was in order to prevent the items from the social capital survey from "contaminating" the interview data. The interviews were digitally recorded in order to facilitate transcribing later. In total, 33 prisoners were interviewed in Mountjoy: 19 prison education participants and 14 non-participants. In Shelton Abbey, 9 interviews were carried out, made up of 7 participants and 2 non-participants. The Shelton Abbey data collection phase was carried out in early July 2011. Five ex-prisoners also took part. These interviews were carried out in the Pathways offices in Dublin in October 2011. The number of prisoners to be interviewed and surveyed in each setting was not set or predetermined; instead it was decided that interviews would be conducted until a saturation point was reached (Bryman, 2016).

Data analysis

Qualitative interview analysis

Following data collection, the data was transcribed from its digitally recorded format and transferred into Microsoft Word documents. This resulted in the production of several hundred pages of interview transcripts. All of the preliminary data gathered was organised into spreadsheet format so as to allow for comparability at a glance and also to allow for it to be accessed with relative ease during the quantitative analysis. In truth, the data analysis began long before the interviews were transcribed. Throughout the data collection phase of the study, notes and reflections were made after each day of data collection. These were recorded in order to help with data analysis later, but the observations also helped in refining the questions that were asked and the points that were elaborated on with each prisoner day to day. Any of the analytical memos made daily during the data collection phase were also written up, specifying whether they were in relation to a particular participant or whether they related to the study in general. The interview data was analysed in line with Miles and Huberman's (1994) three-step approach to qualitative data analysis: data reduction, data display and conclusion drawing and verification. These steps were utilised in the analysis of the interview data.

The transcribed interviews were loaded to NVivo, a popular software tool often used by qualitative research to manage and organise data. The first task was to reduce the data by conducting a preliminary sweep of the interviews. During this phase of the process, each interview was read carefully. Where any issue or theme was observed, a node was created to reflect it. This procedure was followed throughout the entirety of the interviews, and even where a theme appeared to be unrelated to a research question a node was created to reflect it nonetheless. It was possible at that early stage to create a hierarchical structure where relationships appeared to be materialising even during the data collection phase. Once this preliminary sweep of the data had been completed, the researcher set about taking the themes and nodes which had been created and trying to display them in an organised structure so as to be able to observe relationships and categorise themes more effectively. By recoding back and forth several times, it was possible to put a workable structure on the data. This is fulfilling all three of the flows mentioned by Miles and Huberman (1994). Not only does it refine data, reducing its volume and retaining the most relevant parts, the hierarchical structure also ensures that data is displayed in an accessible manner which lends itself to conclusion and verification. This verification and conclusion drawing is ongoing as the data is being reduced and displayed.

The various findings from the interview data will be outlined in the following chapters, particularly Chapter 4 (prison education), Chapter 5 (desistance – narrative theory and cognitive change) and Chapter 6 (desistance – structural theories).

Quantitative survey analysis

Once the surveys were completed, they were scored in accordance with the weighting system and all of the relevant information was entered into a Microsoft Excel spreadsheet. Demographical data was added to the Excel spreadsheet such as ages, offences, relationships, and so on. These variables were given codes which were developed and recording in an accompanying "codebook". The scores for each of the five themes, along with the total score for both social capital and the questions relating to the recognition of prison-based capital, were all entered into the spreadsheet. When the spreadsheet was completed, it was imported into SPSS, a statistical analysis tool in order to test the survey data.

Two particular tests formed the basis of the quantitative data analysis. T-tests are appropriate for use when examining the difference between two groups in relation to one single variable. In the present research, these t-tests were used when examining the difference between the social capital and prison-based social capital scores of those who were and were not participating in prison education. The second type of test relied upon for quantitative data analysis was Pearson and Spearman correlations, which are used to measure the strength of a relationship between two continuous variables. This in turn indicates both the direction of the relationship and the strength of it. These tests were carried out when examining the relationship between social capital and prison-based social capital, for example. The gathering of a significant amount of preliminary data also allowed for a considerable amount of testing on the data, such as in relation to previous occupational history, previous levels of education and so on. The results of the relevant tests will be outlined and discussed in Chapter 7.

Ethical issues and procedures

Informed consent, voluntary participation, anonymity and confidentiality were the key ethical considerations in the study.

Informed consent and voluntary participation

In order to ensure that full, informed and voluntary consent was given by each participant, each prisoner was told about the subject matter of the study and what would be expected of them in terms of participation prior to taking part in the study. Recognising that some prisoners may have issues with literacy, this was done orally. Each prisoner was also provided with an information leaflet prior to consenting to the interview so that they could consider their participation at length if desired. They were reassured that participation was voluntary and that no reward or incentive was being offered for participation, nor would they be at any detriment for declining the invitation to participate in the study. Finally, each prisoner was told that even if they consented to participate they were free to withdraw their consent at any time up to the submission of the research. Any questions or concerns that they may have about the research were answered as honestly and as frankly as possible. Once these formalities had been covered, each prisoner was asked to sign a consent form, containing all of the aforementioned information, to signify that they had given full and free consent to being involved in the research.

Anonymity and confidentiality

In order to ensure anonymity, the researcher formulated pseudonyms for each prisoner and screened the data for any facts or statements which may inadvertently identify the prisoner. The actual name and the pseudonyms were entered onto a password-protected spreadsheet and are therefore available only to the researcher. The use of gatekeepers and the fact that each prisoner who participated came to the interview room dilutes the guarantee of anonymity and confidentiality to a degree. However, the interviews were conducted in strict privacy, out of the earshot of teachers or prison officers.

Limitations of methodology

Despite the careful selection of these methods, there will always be some limitations. The first potential limitation is the issue of self-selection for prison education. The argument may be made that those who are participating in prison education are those prisoners who are already motivated towards change, perhaps having higher levels of self-awareness, agency and social capital even prior to coming to prison education. The inclusion of questions examining the motivations to participate in education goes some way towards answering this concern, as it explores whether the reasons for participating in education are actually with a view to change or achieving goals or whether they are more benign reasons such as escapism. Furthermore, the objective is to explore the connections between the accounts of prisoners and the desistance and social capital framework of literature – the study is not designed to prove causal links between the two. This renders the dangers of self-selection less significant than if this were a purely quantitative study.

This leads to the second potential limitation of the study, that of the exploratory rather than causal nature of the research. The study is not looking to establish causal links between these phenomena, and it is not an intervention-based study. The social capital levels of prisoners when they arrived in prison is unknown. It is also impossible to know what decisions a prisoner had made as they entered prison in terms of change in their own life. This in turn makes showing causality difficult but does not hinder the exploration of the links that exist. Finally, the methods discussed earlier do not encompass a follow-up study. While this is not a methodological impossibility, rather it is a research design decision, it does not allow for those who have participated in education to give a reflective, post-release account of how prison education may have helped them. However, the inclusion of the accounts of five ex-prisoners at various stages of desistance allows an element of retrospection on any supporting role education may have in reintegration and desistance.

Terminology

There is some argument across criminological disciplines regarding the terminology that ought to be used in describing incarcerated persons. While within probation and penal discourse the use of the terms offender and prisoner are common, there are those who feel these are deeply loaded and disrespectful labels. Within this text, in line with my own philosophy, the phrases person, man or woman are used where appropriate. Moreover, those who were participating in prison education are referred to as "participants" and those who were not participating are referred to as "non-participants". However, at times, the words prisoner, ex-prisoner, offender and ex-offender are used where using other words is difficult. There is an effort to keep this to a minimum and, where used, these phrases are not meant in any derogatory sense and are merely descriptive.

Conclusion

Having explained and justified the various decisions and procedures undertaken in the study, a clear picture has been developed of how the research was carried out, the setting within which the research was based, the challenges and obstacles that were faced and the manner in which the data was collected and analysed. The task now is to present these empirical findings throughout the upcoming chapters, in addition to outlining the previous theory and undertaking a detailed discussion of the implications of the findings in this study. The remaining chapters will carry out these tasks, beginning in the following chapter with a detailed look at the prison education literature, before considering the findings in the remaining chapters.

References

Adam, F. and Roncevic, B. (2003) Social Capital: Recent Debates and Research Trends. *Social Science Information* 42, pp. 155–183.

Bryman, A. (2016) *Social Research Methods*. 5th ed. Oxford: Oxford University Press.

Collier, P. (2002) Social Capital and Poverty: A Microeconomic Perspective. In Van Bastelaer, T. (ed) *The Role of Social Capital in Development*. Melbourne: Cambridge University Press.

Costelloe, A. (2003) *Third Level Education in Irish Prisons: Who Participates and Why?* Unpublished Doctoral Thesis, Milton Keynes: Open University.

Creswell, J.W., Plano Clark, V.L., Gutmann, M.L. and Hanson, W.E. (2003) Advanced Mixed Methods Research Designs. In Tashakkori, A. and Teddlie, C. (eds) *Handbook of Mixed Methods in Social and Behavioural Research*. Thousand Oaks: Sage.

Davies, P., Francis, P. and Jupp, V. (2011) *Doing Criminological Research*. 2nd ed. London: Sage.

Denscombe, M. (2017) *The Good Research Guide for Small-Scale Social Research Projects*. 6th ed. Berkshire: Open University Press.

Department of Justice (2019) *Shelton Abbey Visiting Committee Annual Report 2018*. Dublin: Stationary Office.

Farrall, S. (2004) Social Capital and Offender Reintegration: Making Probation Desistance Focused. In Maruna, S. and Immarigeon, R. (eds) *After Crime and Punishment: Pathways to Offender Reintegration*. Devon: Willan Publishing.

Fontana, A. and Frey, J.H. (1994) Interviewing: The Art of Science. In Denzin, N.K. and Lincoln, Y.S. (eds) *Handbook of Qualitative Research*. Thousand Oaks: Sage.

Forrest, R. and Kearns, A. (2001) Social Cohesion, Social Capital and the Neighbourhood. *Urban Studies* 38(12), pp. 2125–2143.

Fukuyama, F. (2001) Social Capital, Civil Society and Development. *Third World Quarterly* 22(1), pp. 7–20.

Irish Prison Service (2009) *Education and Library Services Directory*. Longford: Irish Prison Service.

Irish Prison Service (2020) *Irish Prison Service Annual Report 2019*. Longford: Irish Prison Service.

Lin, N. and Erickson, B.H. (2008) Theory, Measurement and the Research Enterprise on Social Capital. In Lin, N. and Erickson, B.H. (eds) *Social Capital: An International Research Program*. Oxford: Oxford University Press.

Maslauskaite, K. and Mooney, C. (2018) *Doing More with Less: Prisoner Rehabilitation in Ireland*. Paris: Council of Europe Development Bank.

May, T. (2001) *Social Research: Issues, Methods and Process*. 3rd ed. Buckingham: Open University Press.

Miles, M.B. and Huberman, A.M. (1994) *Qualitative Data Analysis: An Expanded Sourcebook*. 2nd ed. Thousand Oaks: Sage.

Morse, J.M. (1991) Strategies for Sampling. In Morse, J.M. (ed) *Qualitative Nursing Research: A Contemporary Dialogue*. Newbury Park: Sage.

O'Reilly, M. (2009) *Report on an Inspection of Mountjoy Prison by the Inspector of Prisons*. Tipperary: Office of the Inspector of Prisons.

Ritchie, J., Lewis, J. and Elam, G. (2003) Designing and Selecting Samples. In Ritchie, J. and Lewis, J. (eds) *Qualitative Research Practice: A Guide for Social Science Students and Researchers*. London: Sage.

Ruston, D. and Akinrodoye, L. (2002) *Social Capital Question Bank: Questions from Social Capital Surveys Included in the Social Capital Survey Matrix*. London: Office for National Statistics.

Chapter 3

Prison education

Exploring the concept

Education is the common thread that runs throughout this book. Given the vast scope of education as a concept, it is difficult to succinctly define and this is an issue that will characterise much of the discussion in this chapter. It is a term that embodies many subjective constructs. Most think of education as formal scholastic or "Socratic" schooling, encompassing primary school, secondary school and perhaps third-level education. Others have taken a much wider view of education. D.H. Lawrence (1922) famously stated that "education should aim to lead out the individual nature in each man and woman to its true fullness". Harris (1999) also reflects this broad notion of education and states that it ought to contribute to a person's happiness and their security and reduce their neurosis and prejudices. Education can also be thought of as a social activity or practice, the purpose of which is to help humans become people (Langford, 1985). The Irish Constitution (1937) also contains a good example of this wider position. In Article 42, the Constitution places a duty on parents to provide "for the religious and moral, intellectual, physical and social education" of their child. In its widest sense, education is about acquiring and using knowledge including cognitive capabilities. Indeed it is these abilities that identify us as humans (Bartlett et al., 2001). Therefore, education in the broad sense is also concerned with the development of the person, which is a feature of the prison education philosophy of many countries.

Prison education is an equally broad concept encompassing the wide range of educational activities that a prisoner may undertake while incarcerated. These educational activities may range from literacy development, to vocational training, to academic education, to arts and cultural development. The most commonly cited aim of prison education is to rehabilitate prisoners. However, this is a somewhat limited view of the value of prison education. Despite taking place in the prison setting, education in prison has the capacity to achieve all of the aspects of education outlined earlier. This chapter will explore these rationales for providing prison education and explore the various philosophies and approaches to its provision. The focus here will be entirely on literature, with a view to providing the theoretical foundation upon which to build the findings and framework of the study in upcoming chapters.

Background to prison education

For a large part of the 20th century the word "correctional" was taken and applied literally. Prisons were correctional facilities, and their function was to "correct" and rehabilitate the offender and the offending behaviour (Dawe, 2007). However, from the 1970s onwards, in the face of rising crime rates, politicians, criminologists and even the public began to question the value of prison-based education and queried its continuing viability (Dawe, 2007). This was further compounded by the "nothing works" slogan, a by-product of the Martinson report (1974) that reviewed over 200 prison programmes and claimed that most were ineffective. Martinson (1974: 25) was highly critical of the studies that supported the success of correctional education and stated that with few and isolated exceptions, the rehabilitative efforts that have been reported so far have had "no appreciable effect on recidivism". Martinson's report, among other things, fed into a sea of public and political opinion that was very unsympathetic towards prisoners and even more unreceptive to the idea of rehabilitation and prison education (Ubah and Robinson, 2003). While the results of Martinson's study were well received by politicians and policy makers looking for ways to cost save in the area of criminal justice, there were those who were critical of Martinson's findings. Palmer (1975), for example, felt that Martinson went in search of a programme that would cure all rather than focusing on one factor such as reducing recidivism which would have been methodologically more sound. A year later, Lipton et al. (1975) released a survey of the results of prison programmes aimed at reforming male offenders between 1945 and 1967, showing that 48% of the programmes recorded a positive outcome of varying degrees. The following decades were characterised by an increasingly punitive approach to punishment which came to be based on the principles of deterrence and retribution, manifest in harsher sentences and mounting pressure to implement mandatory minimum sentences for many offences (Kilcommins et al., 2004). In an increasingly punitive climate, the overriding societal view was that "prison works" (Warner, 2007). The increasing "Culture of Control" (Garland, 2001) adds to this perception, with public opinion fuelling the need for criminal justice policies that are increasingly punitive and tough on crime. The resulting upsurge in incarceration and decline in sympathy for the offender results in a system that ought to prioritise rehabilitation but yet is becoming ever more punitive. With a view to reducing reoffending, such an approach must ultimately be questioned.

In the academic world, in the latter stages of the 1980s and particularly in the 1990s opinions began to change and policy makers began to question "what works" (Cullen and Gendreau, 2001). This shift has prevailed since then, with an ever-increasing interest among researchers about "what works" and a growing likelihood among policy makers to push a more rehabilitative ethos when developing penal policies. Nonetheless, in many jurisdictions the provision of education is provided purely with a view to reducing recidivism and promoting employability in order to reduce crime. While these goals appear to be positive, they tend to lend themselves to a generic approach to educational provision, viewing prison education as treatment. Ultimately they neglect and overlook the various personal effects that education has to offer. While the provision of education is always to be welcomed, no matter what the rationale, the danger is that if the goals of reduced recidivism are not reached, educational offerings may be significantly reduced or withdrawn entirely. However, when education is provided for the sake of the offender, for their own personal interest, personal development or self-actualising goals, it always "works". Prison education today exists against a backdrop of several competing aims – varying greatly depending on the stakeholder and a growing body of research examining the effects of prison education from various perspectives, with most tending to show positive outcomes for those who choose to participate. The following sections will consider the various approaches and philosophies of prison education, in addition to examining the rationales for its provision and the research that exists in relation to its effects.

The rationale for prison education

There are various rationales put forward to support the provision of prison education. Given the significant impact it can have in personal and societal terms, there have also been countless studies investigating its impact. The criticism that could be made of this collective body of research is that the studies tend to investigate the impact of imprisonment by using recidivism rates as a measure. Recidivism bears a substantial cost to society on various fronts. There are the monetary costs of crime such as property damage, replacing stolen property, insurance claims, revenue loss, prosecuting reoffenders (Hellman, 1980) and the cost of their subsequent reincarceration – currently €73,730 per annum in Ireland (Aebi and Tiago, 2020). Society also bears a cost in terms of the emotional hurt to victims and their family, reduced social trust and the secondary impacts of imprisonment for the person's own family (Condry and Minson, 2020). In terms of financial return alone, a UK study found that for every €1 invested in prison education, there was a 2.5% return (Matrix Knowledge Group, 2009). By showing that prison education can be beneficial in reducing reoffending, thus avoiding all of the monetary and societal costs given earlier, it creates justification for the continued funding of prison education.

Warner (2018) criticises the growing tendency of managerialism in the criminal justice and education spheres to focus more on what is measurable, not what is important. Such an approach is increasingly taken to prison education by using recidivism as a measure of its value. This reduces the benefit of prison education to a single outcome (Duguid et al., 1996) and ignores the various other benefits that might accrue to the person. It is also overly causal, presuming that the sole factor responsible for reduced reoffending is the educational intervention (Steurer et al., 2001). Furthermore, it conceptualises education as to a tool to be used in the achievement of penal objectives a way to achieve rehabilitation. Education may be a tool of change, but it is also a tool of human dignity (Munoz, 2009). It aims, among other things, to promote the development of the person, to normalise the prison experience and to minimise the harmful impact of prison upon the person (Council of Europe, 1990). Therefore, this approach of gauging its impact based on a lone indicator has been criticised (Maltz, 2001; Steurer et al., 2001). These competing perspectives have led to extensive discussion in the prison education policy and literature in terms of the true rationale for the provision of prison education.

Following is an overview of the most common rationale put forward for the provision of education, exploring rehabilitation and reduced recidivism rates in the first instance and going on to examine the broader benefits of education for both the person and society. It is not meant as an exhaustive list of all existing studies, as this would be impossible in the confines of this current work. However, it is hoped that what is presented is a comprehensive overview of the main works that support the theoretical framework that underpins this book.

Reduced recidivism

The word "recidivism" comes from the Latin word *recidere*, meaning to fall back (Maltz, 2001), and is the reversion of an individual to offending after they have been convicted of an offence, sentenced and corrected (Maltz, 2001). Recidivism is a significant issue in the criminal justice system, with innumerable studies demonstrating the high rates at which prisoners reoffend. In Ireland, for example, it has been found that up to 62.3% of offenders reoffend within three years of release, with 41.6% of offenders reoffending in the first year post-release (Irish Prison Service, 2013). The United Kingdom has a one-year recidivism rate of 29.2%, rising to 75% within nine years of release (Ministry of Justice, 2020). The United States reports an overall federal recidivism rate of 68% (Nally et al., 2012) and one-year reimprisonment (as opposed to reoffending) rate of 23% (Durose et al., 2014). Reoffending contributes significantly to crime rates and has serious economic and social impacts. The National Economic and Social Forum (2001: 69) has stated that a key way of reducing reoffending is by "*ensuring prisoners have an opportunity to prepare themselves for participation in the community on release*". Education, it appears, can form part of that preparation.

Many studies have found that recidivism rates are positively influenced by participation in prison education. The Three State Recidivism Study (Steurer et al., 2001) is one of the most comprehensive studies undertaken and found a significant reduction in recidivism rates among prisoners who participated in prison education. This study examined the relationship between prison education and recidivism rates across three states in the US, reporting that the rearrest (13%), reconviction (21%) and reincarceration (29%) figures were lower for the correctional education participants as opposed to the non-participants when all three states were combined. More recently, it has been found that participation in prison education reduces reoffending by 13% (Davis et al., 2013). Many other studies have demonstrated similar results, concluding that prison education has an impact on recidivism figures (Hull et al., 2000; Social Exclusion Unit, 2002; Petersilia, 2003; Lochner and Moretti, 2004; Chavez and Dawe, 2007; Anders and Noblitt, 2011; Nally et al., 2012; IPSOS, 2018). Conversely, Cho and Tyler (2010) reported that recidivism rates were not significantly reduced by prison education in their study, but the post-release employment rates were significantly increased through participation in ABE in Florida prisons, as were post-release earnings. An increase in earnings is proposed as having an effect on recidivism due to the increased opportunity cost of crime and the increased loss of income while serving a prison sentence (Lochner and Moretti, 2004). Furthermore, they propose that education makes individuals more risk-averse and less impatient (Lochner and Moretti, 2004).

Callan and Gardner (2005) found that 32% of those who did not participate in VET before release recidivated compared with only 23% of those who did participate in VET (Callan and Gardner, 2005).

It is not just participation itself that is important. The levels at which a prisoner participates in prison education has been directly correlated with a reduction in recidivism rates (Holley and Ensley, 2003). Using reconviction or reincarceration figures, this study found that of the cohort sampled of those who had not reached 9th grade levels of education had a recidivism rate of 53.3%. Those who were educated to between a 9th- and 12th-grade level had a recidivism rate of 50.6%. Those who gained a high school diploma in prison had a much lower recidivism rate of 35.8%. Finally those who pursued higher education such as a college course had the lowest recidivism rate of 28.2% (Holley and Ensley, 2003).

Completion of a full educational programme, while optimal (Cho and Tyler, 2010), is not necessary in order to secure at least some of the benefits (Hull et al., 2000). In a study of 3,000 men and women released from Virginia Department of Corrections institutions, researchers found a reincarceration rate of 20% among programme completers, 40% among programme non-completers and 49% among programme non-participants. In Canada, a similar study found that those who participated in ABE were less likely to recidivate on release (Porporino and Robinson, 1992). ABE completers had a one-year reincarceration rate of 30.1%, and those released before completion and voluntary ABE withdrawals had reincarceration rates of 35.5% and 41.6%, respectively (Porporino and Robinson, 1992). While this shows that those prisoners who actually complete courses in prison tend to recidivate at a lower rate than non-completers, the study was only one year in duration. It has been recommended that any study of recidivism ought to be at least two years in duration to ensure that recidivism rates have the chance to become stable (Chavez and Dawe, 2007).

Those prisoners who are older seem to gain greater benefit from prison education by comparison to younger prisoners undertaking the same programmes.

Defining recidivism as reincarceration, Fabelo (2002) found that prisoners who participated in prison education were 11% less likely to recidivate. The most successful group were those prisoners who were older than 35 and who came to prison unable to read but left prison literate and possibly with other courses also completed. The recidivism rates for these prisoners decreased from 33% to 15% (Fabelo, 2002). While education may be a part of the reason for the reduced recidivism rates, it might also be the case that those prisoners who were older were undertaking education with a view supporting their efforts at desistance, whereas the younger cohort may have had other reasons for participation, such as passing time or alleviating boredom – therefore, the earlier outcomes were pre-decided. Perhaps it is also a reflection of Glueck and Glueck's (1940) theory on how criminals often eventually "age out" of crime.

Finally, third-level education can have a significant impact of recidivism rates. Ouimet-Burke and Vivian (2001) found that prisoners who did not participate in college programmes during incarceration recidivated at a rate of 68.7% over the five-year study period compared to 48.8% of those who participated in college programmes. Despite a seemingly high reincarceration rate for those who participated in college programmes, this study also shows that those who participate in college programmes in prison are likely to remain un incarcerated for a longer period than those who do not participate. The results are encouraging and show the benefits of third level provision in prison. Of course, the provision of college programmes is to be encouraged, particularly for those serving longer sentences. However, this is often limited by constraints such as costs and resources (Costelloe, 2003). A significant issue remains, however, in continuing with and completion of such programmes after release given the considerable costs associated with third-level education.

Critiquing recidivism as a measure of prison education

Many commentators have criticised the "recidivism" approach to measuring the impact of prison education as being reflective of the prevailing punitiveness surrounding criminal justice (Maltz, 2001). The contemporary surge in retributive policy leaves little room for the consideration of interventions that may support the offender, unless of course there is also a measurable benefit to society in return. In most instances, recidivism studies are carried out to determine whether or not to continue funding prison education programmes (Steurer et al., 2001). Those programmes that are not providing enough of a return to society in terms of decreased reoffending rates are deemed to be unworthy of funding. This renders the learner irrelevant. Such a position is also inconsistent with the whole-person approach to educational provision in prisons and ignores the various other rationales and benefits that can be gained through participation in prison education. Costelloe (2003) echoes this, proposing that prison education is not seen as valuable in terms of the individual benefits and must justify its contribution to society through reducing reoffending in order to salvage its existence. As outlined in the Chapter 1, the "what works" approach can result in an overestimation of the causal impact of prison education on reduced reoffending, as it ignores all other contributing factors to the process of moving away from criminality. Finally, this also overlooks the causal chain and does not illuminate the way in which prison education actually works to reduce recidivism. There is no examination of the underlying process, attributing it only to increased employability in most instances – despite the fact that most ex-prisoners find it extremely difficult to secure employment even having undertaken prison education. Given the value of education to self-concept, personality and meaning structures, the mechanisms through which prison education support reduced reoffending are likely to be far more complex than this narrow view suggests. There is a need to explore "how it works" instead of "what works" in order to address these misrepresentations of education's true value in supporting reintegration.

Beyond recidivism: holistic rationales for prison education

Many stakeholders ascribe to the whole-person approach to education, looking at the personal benefits that can be derived from increased educational attainment. While the majority of studies are concerned with recidivism rates, there are other studies that look at more intrinsic factors in measuring the impact of education programmes. The upcoming section will look at the various theories and pieces of literature that support the provision of education in prisons, supporting the more "whole-person" focus of education and looking beyond the acquisition of rehabilitative skills to the other benefits that it can foster (Mezirow, 1991)

Opportunity theory

It is accepted by most criminologists that a majority of crimes are carried out by the poor, undereducated, disenfranchised members of society who have not had the same viable opportunities for legitimate economic success as most (Warner, 2009). This thinking finds its origins in strain theory (Merton, 1938), which suggests that social structures within society may actually foster crime by holding out the same goals to all members of society without each person having equal means of achieving them. Education, and particularly third-level education, is seen as the means of providing these opportunities of equality and social mobility in areas such as employment, further education and access to services in society for example (Nie et al., 1996; Ubah and Robinson, 2003). Society itself places an "inherent value" on the acquisition of knowledge and skills (Eikeland et al., 2009). In an increasingly meritocratic society, those who are educated are often seen as having a greater status in society. Education is also seen to be one of the most significant predictors of social capital (Putnam, 1995,

2000; Brehm and Rahn, 1997; Helliwell and Putnam, 2007; Huang et al., 2009). Those in possession of more social capital tend to be able to identify and pursue greater opportunities that in turn foster the growth of social capital in a cyclical fashion (Nie et al., 1996). It may be that social capital is a link between education and the creation of opportunities within society. Those who are able to either maintain or increase their social capital while in prison are best placed to then identify and act upon opportunities when they arise after release.

Therefore, the education of prisoners is important in ensuring that they can maximise their role and place in society when they are released by developing the whole person (Eikeland et al., 2009). Participation in prison education provides a person with a chance to increase their opportunities when released from prison. For example, Tewksbury and Stengel (2006) found that 35% of the academic participants and 53% of a cohort taking part in vocational education in prison believed that these academic education programmes would help them get a job when released. Furthermore, in the United States the Select Committee on Narcotics Abuse and Control (1993) reported that 70% of inmates interviewed stated that their main reason for participation in prison education was their interest in self-improvement and in giving themselves the best chance of success when they were released. Porporino and Robinson (1992) reported that 79% of the released prisoners in their study were in full-time employment and most of these had found a job within one month of their release from prison. Thirty percent of the interviewed prisoners felt that their ABE acquired skills had helped them a great deal in seeking employment (Porporino and Robinson, 1992). Various other studies have demonstrated a link between prison education and greater employment levels (Fabelo, 2002; Vacca, 2004; Ellison et al., 2017) and educational uptake after release from prison, showing the various pathways and opportunities that education can foster.

There is a need to be cautious here. The narrow view of an opportunity is that it means developing employment opportunities. Education should promote and reinforce the view of opportunity in the broader, more agentic sense of the word. By developing the whole person, education may support the opportunity to take control of their own life, for example, to choose their own actions and determine their own outcomes. While a part of this may include employment, it is also inclusive of the opportunities and chances to create a good life for themselves in all respects.

Moral development theory

Moral development theory proposes that prison education programmes, particularly programmes in the arts such as literature, history, philosophy and sociology, can have a positive effect on prisoners by strengthening their conscience and promoting moral development. This type of broad-based educational approach creates a better understanding of the world around them (Duguid, 1998). It leads naturally to an increased awareness of other's feelings and thoughts and therefore fosters a type of empathy (Morris, 1962). Highlighting the importance of prison education, Duguid (1998) states that "if there is such a dimension of latent humanity in us all then education becomes a potential key, a means of identifying, liberating, and exploring that humanness" (p. 38). Further weight has been added to this view, with Hobler (1999) stating that moral education promotes a less selfish view of situations and people begin to base decisions on moral reasoning instead of solely on self-satisfaction. Participation in education can change a person's personality, outlook, characteristics and interests, promoting open-mindedness in relation to the world (Schuller et al., 2002). When educational programmes are designed to help prisoners with their social skills, artistic development and emotions, they produce drops in recidivism rates, in addition to increasing the problem-solving and critical-thinking capacity of the person (Ripley, 1993). Participating in ABE in prison was found to help prisoners become more concerned about other people's feelings (Porporino and Robinson, 1992). This is important in terms of their future behaviour and decisions relating to offending. Education can also take greater control over their own lives and decision making by challenging their

> taken for granted frames of reference (meaning perspectives, habits of mind, mind sets) to make them more inclusive, discriminating, open, emotionally capable of change and reflective so that they may generate beliefs and opinions that will prove more true or justified to guide action.
>
> (Mezirow, 2000: 7)

People begin to view things in a more objective, open-minded way (Schuller et al., 2002) and base their decisions on these new critical perspectives and understandings.

Studies in this area have shown that prison education can have significant implications for family relationships. Porporino and Robinson (1992) for instance found that 30% of ABE participants stated that it helped them "very much" with their familial relations, particularly with their children. Participating in broad-based prison education also helps to reduce the instances of corporeal punishment of fathers against their children, showing a degree of moral development and consideration on their part (Bushfield, 2004). Parents also reported being less likely to rely on their children for emotional support having participated in prison education (Bushfield, 2004). It is interesting that these results referred to general education, not specific parenting courses where such outcomes might be expected (see positive outcomes in Bushfield, 2004; Gonzalez et al., 2007 for example). Munoz (2009) cautions against focusing on short, treatment-based programmes that seek a particular outcome such as better parenting skills, in favour a more broad-based educational approach to develop all aspects of the person. Such an approach is in line with the recommendation to focus on developing the whole person. By participating in broad-based prison education, the prisoner will still see the benefits across various aspects of their life.

Social psychological development theory

Social psychological development theory suggests that prison education of any form develops cognitive processes, fosters new behavioural patterns (Ubah and Robinson, 2003) and stimulates positive emotions (Schinkel, 2014). Where people are given access to a wide curriculum of prison education programmes, cognitive skills improve, which in turn may help them after release (Keena and Simmons, 2014). This cognitive development eases the mental strains of imprisonment and they are better able to cope with life after release. It is proposed that various aspects associated with classroom learning have an impact on a person's outlook and reforming behavioural patterns (Reuss, 1999). It can build confidence, self-esteem and self-worth (Van Wyk, 2014), all of which are necessary components in working towards a life without crime. Prison education can contribute significantly to a person's well-being, citizenship and social cohesion (Schuller et al., 2002; Pike and Farley, 2018). Furthermore, people learn new, more appropriate ways to interact with people, which strengthens social ties and social networks (Schuller et al., 2002).

VET was shown to increase morale and decrease behavioural problems among prisoners due to increasing self-control (Callan and Gardner, 2005). Porporino and Robinson (1992) examined the impact of ABE on prisoners, finding evidence of wide impacts on the person. In terms of personal changes, 58% reported that when they got mad at someone they were better able to work it out, and 74% felt more in control of themselves (Porporino and Robinson, 1992). The decision to participate in prison education itself shows maturity and a motivation to escape the negative aspects of a prison sentence (Hackman, 1997). The prisoner turns from committing self-defeating acts (crimes) to a constructive activity which shows a willingness to change behavioural patterns, a cause which is furthered by the education itself in a cyclical fashion (Hackman, 1997). Where a student takes an optimistic, diligent approach to learning in prison, they begin *weaving* together their own common sense with new knowledge, life experiences as well as positive, constructive interactions with other persons, and all of this can shape a person's attitude and thus change negative behavioural patterns (Reuss, 1999).

Referring more specifically to cognitive-based programmes of education, Samenow (2001: 275) states that "by identifying specific thinking patterns common to offenders, it is possible to take a more realistic and effective approach to containing and, in some cases, totally eliminating criminal behaviour". While there is a need for caution in relation to programmes that aim to "treat" the offender (Costelloe and Warner, 2008; Behan, 2014), cognitive thinking programmes are becoming increasingly popular additions to the prison curriculum. Studies have also shown that cognitive model approaches for prisoners can reduce recidivism by as much as 74% over 3 to 15 years (Ross and Ross, 1989). Teaching cognitive problem solving skills to prisoners has been shown to help them gain physical, mental and emotion control when in social situations to the extent that there was a 60.3% reduction in the disciplinary action needed (Spradling, 2001). Similarly, Corrective Thinking Training programmes found a significant improvement in cognitive processing among prisoners who participated in the course, with a particular increase in responsible thinking levels (Bye and Schillinger, 2005). The control group in the same study, who were not participating in educational programmes, saw a decrease in their levels of responsible thinking, which appears to demonstrate the harmful effect the prison sentence has on cognitive function (Bye and Schillinger, 2005).

A significant element of social psychological development theory is focused on changing patterns of behaviour through the development of cognitive processes through the use of treatment-based programmes. Benefits such as those results reported in the preceding literature are positive, yet there is also a consensus that cognitive and behavioural programmes do not seem to have any greater impact on reported benefits or outcomes for prisoners than other educational programmes with a broader curriculum. According to Ubah and Robinson (2003), most forms of education can impact cognitive and behavioural processes to bring about change. Academic and vocational education, for example, have been shown to increase levels of self-confidence and self-esteem and belief in a prisoner's own ability to succeed (Callan and Gardner, 2005). Therefore, it is education itself, rather than specific programmes, that produce the social psychological results. Advocating for these narrow "treatment" programmes can be harmful to the overall educational curriculum in prison and are representative of the "what works" influence. The danger is that these will become the mainstay of the education offered, with more mainstream and holistic curriculums being reduced.

Counterbalancing the impact of incarceration

Prison is a deeply anti-social and harmful environment. It has lasting social and psychological impacts for those who experience it. The rationale of using prison education as a means of rebalancing the harmful impact of incarceration was outlined by the Council of Europe (1990), stating that education during a prison sentence is a way of addressing the abnormal and destructive effects of incarceration. Education is a mechanism of normalisation in the alien and criminogenic prison environment. Clemner (1940) for example refers to the process of prisonisation, which in its most simple form is the institutionalisation that happens during the period of incarceration. The inability to exercise autonomy results in a self-depletion of a person's resources that is replaced by harmful prison-based norms, resulting in a further distancing of the person from society and adding increasing strain to their personal relationships. Furthermore, prisoners must suffer the various "pains of imprisonment" (Sykes, 1958).

Sykes (1958) categorised these into five broad "pains" as follows: (1) loss of liberty; (2) desirable goods and services; (3) heterosexual relationships/sexual frustration; (4) autonomy and (5) security. These will be experienced to a greater or lesser extent dependent upon the individual and other factors but will almost always have a detrimental impact by corroding the person's own identity and sense of self, thus exacerbating the mental impact of the prison sentence (Sykes, 1958). Ongoing experience of these pains could have an overall hardening impact on the criminal, thus having a further criminogenic effect (Sykes, 1958). Crewe (2011) has added to this work and notes that while the pains of imprisonment have varied over time due to improvement in prison conditions, there have been other factors such as increased punitiveness, increased sentences and more frequent use of imprisonment that add further pain. Where such pain is aimed at the mind of the person, there is a need for rebalancing this hurt. Opportunities for self-development are key to reducing these pains (Liebling, 2011). Education can be a means of addressing these harmful aspects of imprisonment (Warner, 2007). In light of the foregoing theories, such as moral development theory and social psychological development theory, which both outlined the role that education can play in the development of the person, their personality, their relationships and their life opportunities, it is clear that prison education can have a significant role in mitigating the harshness of the prison sentence. Education can promote a positive outlook, create self-awareness and promote cognitive change. It is therefore a powerful tool when trying to avoid these harms of imprisonment and in minimising institutionalisation throughout the prison sentence.

Improved literacy

Many prisoners struggle with literacy issues (Morgan and Kett, 2003). This curtails their ability to engage with education (Manger and Langelid, 2005) and to seek legitimate opportunities in society (Vandala, 2019) and can therefore be highly criminogenic. Literacy has been linked to recidivism rates, with findings showing that lower levels of literacy are predictive of more persistent levels of reoffending, and those with lower levels of literacy tend to commit more serious offences (Rucklidge et al., 2013). Those who do not possess the basic academic skills that are seen to be prerequisites for participating in society are at a distinct disadvantage and require help frequently (Bartlett et al., 2001). A person's entitlement to education to mitigate these disadvantages provides a strong rationale for the provision of prison education (Warner, 2018).

In the Irish context, 53% of prisoners who participated in a study had literacy levels in the two lowest categories, compared with 22.6% of the general public (Morgan and Kett, 2003). A large number of prisoners had such low levels of skills that it would be impossible for them to meet the challenges of modern life (Morgan and Kett, 2003). Morgan and Kett (2003) recommended that prison education ought to prioritise the educational needs of those prisoners with the lowest level of literacy. Throughout the prison system in most jurisdictions, literacy training is an integral part of the education being offered (Hawley, 2011). However, not all adults wish to attend the school or formal literacy classes, as there is a fear and shame associated with lower literacy levels (Morgan and Kett, 2003). Some programmes have been developed in which literacy is taught in a person's own cell and can be peer-led learning, such as the Toe by Toe programme in Irish prisons (Ahern, 2011). Literacy can also be taught through interaction with other activities and subjects such as vocational programmes and arts, for example (Hurry et al., 2005). These efforts to ingrain and make literacy training more attractive and accessible is not surprising given the links that exist between education and opportunities for success as outlined under the previous headings. The importance of literacy training cannot be understated, not only because of its relevance to further education in prison (Morgan and Kett, 2003) but also given the contribution it can make to the quality of the day-to-day life and the personal development of the person.

Human rights obligations

International obligations relating to the treatment of those in custody impose a duty to provide prison education. Following is a consideration of the framework of laws and standards that exist both internationally and at the European level in relation to prison education. These give an indication of expected best practices and convey the prevailing attitudes among policy makers and legislators in relation to penal matters. They also reflect the various rationales for the provision of prison education that were discussed earlier.

Prison education as an international human right

Prisoners, like all citizens, have a human right to education and training. This right is recognised in various international provisions. In the United Nations report entitled "The Right to Education of Persons in Detention", Munoz (2009) states that while prison education is often provided with a view to reducing recidivism, optimising reintegration and increasing employability, education is far more than a mechanism of change; it is "an imperative in its own right" (p. 4). The report recognises the role of education in fulfilling potential and in personal development. Munoz (2009) points out that while education is to be promoted in prisons, it takes place in an environment that is opposed to its liberating potential. This backdrop of hostility towards education can be a result of broader penal policy objectives based on retribution, deterrence and even rehabilitation that clash with the notion of providing education to prisoners as a human right as opposed to either not at all or simply to reduce recidivism. The report was critical of education that was based entirely on medical, cognitive or opportunistic models that focus on addressing psychological, moral or skills deficiencies, expressing the opinion that they were devoid of human dignity.

In keeping with the recommendations of the Council of Europe (1990), the European Rules 1987 and 2006 and various other documents, the report goes on to recommend that prison education should be aimed at development of the whole person and minimising the negative impact of imprisonment through the provision of a broad curriculum of both formal and informal education including literacy programmes, vocational training, creative and cultural activities, social education and higher education. It also recommended that each state should ascertain the dispositional barriers to participation in education and take measures to help prisoners overcome these barriers, along with ensuring that education activities can be continued after release.

Council of Europe: "Education in Prison Report"

The Council of Europe's (1990) "Education in Prison Report" sets out various recommendations for best practice for the provision of education in the correctional setting and has been the benchmark for the provision of prison education across Europe for several decades. The report takes a broad view of education, as encompassing material that will develop the cultural, creative and social awareness of the person and serve each person's own aspirations. Recommendation 1 states that "(a)ll prisoners shall have access to education, which is envisaged as consisting of classroom subjects, vocational education, creative and cultural activities, physical education and sports, social education and library facilities". Recommendation 1 therefore has a dual role. It stipulates that all prisoners should have access to education, and it also recommends a broad curriculum of activities, conceptualising education in a very expansive manner. This takes a broader view of education, as encompassing material that will also develop the cultural, creative and social awareness of the person and serve each person's own aspirations. It allows the space for other programmes to be introduced in prison schools that might act as gateway subjects to attract learners to the school environment, such as mindfulness and yoga, for example. While adult education is not mentioned in this recommendation, this wider approach to education is in line with the adult education philosophy. King (2019) recommends the revision of this recommendation to include information technology in order to reflect the evolving world into which prisoners will be released. The inclusion of a closing statement "to enable them to reach their full potential" is also recommended (King, 2019: 14), which would reflect the aim of education as being to serve the person, rather than to serve society.

This broad and comprehensive educational approach is also echoed in Recommendation 3, which suggests a "whole-person" approach to education be promoted and that an aim of prison education ought to be to "develop the whole person bearing in mind his or her social, economic and cultural context" (Council of Europe, 1990). This reflects the notion that whatever education curriculum is provided in each jurisdiction, it should be provided with the aim of developing the person and their identity as opposed to simply being provided with a view to reducing recidivism. It would seem to suggest that courses or curricula that consist of programmes aimed at behavioural change or employability are not the optimal form of education – in isolation at least. Rather, education that focuses on social and cultural aspects of the person are also to be encouraged in order to facilitate the development of the learner and address their own personal needs. These recommendations reflect the notion that educational provision should be aimed at developing the person and their identity as opposed to simply being provided with a view to reducing recidivism or as a form of "treatment". In calling for a form of social education to support the person in prison and on release, it takes a holistic view to minimising both the harms of imprisonment and the barriers to reintegration. This category is very broad and could potentially include modules such as communications, healthcare, independent/home living (cooking, cleaning, budgeting, low-level maintenance skills), societal values and norms and coping skills. The provisions of the report are indicative of the whole-person approach to education, rather than simply providing skills that are linked to treatment, employability or reducing recidivism.

Recommendation 7 calls for the use of "*appropriate adult education methods*" by teachers. The report does not clarify exactly what is meant by "appropriate" methods. The concept of adult education is explored in detail later in this chapter, but this phrase appears to refer to those forms of education that address the needs, goals and development of the person, relevant to their own experience (Knowles, 1970). It could be argued that a significant part of achieving this is having access to a wide array of resources outside of the classroom that support learning, such as a well-stocked library that prisoners should have access to at least once a week.

Finally, Recommendation 13 suggests that social education should be included in the prison curriculum so as to enable the prisoner to manage daily life both inside and outside of prison. This demonstrates the broader thinking around prison education, that it is not simply a tool of reintegration, but it exists to support the person during their prison sentence and to manage life after release. It also reflects the need to teach core life skills and social skills as opposed to relying solely on more traditional school subjects. This category is very broad and could potentially include education that addresses any of the needs that a prisoner would have after release. These could be communications, healthcare, independent/home living (cooking, cleaning, budgeting, low-level maintenance skills), societal values and norms and coping skills for the various hurdles they will face when released. Again this is indicative of the "whole-person" approach to education, rather than simply providing skills that are linked to employability or reducing recidivism.

These recommendations are comprehensive and have been instrumental in providing a model of best practice to those developing prison education curriculum in recent decades. However, the report is becoming outdated and there is a growing need to update these recommendations to reflect advances in modern society such as the inclusion of ICT, for example, to enable prisoners to optimise their ability to actively engage with society after release. This is particularly important for those who have served longer sentences.

Council of Europe: European Prison Rules 1987 and 2006

The 1987 and 2006 European Prison Rules set out the rules for the government and running of prisons in Europe. These rules exist as a model of best practice as opposed to an enforceable set of rules. While they refer to the entirety of the prison system, there are several principles contained therein that are relevant to the development of a philosophy of rehabilitation and education in prisons. While the rules are prisoner-centred in nature, there is evidence of a growing degree of punitiveness notable in the tone of the 2006 version of the rules.

Taking the earlier version of the rules as a starting point, Rule 3 sets out the purpose of the rules and recognises a desire for prison interventions to preserve the self-respect of the person and to "develop their sense of responsibility and encourage those attitudes and skills that will assist them to return to society with the best chance of leading law abiding and self-supporting lives after their release". This ethos is reinforced later by Rules 64 and 65, which highlight the type of treatment a prisoner should expect beyond their daily routine that might serve to minimise these negative effects of the prison sentence. Rule 64 insists that the deprivation of liberty itself is the punishment and imprisonment should not create further punishment than this. Rule 65 carries on this humanistic approach, insisting that human dignity should be upheld and efforts be made to minimise the harms of imprisonment, to strengthen links with community and family and to provide opportunities to develop skills and aptitudes that improve the person's prospects of reintegration.

Reading the three rules together, Warner (2002a) sums up these ideas as follows:

1. The experience of incarceration has damaging consequences for the person and this ought to be minimised;
2. the prisoner's self-development ought to be facilitated by the prison and opportunities should be made available to the prisoner to do so; and
3. a proactive approach to reintegration and supporting themselves in a law-abiding manner when released should be fostered within the prison system.

These ideas are in line with the adult education philosophy. Rule 65 appears to look towards the person, rather than the "offender" and recognises that the person should be afforded dignity and respect (Costelloe and Warner, 2003). Punishment ought to be limited to the deprivation of liberty and not the stripping of self-dignity through degradation, humiliation or abuse (Costelloe and Warner, 2003). Prison undoubtedly causes a great degree of harm to the person, with Liebling and Maruna (2005) proposing that during the prison sentence a prisoner experiences harm in the form of fear, anxiety, loneliness, trauma, depression, injustice, powerlessness, violence and uncertainty. The recognition of such harm in the rules and the expressed ideal that this ought to be minimised is a positive for the promotion of prison education. This idea of the detrimental impact of imprisonment challenges the notion that "prison works" (Costelloe and Warner, 2003). Costelloe (2003) questions whether the aim of minimising the harmful impact of imprisonment acts as a way of normalising prison life and as such this aim should be rejected. However, the one of the greatest harms of the prison sentence is institutionalisation, where the prison environment is normalised. Perhaps the best way in which prison education minimises the harms of imprisonment is by protecting against this institutionalisation and normalising of life in prison. It is proposed that this is a result of the insulating effect of prison education against the assimilation of the person into prison culture and through the protection of their social capital levels. It maintains a distance between the prisoner and the more harmful elements of prison life, creating both a physical and mental distancing between the prisoner and the world of the prison. In fact, whether we reject the aim or not, prison education nonetheless minimises the harm of imprisonment through these mechanisms; there is little that can be done to stop that. The outcomes of the research presented later in this book show that prison education and time in the school can act as a barrier to the more negative aspects of the prison. It appears that a combination of the education and spending time in a space that is perceived by participants to be external to the prison allows the promotion of positive changes in the way the person thinks of and sees themselves and the world. While this is a simplistic overview of the findings and the various ways in which prison education protects against the harms of imprisonment are explored in far greater details later in this book, prison education makes the prison sentence more bearable but it does not normalise it.

While the updated 2006 rules reinforce the requirement that education and training be provided to those in prisons throughout Europe, this iteration does not appear to be as person-centred as the 1987 version of the rules. The overall impression is that the 2006 rules are primarily concerned with reintegration and rehabilitation, to the exclusion of the concepts of respect and dignity for the prisoner. For example, Rule 6 recommends the prison sentence be managed in such a way as to facilitate reintegration after release. Furthermore, Rule 102.1 (the equivalent of Rule 65 in the 1987 version) states that the regime for sentenced prisoners shall be designed to help them live a responsible and crime-free life. While Article 5 calls for the normalisation of prison life and Rule 102.2 reflects the minimisation of harm in line with Rule 64 of the 1987 rules, it appears that any references to self-respect, dignity and person-centred approach to treatment have been removed. This reflects the increasingly punitive attitudes in criminal justice systems throughout Europe and internationally.

Prison education: approaches and philosophies

What is prison education?

The previous section explored the rational for the provision of prison education and outlined some of the most important reasons for the provision of education in prisons. However, it also showed a lack of a single, agreed aim of prison education. Such uncertainty regarding what prison education should or should not achieve leads to issues with delivery and curriculum development. Hawley (2011) asks whether prison education should be conceptualised as entirely classroom-based learning or whether it should be wider, including life skills, vocational training and so on. The approach varies from one country to another depending on penal objectives, resources and the model of prison education (Langelid et al., 2009) adopted by that country. Many countries offer both training and education in their prisons. These should be treated differently according to Costelloe and Warner (2014) given that training is provided with a view to providing employment-based skills, whereas education is about understanding something and the value that accrues to the person from that knowledge and understanding. Education is more about critical reflection and analysis and applying knowledge in a variety of scenarios. Training is focused on particular employment-based scenarios. For example, training as a block layer will provide skills that will serve the person on a building site but is not concerned about the application of wider soft skills such as critical thinking or self-awareness. Education is more concerned with the "other" learning associated with knowledge acquisition, such as the analytical ability and insight into one's own self that can support the person every day. For this reason, Costelloe and Warner (2014) contend that education that focuses too greatly on employability is not education as it is conceptualised in the adult education philosophy or the approach to prison education envisaged in the Council of Europe (1990) recommendations. The approach that each state adopts in relation to prison education is often a general reflection of the prevailing penal attitude of that state. In Ireland, for example, there is a clear distinction between education and training (Maslauskaite and Mooney, 2018). Education is provided by an external education and training board, whereas training is provided by trained prison officers (Maslauskaite and Mooney, 2018). The provision of treatment-based programmes as a form of education is also questioned. These are generally more therapeutic than educational in nature and aimed at fixing a particular character flaw or a criminogenic aspect of the personality. Munoz (2009) cautioned against the representation of these treatment-based programmes as education in prisons. His report was highly critical of such forms of education, expressing the opinion that medical, cognitive or opportunistic models that focus on addressing psychological, moral or skills deficiencies were devoid of human dignity. This reluctance towards viewing treatment-based programmes as education is also reflected in Parson and Langenbach's (1993) decision to use GED participants rather than those from substance abuse or self-help programmes in their study since the latter do not satisfy the criteria of education in that they do not take the same sustained, time-consuming and systematic effort that a GED programme would. It is therefore concerning that there appears to be a growing reliance on treatment-based programmes of "education" and on skills-based programmes. In some ways, this might be a response to two related issues. First, there is a growing demand to move towards education that satisfies the goals of rehabilitation and reduced reoffending through skills development and employment readiness. For this reason, training programmes are an attractive option for satisfying this aim. Second, society is becoming increasingly evidence-based. There is a desire to ensure that funds are applied only to those programmes that are proven effective. Vocational training and treatment-based programmes are far easier to examine empirically, since the outcome is defined and certain. Therefore, these courses yield the empirical results that are desired by funders but that can be far more difficult to gain in studies examining traditional education. In this way, the "what works" movement can undermine the provision of education its true form. The adult education approach that is favoured by the Council of Europe (1990) and that is the foundation of the philosophy of prison education in many jurisdictions advocates for education that is broad in its scope, encourages critical reflection and focuses on the both knowledge but also the accrual of soft skills that are applicable to all aspects of a person's life. In many ways this is education in its true form. This concept will be explored later.

The adult education approach

Recommendation 7 of the COE's (1990) Education in Prison report calls for "adult education methodologies and practices" to be used in prison schools. One of the earliest theorists to explore the concept of adult education stated that its purpose is "to put meaning to the whole of life" (Lindeman, 1926: 5). Adult education is often described as "second chance" education, giving adults the chance to re-access education to address deficits in past schooling or to diversify or up skill in their current field. It is viewed as a means of empowerment that facilitates a person in reaching their full personal and educational potential. Article 3 of the Hamburg Declaration describes adult education as a mechanism whereby adults "develop their abilities, enrich their knowledge and improve their technical or professional qualifications or turn them in a new direction to meet their own needs and those of their society". The aim of adult education was outlined by UNESCO (2019) as "to equip people with the necessary capabilities to exercise and realise their rights and take control of their destinies. It promotes personal and professional development, thereby supporting more active engagement by adults in their societies, communities and environments". These aspects of the adult education approach are also reflected in Ireland's Department of Education and Science (2000) white paper on adult education that outlines six sociopersonal areas that are strengthened by the adult education approach. These are (1) consciousness raising; (2) citizenship; (3) cohesion; (4) competitiveness; (5) cultural development; and (6) community development (Department of Education and Science, 2000). The first three of these elements relate to the individual and the second three relate to the wider, societal benefits of adult education approaches. In terms of the individual benefits, conscious raising conceptualises adult education as an empowering process of personal development and self-discovery, enabling a person to reach their full human potential. This is achieved by creating links between their individual experience and wider structural factors, which will become quite relevant in the discussion of structural theories of desistance in Chapter 6. Citizenship is enhanced through the individual's capacity to engage more proactively in society and begin to actively participate in the overall shaping of society as they grow in self-confidence, awareness and social responsibility. Increased social capital and the empowerment of those who have experienced social disadvantage are implications of greater cohesion (Department of Education and Science, 2000).

The remaining three benefits of adult education are broader in nature and relate to the increased competitiveness that results from a more skilled workforce, the greater depth of culture brought about by more educated and reflective citizens, and the community development that is facilitated when all citizens, particularly those who were previously marginalised, take a more active role in civil life (Department of Education and Science, 2000). Each of these elements can be seen to link back to the various rationales put forward as supporting the provision of prison education earlier in this chapter.

Article 3 of the Hamburg Declaration outlined earlier refers to the power of adult education to act as a mechanism for turning people in a new direction. This is echoed in Mezirow's theory of transformational learning (1991), an important part of the adult education framework of literature. This theory proposes that every person's outlook and perspective are defined by their own meaning structures. Meaning structures are made up of both meaning schemes and meaning perspectives. Meaning schemes include a person's knowledge, values and beliefs. Meaning perspectives are made up of a person's world view, their understanding of social structures, moral dimensions such as the ability to know right from wrong and points of view, among other things (Mezirow, 1991). Transformational learning theory and perspective transformation are concerned with how these meaning structures and their various elements are revised within a person through learning. By changing how a person views the world, their values and moral understandings, it may be possible that their behaviours will ultimately change. When applied to the prison education context, perhaps their offending behaviour will cease. Mezirow (1997) also suggests that the goal of adult educators must be to guide learners to transform to grow, to mature intellectually and to change through critical reflection of one's beliefs and values. This relates more to self-directed learning, as opposed to directed learning.

Self-directed learning is an important aspect of adult education, and there are several reasons that fostering self-directed learning is important (Knowles, 1975). One of these reasons is that self-directed learning mirrors the processes of psychological development. As people mature, lives become increasingly self-directed and people take more responsibility for their own direction. This process can be promoted and developed through the process of adult education (Knowles, 1975). Self-directed learners do not wait to be taught by a teacher but rather are also capable of taking the initiative (Knowles, 1975). This promotes a greater level of self-responsibility in a person's approach to learning, and this is also an important skill in other aspects of a person's life. The concept of self-direction might also be applied to the ability of offenders to self-direct their own lives, by taking responsibility for their choices and paths and their own life changes. While prison education is mainly teacher-led, there is a strong element of self-direction in the primary decision to attend the prison school and overcome the various institutional barriers that exist to attending the school each day. Furthermore, this is also related to the idea of social psychological development theory, which claims that education fosters maturity, responsibility and new attitudes which are also in line with Mezirow's (1991) theory of transformational learning.

There are several important points that arise in light of the foregoing points on the adult education approach that are important in the context of the prison setting. First is the broad nature of adult education; it is not merely formal classroom-based learning but all practices that develop the abilities, knowledge and personality of a person. This is in line with the broad, holistic approach to prison education that is widely recommended (see for example Munoz, 2009; Council of Europe, 1990). Second, the aims and purposes of adult education outlined earlier all reflect the idea of enhancing the ability of the person to engage more actively as a citizen, such as through civic engagement and strong roles within their community (Department of Education and Science, 2000; UNESCO, 2019). This is particularly relevant to the notions of opportunity theory and social psychological theory explored earlier in this chapter as being rationales for the provision of prison education. Furthermore, this also relates directly to the concept of social capital and the ability to both participate in society and draw on the resources with the community in a reciprocal fashion, all of which are important aspects of social bonds theory in the desistance literature. Costelloe (2003) calls for a more social capital than human capital based approach to prison education, which could be seen to be satisfied through the adult education philosophy in prison schools. The final point that is pertinent to prison education is the notion of adult education as a possible turning point in the lives of those who undertake it. The revision of meaning structures, transforming the way a person views the world or changing morals and values (Mezirow, 1997) are again echoed in the various theories outlined earlier in this chapter, such as moral development theory (Morris, 1962; Duguid, 1998; Hobler, 1999) and social psychological development theory (Reuss, 1999;

Ubah and Robinson, 2003). In terms of desistance, this is perhaps the most important benefit of the adult education approach. However, any such transformations may be undermined by emerging into a society where opportunities are taken away from them and obstacles are placed in their path by reason of their past offending. In fact, the most significant critique of this theory in terms of prison education is that it fails to take account of the society into which prisoners return (Costelloe, 2003). While transformations may occur in the prisoner, these transformations are not always recognised or facilitated by society. This point by Costelloe (2003) is apt, considering the increasing punitiveness of society and the increasing demonisation of the offender. Prisoners may benefit fully from the education they undertake in prison. This point will be elaborated upon later in this chapter and in subsequent chapters, particularly when looking at the narratives of those interviewed who were very mindful of the impact stigma and prejudice they would face when they were released.

The adult education philosophy underpins the provision of prison education in many countries across Europe, in line with the recommendations made by the Council of Europe in the Education in Prison Report (1990) and the European Prison Rules (1987, 2006) and by Munoz (2009) in the UN Report on the Right to Education in Detention. The foregoing section outlines the justification for this. The idea of adult education as a journey and process for the learner rather than a specific outcome, with transformational capacity through enhancing the whole person, sits well with the various rationales for the provision of education in prisons. It will also be shown in later chapters that these points align well with many aspects of the desistance literature. While this approach is increasingly vulnerable to punitive influences, a continued adherence to the principles of adult education in the provision of education in prison is to be favoured in the best interests of the person. The next section will look at the ways in which this approach is being threatened by changes in modern penal discourse.

Competing aims of prison education

The existence of a formalised set of rules, standards and recommendations within European and international legal discourse does not of itself mean that every country has a similar approach to prison education. There are many different schools of thought in relation to the philosophy, purpose and provision of prison education, both in Europe and beyond. In fact, it could also be said that the concept of "education" in prisons of itself causes confusion, with many jurisdictions having a significant divergence in their educational offerings in prison, ranging from short, treatment-based behavioural programmes to mainstream school subjects, vocational programmes or arts and self-development modules. It may be any one of these in isolation or it may be a mix of all of these and more depending on the jurisdiction. The provision of education in prison is a basic human right (Munoz, 2009), and beyond this there are various other reasons for its provision, depending on the perspective of the particular stakeholder or jurisdiction in question (Hawley, 2011). All of this makes it difficult to ascertain one particular aim of prison education or rationale for its provision.

The Council of Europe's Education in Prisons Report (1990), the European Prison Rules (1987, 2006) and the Report of the Special Rapporteur on the Right to Education (Munoz, 2009), along with other pieces of literature, reflect the various purposes of prison education. On the one hand, the "what works" movement views prison education as a tool of rehabilitation, to provide prisoners with the skills required to reintegrate successfully into society on release and gain steady employment. However, there are others who believe education should be provided purely as a human right, as a means of personal, whole-person development and as a means of mitigating the immense personal harm caused by serving a sentence of imprisonment. Hawley (2011), for example, points out the dichotomy that exists in relation to the aims of providing prison education. She terms the opposing perspectives the esoteric and prosaic view. The esoteric view of educational provision refers to the idea that the purpose of prison education is to lessen the harmful impacts of imprisonment on the person (Council of Europe, 1990; Costelloe and Warner, 2008; Behan, 2008). The prosaic view sees education in its more structural sense, aiming to up skill prisoners and ready them for reintegration and employment (Hawley, 2011). This is also noted by Munoz (2009), who reflects the dual esoteric and prosaic views together where he states that education should be aimed at the full development of the person but also to minimise the harms of incarceration and to improve their chances of a successful reintegration and increase self-esteem and morale.

The aims of education are diverse, and the perspective held in relation to the purpose of education will often depend on the stakeholder in question, rather than the jurisdiction's policy. Educators and teachers traditionally view education in the esoteric sense, seeking to enhance the "whole person", to strengthen their mind, enhance their knowledge and help them to minimise the harms of imprisonment (Warner, 2002a; Hawley, 2011). From this perspective, prison education is intrinsic in nature because its value is not connected to any external validatory measure. From the outset, prison education was envisaged as being inclusive of a curriculum that included arts, languages, critical thinking and philosophy in order to promote the emergence of a "citizen" from prison when the sentence was served (MacCormick, 1931). Examples of such an approach can be found in the policy documents published in the states that aspire to this type of education. For example, the preface to the Norwegian policy document "Another Spring" (Norwegian Ministry of Education and Research, 2005: xi) acknowledges that protecting the civil rights of prisoners is key for a successful return to society and further states that education "is meant to help to cultivate, assist in coping with society and becoming self-reliant and impart knowledge, enabling the individual to make the most of his talents and contribute to wealth creation in Norwegian society". Austin H. MacCormick

(1931: 11) wrote "consider the prisoner as primarily an adult in need of education and only secondarily as a criminal in need of reform".

By contrast, reflecting the "what works" approach, prison staff, policy makers, politicians and funders often tend to believe education is provided with a view to more extrinsic rewards – such as successful reintegration and ultimately employment (Hawley, 2011). Costelloe and Warner (2014) draw attention to the contrast that exists between the two perspectives by comparing the tone of the Norwegian document "Another Spring" (outlined with accompanying quote earlier) with the UK document "Reducing Reoffending through Skills and Employment" (Department of Education and Skills, 2005), which was published in the same year and views education as a means of reducing reoffending and increasing employability of the offender. It appears that in many countries, at a governmental level at least, the rationale for the provision of prison education is to reduce future crime rates, rehabilitate and increase employability – thus entering into a cost-benefit analysis of educational provision in the hope of a significant return in terms of the reduced cost of crime due to lower recidivism. Indeed, such an approach seems to be echoed in the newest version of the European Prison Rules 2006, where the sentence and treatments are directed towards the reintegration of the offender.

While rehabilitation and reduced recidivism are worthy aims of education, since the offender still benefits from the intervention, Warner (2007) warns against relying on education as just a rehabilitative tool. Prison education can help in minimising the damaging impact incarceration has on the prisoner (Council of Europe, 1990; Warner, 2002a). However, maintaining humanisation and citizenship in such an abnormal situation can be extremely difficult. Education is one of the ways in which a prisoner can escape prison life and the prison mindset during their sentence. By keeping the prison curriculum close to that which they could access externally, it ensures some degree of normality and of course facilitates further learning on release in line with the adult education approach. The perspective adopted in each individual state is also often a reflection of where each country lies on the care custody continuum. Those states that tend more towards the provision of education for holistic and intrinsic reasons will generally have more of a "care orientation" throughout their entire penal system. On the contrary, the further a state is orientated towards the provision of education to serve extrinsic benefits the more evidence there will be of a "custody-heavy orientation" visible throughout their penal system.

Reports issued by state bodies and research carried out in various jurisdictions give some indication of the approach taken in each state, and while this varies from country to country, due to the existence of Council of Europe Recommendations (1990) and European Prison Rules 1987 and 2006, the provision around Europe tends to encompass a broad curriculum. The form of education offered and the tone of official governmental reports often give a good indication of the attitude to and main aim of education in that state – though of course this may differ from the philosophies and the type of education the teachers themselves aspire to in the classroom. Following is a very brief overview of the main approaches in the European context.

England

The official position taken by government and policy makers in the United Kingdom reflects the more narrow perspective that is cautioned against by Costelloe and Warner (2014). The 2005 report "Reducing Reoffending through Skills and Employment" seeks to tackle reoffending through training in skills to promote employability. The key aims are to

> improve offenders skills and job prospects . . . build a modern correctional system, focused on rehabilitation, working in partnership with employers and those able to provide high-quality training . . . with more relevant skills training led by employer needs.
>
> (Department of Education and Skills, 2005: 5)

The language used throughout the report alludes to a system that is motivated by public safety and crime reduction. While these are worthy aims, the person is lost, with the focus of education placed on employability for rehabilitation and meeting employer needs. This has been reinforced recently with the publication of the Ministry for Justice Departmental Plan 2019–2022, where they key objective is set out as being to reduce reoffending and improve the life chances of prisoners. This is to be achieved through access to education, training and employment for prisoners during their sentence, with a view to developing competencies and skills to maximise the chances of securing stable employment after release (Ministry of Justice, 2019). The ministry also acknowledges that education can have a transformative effect on the perspective of the person that helps them come to see themselves and the world differently, which in turn reduces reoffending (Ministry of Justice, 2019). This is further evidence of a narrow view of education, provided to reduce reoffending. Even while talking of the broader benefits of education for the person, these benefits are only important insofar as they result in a reduction in offending.

On a more positive note, one of the most important developments in the United Kingdom in relation to prison education in recent years was the 2016 report by Sally Coates that reviewed the provision of education in English prisons and made many important recommendations. She stated that education should be provided for individuals to unlock potential, gain employment and become assets to their communities. Reflecting the holistic rationale for the provision of education, she proposed that education be composed of basic skills, vocational skills, personal and social development, art, music, sport and ICT, among other things (Coates, 2016). This broad curriculum is indicative of a "whole-person" approach to education and in line with the European Prison Rules 2006 and the recommendations in the Council of Europe's

(1990) Education in Prisons Report. When compared with the ethos of the Ministry for Justice in their 2019–2022 plan, it demonstrates the competing perspectives of the various actors involved in prison education. However, it appears at the governmental level, at least, the focus is on the provision of education as a means of reducing reoffending.

Scandinavia

Many of the Scandinavian countries reflect the dual purposes of education in their approaches. The Norwegian government views education as both a human right and a means of preventing recidivism (Norwegian Ministry of Education and Research, 2005). Denmark's approach, while acknowledging the requirement that prison time be as "normalised" as possible in order to minimised the harmful effects of imprisonment, also sees the provision of prison education as being a means of rehabilitation (Raundrup, 2009). In Finland, the provision of prison education is geared towards the reintegration of the prisoner into society after release (Karsikas et al., 2009). However the Finnish "Principles of Enforcement of Prison Sentences" state that imprisonment is the deprivation of liberty and any punishment or harm beyond that ought to be minimised. It is also maintained that prison education can promote personal growth and development, improve individuals' ability to cope in society and facilitate a crime-free life (Karsikas et al., 2009). This approach by Finland again reflects the dual purpose of educating for both the person and society.

Denmark appears to embraces the idea of normalisation of treatment in prison (Raundrup, 2009). One of the principles of imprisonment in Denmark, particularly in relation to treatment of prisoners, is that time spent in prison be as "normal" as possible so as to avoid the harmful effects of imprisonment (Raundrup, 2009). In terms of normalisation, Denmark's Prison and Probation Directorate stipulates that a broad range of educational options be available to prisoners that can be adapted to the needs of prisoners where necessary and that prisoners should be allowed day release where appropriate to pursue education in the community (Raundrup, 2009). This demonstrates the way in which education can overcome the often insurmountable wall that appears to exist between prison and society and minimises the distance between the prisoner and the society into which they will be released. This perspective represents a very person-centred approach to prison education at a governmental level which appears to be far more esoteric than most other states outlined.

Ireland

The standards and vision for prison education in Ireland are contained in the Joint IPS/ETBI Education Strategy 2019–2022. The is aim to provide education that "helps people in custody cope with their sentence, achieve personal development, prepare for life after release and establish an appetite and capacity for lifelong learning" (Irish Prison Service, 2019: 1). The focus is on the provision of programmes that are relevant, holistic and multidisciplinary and prioritise those with basic education needs (Irish Prison Service, 2019). A balance between practical and accredited education along with personal development opportunities is also seen to be an important aspect of education provision under the strategy. The mission is to "provide a programme that is quality assured, learner centred and that facilitates lifelong learning while helping persons in custody respond to their sentence through personal development and positive renewal" (Irish Prison Service, 2019: 2). These goals are very person-centred, focused on the needs of the person and their own development. The influence of both the Council of Europe's Education in Prisons Report (1990) and the European Prison Rules (1987, 2006) are evident in the approach set out in the document. The focus on coping with the sentence is the primary aim, in line with the Council of Europe's (1990) call for education to minimise the harmful impact of the prison sentence. Moreover, the aim of providing broad, holistic and multidisciplinary education reflects the whole-person and adult education approaches to prison education. It appears that the strategy is heavily influenced by the standards set out in the European framework relating to prison policy. There is also a notable absence of any references to rehabilitation or reduced reoffending in the strategy which is extremely positive in demonstrating the person-centred approach to education being advocated in Irish prisons.

However, organisational aims, much like international standards, are often aspirational and grandiose statements, routinely overlooked in the day-to-day affairs of an organisation. In theory, while the education policies of most countries are in line with the European rules (1987, 2006) and recommendations (1989), to a greater or lesser extent, the question is whether these aims are actually being met on the ground and in practice. Regardless of the approach suggested in strategies, plans and policy documents, the most important philosophies will be those of the teachers and prison officers in each prison and school. Their attitudes will ultimately set the ethos of education in their own schools and classrooms. It is important, therefore, that officers and teachers reflect on their own philosophies. While the aims of education might be competing, there is scope in every classroom to ensure that the holistic, person-centred approach prevails and that each student is given the space to take what they need from education, rather than having their experience be predetermined by penal aims and provisions.

The influence of punitiveness

While many states officially subscribe to the notion that they provide education for the dual purposes of enhancing the whole person and also promoting resettlement and employment, these are often the official policies adopted by the country and can be just aspirational in nature. While those responsible for providing education might adhere to the holistic and person-centred views in the classroom and aim to provide education in line with the recommendations, this is not to say that they are not hindered in doing so. In increasingly punitive societies, the provision of education in line with these principles is becoming more difficult as a clash of interests occurs. Many countries are experiencing what Garland (2001) termed the "culture of control" and its associated punitive response to crime, described aptly by Warner (2018: 3) as "penal climate change". In an effort to control crime rates, the need to be tough on crime and satisfy public opinion operates to the detriment of logical and theory-based penological decisions by those responsible for implementing criminal justice policies. In fact, while there is often an associated drive to find "what works", many policy makers ignore the evidence in order to satisfy a growing punitive discourse (Warner, 2018).

Increased incarceration, the upsurge in retributive rather than rehabilitation-led policies and the return of the victim with the consequent demonisation of offenders are all indicators of the culture of control (Garland, 2001). Under this model of penality, the care custody continuum is significantly skewed towards the custody element, with little but policy-based lip service and the goodwill and efforts of some dedicated people on the care side to soften the impact of these policies. Warner (2002b) refers to the Anglo-American model of imprisonment as being characterised by similar features, such as the negative stereotyping of prisoners, vengeful attitudes and marked increases in the use of imprisonment as a sanction. These features of the current approach to punishment are in stark contrast to the objectives and approaches outlined in relation to the provision of prison education and as such illustrate the competing and sharply delineated interests of prison educators and criminal justice administrators in many countries. The difficulty of this is noted by Warner (2002b: 738), where he states that "the more oppressive and demeaning the penal context in which education is offered, the more difficult it will be for that learning to be genuinely 'transformative' and 'emancipatory'; but it is not impossible". Such an approach is pointed out several times in the preceding section. The move away from the provision of education for the good of the person, to allow them to gain the education that they did not receive as a young person or to develop a personal interest or to give themselves opportunities or simply to open their own mind is deeply concerning. In order for education to achieve its person-centred aims, policy ought to favour "helping over punishment and be socially inclusive, rather than reinforce the demonisation of people held in prison" (Warner, 2018: 42). A move to use education as a tool of criminal justice as a method of satisfying a voting public that crime is being dealt with, that criminals are being "fixed" and that crime rates are being brought down is too narrow a scope for something so potentially powerful as education. At the centre of this conflict is the person, a person who has committed an offence and has served their time. Using treatment programmes dressed up as education is in many ways a mechanism to suppress the person by serving as a constant reinforcement of the more negative aspects of their life, to the point that they remain focal. Broad and well-resourced educational provision serves as a positive activity in the day and life of the person in prison and with time can help the person immensely in terms of mindset, confidence and so on. This results in them leaving prison feeling like they have or are doing something positive for themselves. When education is used as a means to an end, such as to get a job or reduce offending, and that goal is not met within the expected timeframe the offender again can have a sense of failing in their efforts, which can lead them again to a negative spiral.

What happens outside of prison often has as significant an impact as that which happens during the sentence. Because of this punitiveness that prevails in society, Costelloe (2014) is sceptical of the "transformative" capabilities of prison education. Adult education and prison education have the capacity to transform the individual, yet the society into which they ultimately return will be unlikely to have become any less punitive and is unlikely to recognise the transformation of the offender (Costelloe, 2014). In many ways, this reinforces the need for education to be broad and holistic, rather than focusing on employability and skills training. Not having a job will be only one of the hurdles that a person faces on release. Being able to navigate the barriers to reintegration in addition to withstanding the prejudice that will be faced at every level of their engagement with society will be a necessity. The adult education approach and the provision of a wide curriculum is optimal to the creation of social capital. It assists in the subsequent creation of social bonds and networks and a willingness towards societal participation, which in the face of such punitiveness and prejudicial attitudes in society could better serve the reintegrating prisoner than a completely human capital– and skills-based approach to education. Of course, ideally transformation of society's approaches and views, along with the transformed perspective of the offender, would work to better facilitate reintegration and support the person's transformation. However, such societal reform is too great an issue for the confines of this research and too great an issue to be tackled by prison education alone. However, prison education is concerned with the person, and every effort should be made to equip the person with the appropriate skills to succeed in the punitive society they will face on release.

Conclusion

Prison education is the thread that runs through this book, and as such this chapter has explored the literature that underpins the concept, giving a foundation upon which to build the forthcoming chapters and provide context to the findings that will be presented in the remaining chapters. Prison education is a broad concept, with many views, philosophies and approaches to its conceptualisation. In exploring its historical development at the outset of the chapter, it was possible then to see the emergence of the debates that have characterised prison education discourse to the present day. The competing views on the philosophies and purposes are central to these debates. A notion that also characterised this chapter is the idea that education in prison can be truly transformatory. While much of the research has focused on reduced recidivism rates and that is problematic in some respects, it also shows that crime is not a career and criminal careers end, perhaps even quicker for those who undertake education. Moreover, those studies that looked at other aspects of prison education showed that it can transform the way a person sees the world and encourage empathy, self-awareness and self-reflection. It can change behaviours and outlooks. These are the emancipatory aspects of prison education that are envisaged by the broad, whole-person approaches. An important point to address is the competing approaches to education, both the esoteric and prosaic views of education. A caution is offered against the narrowing of education just to a means of rehabilitation. The penal landscape is an unsympathetic and often unforgiving place, a mirror of some aspects of society that the person must navigate on release. This chapter concluded by recommending that this penality be shunned in prison education discourse in favour of ensuring that the broad and person-centred approach to education be maintained within prison schools for the benefit of those who are undertaking it. All of these points will be pertinent to the material presented in upcoming chapters and will be drawn upon several times in drawing together the study findings and framework.

References

Ahern, D. (2011) *How Toe by Toe Works*. Dublin: Independent Monitor.

Anders, A.D. and Noblitt, G.W. (2011) Understanding Effective Higher Education Programs in Prisons: Considerations from the Incarcerated Individuals Program in North Carolina. *Journal of Correctional Education* 62(2), pp. 7–23.

Bartlett, S., Burton, D. and Peim, N. (2001) *Introduction to Education Studies*. London: Paul Chapman Publishing/Sage.

Behan, C. (2014) Learning to Escape: Prisoner Education, Rehabilitation and the Potential for Transformation. *Journal of Prison Education and Reentry* 1(1), pp. 20–31. doi:10.15845/jper.v1i1.594.

Behan, C. and O'Donnell, I. (2008) Prisoners, Politics and the Polls: Enfranchisement and the Burden of Responsibility. *The British Journal of Criminology* 48(3), pp. 319–336. doi:10.1093/bjc/azn004.

Brehm, J. and Rahn, W. (1997) Individual-Level Evidence for the Causes and Consequences of Social Capital. *American Journal of Political Science* 41(3), pp. 999–1023. doi:10.2307/2111684.

Bushfield, S. (2004) Fathers in Prison: Impact of Parenting Education. *Journal of Correctional Education* 55(2), pp. 104–116.

Bye, L. and Schillinger, D.A. (2005) Evaluation of a Cognitive Thinking Program. *Journal of Correctional Education* 56(3), pp. 202–215.

Callan, V. and Gardner, J. (2005) *Vocational Education and Training Provision and Recidivism in Queensland Correctional Institutions*. Adelaide: NCVER.

Chavez, R. and Dawe, S. (2007) International Research and Trends in Education and Training Provision in Correctional Settings. In Dawe, S. (ed) *Vocational Education and Training for Adult Prisoners and Offenders in Australia*. Adelaide: National Centre for Vocational Education Research.

Cho, R.M. and Tyler, J.H. (2010) Does Prison-Based Adult Basic Education Improve Post-Release Outcomes for Male Prisoners in Florida? *Crime & Delinquency* 59, pp. 975–1005.

Clemmer, D. (1940) *The Prison Community*. New York: Holt, Rinehart and Winston.

Coates, S. (2016) *Unlocking Potential: A Review of Education in Prisons*. London: Ministry of Justice.

Condry, R. and Minson, S. (2020) Conceptualizing the Effects of Imprisonment on Families: Collateral Consequences, Secondary Punishment, or Symbiotic Harms? *Theoretical Criminology*, pp. 1–19. doi:10.1177/1362480619897078.

Costelloe, A. (2003) *Third Level Education in Irish Prisons: Who Participates and Why?* Unpublished Doctoral Thesis, Milton Keynes: Open University.

Costelloe, A. (2014) Learning for Liberation, Teaching for Transformation: Can Education in Prison Prepare Prisoners for Active Citizenship? *Irish Journal of Applied Social Studies* 14(1), Article 4. doi:10.21427/D7TM7H.

Costelloe, A. and Warner, K. (2003) Beyond 'Offending Behaviour': The Wider Perspectives of Adult Education and the European Prison Rules. *9th EPEA Conference on Prison Education*, Langesaud, Norway, June 2003.

Costelloe, A. and Warner, K. (2008) Beyond 'Offending Behaviour': The Wider Perspectives of Adult Education and the European Prison Rules. In Wright, R. (ed) *In the Borderlands: Learning to Teach in Prisons and Alternative Settings*. San Bernardino: California State University.

Costelloe, A. and Warner, K. (2014) Prison Education across Europe: Policy, Practice, Politics. *London Review of Education* 12(2), pp. 175–183. doi:10.18546/LRE.12.2.03.

Council of Europe (1987) *European Prison Rules*. Strasbourg: Council of Europe.

Council of Europe (1990) *Education in Prison: Recommendation No. R (89) 12*. 13th October 1989. Strasbourg: Council of Europe.

Council of Europe (2006) *European Prison Rules*. Strasbourg: Council of Europe.

Crewe, B. (2011) Depth, Weight, Tightness: Revisiting the Pains of Imprisonment. *Punishment & Society* 13(5), pp. 509–529. doi:10.1177/1462474511422172.

Cullen, F.T. and Gendreau, P. (2001) From Nothing Works to What Works: Changing Professional Ideology in the 21st Century. *The Prison Journal* 81, pp. 313–338.

Davis, L.M., Bozick, R., Steele, J.L., Saunders, J. and Miles, J.N.V. (2013) *Evaluating the Effectiveness of Correction Education: A Meta-Analysis of Programmes That Provide Education to Incarcerated Adults*. Santa Monica: RAND Corporation.

Dawe, S. (2007) *Vocational Education and Training for Adult Prisoners and Offenders in Australia*. Adelaide: National Centre for Vocational Education Research.

Department for Education and Skills (2005) *Reducing Re-Offending Through Skills and Employment*. Norwich: The Stationery Office.

Department of Education and Science (2000) *Learning for Life: White Paper on Adult Education*. Dublin: Stationary Office.

Duguid, S. (1998) Policy, Praxis and Rehabilitation: Prison Education in Canada 1945–1995. In Forster, W. (ed) *Education behind Bars: International Comparisons*. Leicester: National Institute of Adult Continuing Education.

Duguid, S., Hawkey, C. and Pawson, R. (1996) Using Recidivism to Evaluate the Effectiveness of Prison Education Programmes. *Journal of Correctional Education* 47(2), pp. 74–85.

Durose, M.R., Cooper, A.D. and Snyder, H.N. (2014) *Recidivism of Prisoners Released in 30 States in 2005: Patterns from 2005 to 2010*. Washington: U.S. Department of Justice.

Eikeland, O.J., Manger, T. and Asbjørnsen, A. (eds) (2009) *Education in Nordic Prisons: Prisoners' Educational Background, Preferences, and Motivation*. Copenhagen: Nordic Council of Ministers.

Fabelo, T. (2002) The Impact of Prison Education on Community Reintegration of Inmates: The Texas Case. *Journal of Correctional Education* 53(3), pp. 106–110.

Garland, D. (2001) *The Culture of Control: Crime and Social Order in Contemporary Society*. Chicago: University of Chicago Press.

Glueck, S. and Glueck, E. (1940) *Juvenile Delinquents Grown Up*. New York: Commonwealth Fund.

Gonzalez, P., Romero, T. and Cerbana, C.B. (2007) Parent Education Program for Incarcerated Mothers in Colorado. *Journal of Correctional Education* 58(4), pp. 357–373.

Hackman, K.M. (1997) Correctional Education: Challenges and Changes. *Journal of Correctional Education* 48, pp. 74–78.

Harris, K. (1999) Aims! Whose Aims? In Roger Marples (ed) *The Aims of Education*. London: Routledge.

Hawley, J. (2011) *Prison Education and Training in Europe: A Review and Commentary of Existing Literature, Analysis and Evaluation*. Birmingham: GHK.

Helliwell, J.F. and Putnam, R.D. (2007) Education and Social Capital. *Eastern Economic Journal, Eastern Economic Association* 33(1), pp. 1–19.

Hellman, D.A. (1980) *Economics of Crime*. New York: St. Martins Press.

Hobler, B. (1999) Correctional Education: Now and in the Future. *Journal of Correctional Education* 50, pp. 102–105.

Holley, G. and Ensley, D. (2003) *Recidivism Report: Inmates Released from Florida Prisons July 1995 to June 2001*. Florida: Department of Corrections.

Huang, J., Maassen van den Brink, H. and Groot, W. (2009) A Meta-Analysis of the Effect of Education on Social Capital. *Economics of Education Review* 28(4), pp. 454–464. doi: 10.1016/j.econedurev.2008.03.004.

Hull, K.A., Forrester, S., Brown, J., Jobe, D. and McCullen, C. (2000) Analysis of Recidivism Rates for Participants of the Academic/Vocational/Transition Education Programmes Offered By the Virginia Department of Correctional Education. *Journal of Correctional Education* 52(2), pp. 256–262.

Hurry, J., Brazier, L., Snapes, K. and Wilson, A. (2005) *Improving the Literacy and Numeracy of Disaffected Young People in Custody and in the Community: Summary Interim Report of the First 18 Months of the Study*. London: Institute of Education, University of London.

IPSOS (2018) *Evaluation of Prisoner Learning: Initial Impacts and Delivery*. London: Ipsos MORI Social Research Institute.

Irish Prison Service (2013) *Irish Prison Service Recidivism Study 2013*. Longford: Irish Prison Service.

Irish Prison Service (2019) *Joint Irish Prison Service/Education and Training Boards Ireland Prison Education Strategy 2019–2022*. Longford: Irish Prison Service.

Karsikas, V., Kuivajarvi, K. and Maki, M. (2009) Finland. In Langelid, T., Maki, M., Raundrup, K. and Svensson, S. (eds) *Nordic Prison Education: A Lifelong Learning Perspective*. Copenhagen: Norden.

Keena, L. and Simmons, C. (2014) Rethink, Reform, Reenter: An Entrepreneurial Approach to Prison Programming. *International Journal of Offender Therapy and Comparative Criminology* 59(8), pp. 837–854. doi:10.1177/0306624X14523077.

Kilcommins, S., O'Donnell, I., O'Sullivan, E. and Vaughan, B. (2004) *Crime, Punishment and the Search for Order in Ireland*. Dublin: IPA.

King, J. (2019) *Review of European Prison Education Policy and Council of Europe Recommendation (89) 12 on Prison Education*. The Hague: EuroPris.

Knowles, M. S. (1970) *The Modern Practice of Adult Education: Androgogy Versus Pedagogy*. New York: New York Association Press.

Knowles, M. (1975) *Self-Directed Learning: A Guide for Learners and Teachers*. New York: Associated Press.

Langelid, T., Mäki, M., Raundrup, K. and Svensson, S. (eds) (2009) *Nordic Prison Education: A Lifelong Learning Perspective*. Bergen: Norden.

Langford, G. (1985) *Education, Persons and Society: A Philosophical Enquiry*. London: MacMillan Publishers Ltd.

Lawrence, D.H. (1922) *Fantasia of the Unconscious*. New York: Thomas Seltzer.

Liebling A. (2011) Moral Performance, Inhuman and Degrading Treatment and Prison Pain. *Punishment & Society* 13(5), pp. 530–550. doi:10.1177/1462474511422159.

Liebling, A. and Maruna, S. (2005) Introduction: The Effects of Imprisonment Revisited. In Liebling, A. and Maruna, S. (eds) *The Effects of Imprisonment*. Cullompton: Willan Publishing.

Lindeman, E. (1926) *The Meaning of Adult Education*. Montreal: Harvest House.

Lipton, D.S., Martinson, R. and Wilks, J. (1975) *The Effectiveness of Correctional Treatment: A Survey of Treatment Valuation Studies*. New York: Praeger Press.

Lochner, L. and Moretti, E. (2004) The Effect of Education on Crime: Evidence from Prison Inmates, Arrests, and Self Reports. *The American Economic Review* 94, pp. 155–189.

MacCormick, A. (1931) *The Education of Adult Prisoners: A Survey and a Program*. New York: The National Society of Penal Information.

Maltz, M.D. (2001) *Recidivism*. Orlando: Academic Press.

Manger, T. and Langelid, T. (2005) *Læring bak murene: Fengselsundervisningen i Norge* [Learning behind Bars, Prison Education in Norway]. Bergen: Fagbokforlag.

Martinson, R. (1974) What Works?: Questions and Answers about Prison Reform. *The Public Interest* 35, pp. 22–55.

Maslauskaite, K. and Mooney, C. (2018) *Doing More with Less: Prisoner Rehabilitation in Ireland*. Paris: CEB.

Matrix Knowledge Group (2009) *Lifelong Learning and Crime: An Analysis of the Cost Effectiveness of in-Prison Educational and Vocational Interventions: IFLL Public Value Paper 2*. Leicester: National Institute for Adult and Continuing Learning (NIACE).

Merton, R.K. (1938) Social Structure and Anomie. *American Sociological Review* 3(5), pp. 672–682.

Mezirow, J. (1991) *Transformative Dimensions of Adult Learning*. San Francisco: Jossey-Bass.

Mezirow, J. (1997) Transformative Learning: Theory to Practice. *New Directions for Adult and Continuing Education* 74, pp. 5–11.

Mezirow, J. (2000) Learning to Think Like an Adult: Core Concepts of Transformation Theory. In Mezirow, J. (ed) *Learning as Transformation: Critical Perspectives on a Theory in Progress*. San Francisco: Jossey-Bass.

Ministry of Justice (2019) *Ministry of Justice Single Departmental Plan 2019–2022*. London: Ministry of Justice.

Ministry of Justice (2020) *Proven Reoffending Statistics Quarterly Bulletin, England and Wales, January 2018 to March 2018*. London: Home Office.

Morgan, M. and Kett, M. (2003) *The Prison Adult Literacy Survey: Results and Implications*. Dublin: Irish Prison Service.

Morris, C.W. (1962) *Mind, Self and Society: From the Standpoint of Social Behaviourist*. Chicago: University Press of Chicago.

Munoz, V. (2009) *The Right to Education of Persons in Detention*. A/HRC/11/8, 2nd April 2009. New York: Human Rights Council.

Nally, J., Lockwood, S., Knutson, K. and Ho, T. (2012) An Evaluation of the Effect of Correctional Education Programmes on Post-Release Recidivism and Employment: An Empirical Study in Indiana. *The Journal of Correctional Education* 63(1), pp. 69–88.

National Economic and Social Forum (2001) *The Reintegration of Prisoners: Forum Report No. 22*. Dublin: National Economic and Social Forum.

Nie, N.H., Junn, J. and Stehlik-Barry, K. (1996) *Education and Democratic Citizenship in America*. Chicago: University of Chicago Press.

Norwegian Ministry of Education and Research (2005) *Education and Training in the Correctional Services 'Another Spring': Short Version of Report No. 27 to the Storting*. Oslo: Norwegian Ministry of Education and Research.

Ouimet-Burke, L. and Vivian, J.E. (2001) The Effect of College Programming on Recidivism Rates at Hampden County House of Correction: A 5-Year Study. *Journal of Correctional Education* 52(4), pp. 160–162.

Palmer, T. (1975) Martinson Revisited. *Journal of Research in Crime and Delinquency* 12, pp. 1–23.

Parson, M. and Langenbach, M. (1993) The Reasons Inmates Indicated They Participate in Prison Education Programmes: Another Look at Boshiers PEPS. *Journal of Correctional Education* 44(1), pp. 38–41.

Petersilia, J. (2003) *When Prisoners Come Home: Parole and Prisoner Reentry*. New York: Oxford University Press.

Pike, A. and Farley, H. (2018) Education and Vocational Training: Why the Differences Are Important. *Advancing Corrections: Journal of the International Corrections and Prisons Association* 6, pp. 81–93.

Porporino, F.J. and Robinson, D. (1992) *Can Educating Adult Offenders Counteract Recidivism?* Ontario: Correctional Services of Canada.

Putnam, R.D. (1995) Bowling Alone: America's Declining Social Capital. *Journal of Democracy* 61, pp. 65–78.

Putnam, R.D. (2000) *Bowling Alone: The Collapse and Revival of American Community*. New York: Simon and Schuster Paperbacks.

Raundrup, K. (2009) Denmark. In Langelid, T., Maki, M., Raundrup, K. and Svensson, S. (eds) *Nordic Prison Education: A Lifelong Learning Perspective*. Copenhagen: Norden. doi:10.6027/TN2009-536.

Reuss, A. (1999) Prison(er) Education. *The Howard Journal of Criminal Justice* 38(2), pp. 113–127.

Ripley, P. (1993) *Prison Educations Role in Challenging Offending Behaviour*. Mendip Papers, MP 047, ED 379405. Bristol: Staff College.

Ross, R.R. and Ross, B.D. (1989) Delinquency Prevention through Cognitive Training. *Educational Horizons* 67(4), pp. 124–130.

Rucklidge, J.J., McLean, A.P. and Bateup, P. (2013) Criminal Offending and Learning Disabilities in New Zealand Youth: Does Reading Comprehension Predict Recidivism? *Crime & Delinquency* 59(8), pp. 1263–1286. doi:10.1177/0011128709336945.

Samenow, S.E. (2001) Understanding the Criminal Mind: Phenomenological Approach. *Journal of Psychiatry and Law* 29(3), pp. 275–293.

Schinkel, M. (2014) *Being Imprisoned*. London: Palgrave McMillan. doi:10.1057/9781137440839.

Schuller, T., Brassett-Grundy, A., Green, A., Hammond, C. and Preston, J. (2002) *Learning, Continuity and Change in Adult Life*. Wider Benefits of Learning Research Report No. 3. London: Centre for Research on the Wider Benefits of Learning.

Select Committee on Narcotics Abuse and Control (1993) *Federal Prisons: Inmate and Staff Views on Education and Work Training Programmes*. Washington: House of Representatives.

Social Exclusion Unit (2002) *Reducing Re-Offending by Ex-Prisoners*. London: HMG Cabinet Office.

Spradling, T.M. (2001) *A Study to Determine If Cognitive 'Problem Solving Skills for Offenders' Is an Effective Method for Reducing Inmate Infractions in a Maximum-Security Level Institution*. Unpublished Masters Thesis. Salem: Educational Resources Information Centre.

Steurer, S.J., Smith, L. and Tracy, A. (2001) *Three State Recidivism Study*. Washington: United States Department of Education.

Sykes, G.M. (1958) *The Society of Captives*. Princeton: Princeton University Press.

Tewksbury, R. and Stengel, K.M. (2006) Assessing Correctional Education Programmes: The Students' Perspective. *Journal of Correctional Education* 57(1), pp. 13–25.

Ubah, C.B.A. and Robinson, R.L. (2003) A Grounded Look at the Debate over Prison-Based Education: Optimistic Theory versus Pessimistic Worldview. *The Prison Journal* 83, pp. 115–129. doi:10.1177/0032885503083002001.

UNESCO (2019) *Leave No One behind: Participation, Equity and Inclusion, 4th Global Report on Adult Learning and Education*. Hamburg: UNESCO Institute for Lifelong Learning.

Vacca, J.S. (2004) Educated Prisoners Are Less Likely to Return to Prison. *Journal of Correctional Education* 55(4), pp. 297–305.

Vandala, N.G. (2019) The Transformative Effect of Correctional Education: A Global Perspective. *Cogent Social Sciences* 5(1), p. 1677122. doi:10.1080/23311886.2019.1677122.

Van Wyk, S.A. (2014) *From Incarceration to Successful Reintegration: An Ethnographic Study of the Impact of a Halfway House on Recidivism amongst Female Ex-Offenders*. Unpublished Masters Thesis. Cape Town: University of Stellenbosch.

Warner, K. (2002a) Widening and Deepening the Education We Offer Those in Prison: Reflections from Irish and European Experience. *Journal of Correctional Education* 53, pp. 32–37.

Warner, K. (2002b) Penal Policy and the Adult Education of Prisoners. In O'Mahony, P. (ed) *Criminal Justice in Ireland*. Dublin: Institute of Public Administration.

Warner, K. (2007) Against the Narrowing of Perspectives: How Do We See Learning, Prisons and Prisoners? *Journal of Correctional Education* 58(2), pp. 170–183.

Warner, K. (2009) 'Resisting the New Punitiveness: Penal Policy in Denmark, Finland and Norway and Some Implications for Education. *European Prison Education Association Conference*, Protaras, October 2009.

Warner, K. (2018) Every Possible Learning Opportunity: The Capacity of Education in Prison to Challenge Dehumanisation and Liberate 'the Whole Person'. *Advancing Corrections, Journal of the International Corrections and Prisons Association* 6, pp. 32–45.

Chapter 4

Prison education

Motivations, barriers and experiences

The previous chapter outlined the various advantages of undertaking education while in prison. It is a means of rebalancing an educational deficit, of opening the mind to new ways of thinking, of developing the personality, of providing opportunities, of fostering community engagement and of reducing reoffending, among other things. Chapter 3 also highlighted that these benefits are also dependent upon the type of education offered or the philosophy and approach taken in that particular prison or state. Regardless of the benefits of education, the curriculum offered or the philosophies of those who provide prison education, none of this is relevant without the participation of those at whom the education is ultimately aimed. The typical person in prison is undereducated by comparison to the general population and will most likely have left school at an early age with few or no qualifications – in fact many have difficulty with even the basics of numeracy, reading and writing (Morgan and Kett, 2003). This deficit will likely have contributed to various social disadvantages including lower income, lower standard of living, limitations on social mobility, relational instability and a greater likelihood of substance abuse and homelessness, for example, all of which can also be criminogenic factors. Prison education therefore provides an important opportunity for those serving prison sentences to use this time to address any shortfalls in their past educational attainment and potentially address any of these issues that this deficit may have caused in their past. Prison education is based on an ethos of attraction rather than promotion, and a person must voluntarily decide to engage. Understanding what motivates a person to participate and to subsequently continue with prison education in the long term is paramount to ensuring that education meets both the desired goals and potentially the unknown needs of those who undertake it. Furthermore, having an understanding of the barriers to participating in education is equally important in reducing the obstacles and ensuring that as many as possible can engage with education during their sentence. This chapter will explore the previous literature in relation to each of these points, along with the narratives of prisoners in relation to these themes. This chapter will also outline the various findings in relation to other aspects of prisoners' experiences of education, concluding with a discussion of the meaning and implications of the findings in terms of educational philosophy, policy, reintegration and the desistance framework.

Prison education participation rates

In Ireland, prison education participation rates vary greatly from one prison to another. The highest participation rate of 76.5% is recorded in Loughan House, an open prison with good educational facilities (Maslauskaite and Mooney, 2018). Therefore, it is to be expected that participation rates would be highest in the prisons of this type. Ireland's second open prison, Shelton Abbey, where some of the interviews for this research were carried out, has a participation rate of 56.5%, which is quite a bit lower than Loughan House (Maslauskaite and Mooney, 2018). The lowest participation rate of 20.4% is in Cloverhill Prison, which is a remand prison, and given the transient population and profile of the men in this prison, a low participation rate is to be expected. Of the medium-security closed prisons that are the mainstay of the Irish prison system, the rate varies from 20.5% in Mountjoy, which was the main data collection site in this research, to 55.5% in Wheatfield Prison. Both are located in Dublin and have similar populations. The majority of prisons of this type reflect participation rates of approximately 45% (Maslauskaite and Mooney, 2018). The participation rates appear to be inclusive of those prisoners who are only participating on a part-time basis, in addition to those who are engaging at a high level. For that reason, the figures tend to demonstrate a low to moderate participation level among Irish prisoners. In England and Wales, it is estimated that 33% of prisoners engage in prison education at some point during their sentence (Natale, 2010). However, the numbers engaging with education during their sentence are declining. Those undertaking academic qualifications in maths and English fell by 40% and 47%, respectively, between the 2010/2011 and 2017/2018 academic years (Atkins et al., 2019). In the same period, a drop of 36% was reported in programmes with more of a treatment orientation such as domestic violence and violent offending reduction courses (Atkins et al., 2019). In the United States, it is reported that 25% of prisoners participate in academic education while in prison and 32% undertake some form of vocational training, though this figure is representative of those who began courses, rather than those who completed education courses (Wolf Harlow, 2003). Given the various benefits that can accrue from participation in prison education and the fact that a significant proportion of prisoners will have low levels of previous education, these figures appear to be quite low. The answers to encouraging greater levels of participation may lie in understanding more about why prisoners are motivated to participate in education and the barriers that exist for those who do not participate. Both of these questions will be considered in detail later.

Motivations for participation in prison education

Motivation refers to the factors that cause a person to do or not do something (Broussard and Garrison, 2004) and is a combination of beliefs, perceptions, values, interests and actions (Lai, 2011). Motivation towards education is often conceptualised as two ends of a continuum with intrinsic and extrinsic at either end (Deci and Ryan, 1985). Intrinsic motivations towards a task will be to serve no other end than to engage in the action itself or for some element of personal development. Deci et al. (1999) suggest that intrinsic motivation creates enthusiasm for activity based on the personal rewards that result from deliberate and effective actions. Extrinsic motivations are those with an external reward such as employment or greater income, for example. Those who participate in education for intrinsic reasons tend to be far more engaged than those who are being pushed by extrinsic reasons (Deci et al., 1999). Of course there can be overlap between the two. Educators tend to view intrinsic motivation as being more desirable, as it results in better learning outcomes for learners than those motivated by external rewards, due to a person being more likely to apply themselves, to be persistent, to enjoy the challenge and to want to master their particular area of study (Gottfried, 1990). Chapter 3 touched on this when examining the approaches to prison education, which can also be guided by esoteric or prosaic aims. The esoteric view aims to provide education that will provide personal benefits for the person, with the prosaic view focused on the advantages of education that are linked to external reward (Hawley, 2011). The widely recommended holistic approach to prison education is in line with the esoteric view. The call for the provision of broad, person-centred education is further reinforced by the fact that prisoners are more likely to be motivated by and engage with education that has some intrinsic value to them, which will potentially result in higher levels of participation in education. Motivations are therefore an important issue.

One of the earliest studies examining prisoners' motivations to participate in prison education was Boshier's (1983) study in which he developed the PEPS (Prison Education Participation Scale). The results demonstrated that the most important factors in motivating prisoners to participate in prison education were (1) cognitive interest; (2) personal control; (3) self-preservation; (4) outside contact; and (5) self-assertion. Parsons and Langenbach (1993) later questioned the validity and replicability of this study due to the relatively small sample size and sought to revisit the study with a view to replicating and retesting the hypothesis, albeit with a larger sample. The findings were categorised differently and reduced to four categories or "orientations". The most common motivation found among prisoners was the goal orientation (Parsons and Langenbach, 1993). Goal-orientated participants were those who used education as a means to an end and were seeking to achieve a particular outcome. They were extrinsically motivated by an aim such as post-release employment or success, for example. Those of an activity orientation are motivated by social factors, such as getting out of the cell to meet other prisoners or teachers or engaging with friends and relieving the boredom of prison life (Parsons and Langenbach, 1993). The next most common category was cognitive control, which is concerned with satisfying an inquisitive mind, the acquisition of knowledge or feeling fulfilled. Those who were characterised by this orientation were learning simply for the sake of learning; they were motivated by education itself or learning a new skill (Parsons and Langenbach, 1993). This is seen to be the best form of learning, as the person is intrinsically motivated and is more likely to continue participating over the entirety of their sentence and complete the courses they undertake (Deci et al., 1999). Avoidance posture as a motivation for education is characterised by a desire to get away from certain elements of the prison life. Avoidance had the lowest mean scores in the research and therefore was the least likely motivation for participation in prison education (Parson and Langenbach, 1993). While on the face of it, this can appear to be an extrinsic motivation, this category can also represent deeply intrinsic reasons for participating in education such as a desire to avoid certain situations that may undermine their plan to stay away from drugs or anti-social peers, for example.

Future planning, preparation for release and competence/skill building

These early findings of Parson and Langenbach (1993) were further supported by the motivations discovered in several other studies (Stana et al., 1993; Costelloe, 2003; Skaalvik et al., 2003; Diseth et al., 2008; Manger et al., 2010; Manger et al., 2013; Roth and Manger, 2014; Behan, 2014) which all found that one of the most common reasons for participating is preparation for reentry or future planning. Diseth et al. (2008), for example, found that motivations could be categorised as follows: (1) prepare for life after release; (2) social reasons; and (3) acquire knowledge and skills. This was reinforced by Manger et al. (2013) and Roth and Manger (2014), though they adjusted the latter two categories slightly to "social reasons and reasons unique to the prison context" and "competence building". This reflects the fact that soft skills are also an essential part of the competencies developed through education. Each study found that categories 1 and 3 respectively were the most likely motivators for participation. They also found a significant overlap between those who mentioned future planning and those who mentioned competence building since competence building is seen by many as being a requirement for future success. In particular, those prisoners with longer sentences tended to be participating with a view to future planning and competence (Roth and Manger, 2014). The more of their sentence that had passed, the more likely they were to value future planning (Roth and Manger, 2014). This is likely to be a result of an impending release date focusing the mind, with prisoners becoming more aware of the challenges they will soon face and wishing to prepare to meet those obstacles. A fourth category is suggested by Eriksson and Samuelson (2007) called "social and emotional needs" – in Roth and Manger (2014) this is included as part of social reasons and reasons unique to the prison context. This may be flawed, as it discounts an element of self-developmental aspirations that may be part of the "emotional need" motivation to participate. Social and emotional education may also be a fundamental part of competence building since competence should not relate to work skills alone but a person's capacity to participate in all aspects of life.

A Scandinavian study (Eikeland et al., 2009) of five countries examining the motivations to participate in prison education gave a range of possible reasons and asked prisoners to rank them. The study found that the primary motivation for prisoners in all five countries was to spend their time constructively. To pass an exam or improve previous education was only listed in the top four in two of the five countries. Other reasons included to make serving time easier, to bridge their educational gap for when released or to satisfy a desire for learning.

The most recent study by Behan (2014) found getting education and up skilling to be the most likely reason for participating in education.

Escape

Several studies have reported conflicting results in relation to the extent of educational escapism as a motivator for participation. Research in Ireland carried out by Costelloe (2003), focusing on participation in third-level courses by prisoners, found that this was the most likely motivation for prisoners in that study. This study categorised motivations for participation into both push and pull factors. Push factors were those factors that result in prisoners seeking out the school based on a conscious decision to distance themselves from some aspect of the prison, rather than a decision based on a desire to participate in education. Therefore, they are motivated by an impulse or reaction to other factors and not education *per se*. These factors tend to be unique to the prison context, such as avoiding the boredom of prison, creating distance between themselves and certain other prisoners or avoiding drugs, for example. Push factors are most often the motivation for prisoners with weak educational backgrounds (Costelloe, 2003). Alternately, those with stronger educational backgrounds are usually motivated by pull factors (Costelloe, 2003). Pull factors are those that draw a prisoner towards education on the basis of a conscious decision that education can help them. There is an assumption that those motivated by pull factors are acting rationally and intentionally based on some intrinsic or extrinsic goal. These goals may include improving employment prospects, using their time in prison constructively, making their families proud, or picking up on a previous interest. This is similar to Skaalvik et al. (2003), cited by Langelid et al. (2009), where it was found that prison education participants tend to fall into two categories in terms of motivation. One group are achievement-based, participating in education in order to achieve a goal such as gaining knowledge or skills that will help in daily life or after release. The second motivation is avoidance-based, where prisoners participate to avoid prison work, boredom or some other intolerable aspect of prison life (Skaalvik et al., 2003).

The finding in relation to the prevalence of escapism as a motivator to participate in education reinforced Forster's (1990) findings that the initial motivations to participate relate to the prison context itself (such as to avoid prison work). According to Forster (1990), the educationally deprived inmate is "pushed" towards education and shortly becomes aware of this own lack of education and the impacts this may have had on his life, which can in turn convert his motives to more "pull" based reasons. More recently, Behan (2014) found that this is the second most likely motivation for those who are participating in education, hoping to break the monotony and boredom of prison. These studies conflict with the finding of Manger et al. (2013), who found that escapism and avoidance were the least likely reason for participation in education. Of course, these studies were carried out on different populations and in different countries, and this may be representative of a culture difference in both the penal and educational contexts of each state.

Previous education, age and sentence length

Previous levels of education have been found to play a role in motivation towards prison education. The more educated a person is, the more motivated they will be to participate in prison education (Diseth et al., 2008), particularly for intrinsic reasons (Manger et al., 2013). Those prisoners who have low levels of education when entering prison are less motivated towards education, and when they do come to education it is for reasons such as the alleviation of boredom and getting away from prison life (Forster, 1990). Those who have higher levels of educational attainment when coming to prison tend to be much more motivated towards study in prison, knowing what they want to study and embracing the educational process (Forster, 1990). Those with lower levels of educational achievement were more likely to be participating in education based on push factors and avoidance motives, whereas those who were well educated tended to be motivated by the value of education on release or resettlement or just for the sake of education (Costelloe, 2003).

Perhaps this is due to prisoners with stronger educational backgrounds having confidence in the power of education or being aware of what education can achieve. Those with lower levels of education do not see the value of education to begin with and perhaps begin education for no other reason than to alleviate boredom, seeing it as something to do as opposed to an entity that can provide significant personal benefits. This view appears to be supported by Forster's (1981) finding that many prisoners, particularly those from weaker educational backgrounds, begin education to alleviate boredom. However, there is often a fluidity to motivations for learning and those who are motivated by one factor at the outset subsequently find other motivators to continue with education (Forster, 1981). Finally, for those prisoners who had good levels of education coming to prison, education in prison is often seen as the only part of their former life they can continue (Forster, 1990).

Age has a significant influence on participation in prison education (Manger et al., 2013). Younger participants were more likely to engage with education and tend to be motivated by education's capacity for future planning and to improve life after release more than older participants (Manger et al., 2013; Roth and Manger, 2014). This may be because low educational attainment is more prevalent among younger prisoners, causing them to reflect on the importance of education their future prospects if they wish to have legitimate income and a good life, therefore seeking out ways to improve their chances of success. Those who are older may be inclined to see education and school as being for the young and lack confidence in their ability to begin to learn at their later stage in life. Furthermore, younger inmates also tended to use education as a means of gaining education; older prisoners tend to access education in order to make prison life a little less boring and to make prison life easier (Manger et al., 2013).

The evidence in relation to the impact of sentence length on the motivations of prisoners to participate has been conflicting. A study carried out in the United States found that those prisoners who had served more than half of their sentence study were more likely to be participating in prison education (Jackson and Innes, 2000). This was not borne out in a later Norwegian study where sentence length, sentence served and previous incarceration did not affect the social reasons and escapism motive (Manger et al., 2013). Short sentences also appeared to discourage participation in education since prisoners of often see little value in starting a course when they will not be in prison for a long period of time (Eikeland et al., 2009). It is speculated that this may be due to the fact that they view education in its traditional sense where it is a long-term commitment, rather than also being facilitated through shorter and more focused courses of study (Eikeland et al., 2009)

Worthy motivations and motivational evolution

Escapism and other factors unique to the prison context can be categorised as push type motivations (Costelloe, 2003). One criticism of push factors is that the person simply "ends up" in education, rather than having made an intentioned decision to do so. Therefore, the motivations to participate may be outside of the person's own conscious awareness. This may be reflective of a lifetime attitude towards decision making that has ultimately led them to criminality. The lack of conscious choice and the tenancy to be led or pushed or to drift into a situation as a response to other factors can be a cause of delinquency. Indeed, this is the anthesis of agency, control and self-determinism that are crucial to desistance (Maruna, 2001). Pull factors result in participation based on a very conscious decision. Where a person makes this conscious decision, they tend to be more engaged and more likely to continue with their studies (Roth and Manger, 2014). It would seem that engaging in education on the basis of pull factors is far more desirable. While this may be true, regardless of motivation, any time spent in the prison school will be advantageous.

It is important to look behind these push factors to the reasons that a person is seeking to escape the negative aspects of prison life. These negative aspects may be as benign as escaping the monotony of the prison, and it is often viewed as the least worthy reason to participate in education. However, when one considers the other more harmful aspects of prison life that a person may wish to escape, such as drug use or gang affiliation, education may be a route to distance themselves from past mistakes and in such a case education that might on the surface appear to be avoidance-orientated may in fact be goal-orientated. Both would be characterised as extrinsic motivations, but upon consideration may be coming from a deeply intrinsic rationale, involving a significant effort to move away from crime. Therefore, any motivation for education is still motivation, and those who participate will undoubtedly benefit in at least some way.

Avoidance and push motives can lead to participation, which can in turn change the reasons that prisoners stay participating in education (Costelloe, 2003). Motivations that may have originally been embedded in push factors can subsequently evolve into pull factors through developing interests in future education when a person sees what education has to offer (Costelloe, 2003). Prisoners who are primarily motivated by push factors tend to be educationally disadvantaged and may have previously avoided education due to low levels of motivation, self-esteem and self-efficacy. These prisoners may subsequently change their motivations on foot of a positive experience (Manger et al., 2013; Behan, 2014). Behan (2014) found that those who were originally motivated by the boredom of prison subsequently reported continuing with a view to preparing for release or because they enjoyed the personal transformational effects of education. If not for these push factors, they may never have accessed education. Motivations can also change as students progress in education, as the educational experience may unearth motivations that were previously buried within the person and are only realised through participation (Forster, 1990).

The prison school and staff have a role to play in transforming the views of those motivated by the prison context to motives that are aligned with educational, personal development needs and goals in order to maintain the motivation of marginalised learners (Hawley, 2011). Prison teachers need to be knowledgeable of the factors that can result in a transformation of the inmates motives from those unique to the prison context to motives that are more intrinsically based, which can thus produce a more enhanced learning for the student and increase their appetite for future learning (Hawley, 2011).

Findings: motivations to participate in prison education

In the current study, the participants were asked about their motivations to participate in prison education from two perspectives. First, they were asked about the original reason they became involved in prison education and they were also asked why they continued to participate. This was to reflect the evolution of motivations over time, as indicated by Costelloe (2003) and Forster (1990). This led to an interesting aspect of the study, showing a contrast between the original and ongoing motivations for participation. In line with the semi-structured interview approach, prisoners were allowed to talk freely about the reasons for participating in education, they were not limited to one answer and several prisoners had dual reasons for getting involved. In line with Costelloe (2003) and Forster (1990), the most common reason for becoming involved in prison education in Ireland was to escape some element of prison life, such as the boredom or some anti-social element of prison life. Other reasons for participation included to increase their levels of education, to support post-release goals or to pursue an interest in a particular subject. Embellishment of their prison record was also mentioned by a very small number of prisoners.

Escape from boredom and the prison environment

The most common reason for participating in prison education was to alleviate boredom and escape the prison environment. In line with the findings of Costelloe (2003) and Forster (1990), who both found that escape was the most common reason for participating in prison education, many of the prisoners named this as the primary reason they had originally come to the school.

Boredom

Participants stated that they found it hard to engage in the same routine every day with little in the way of mental stimulation. The school was a way to break the boredom of the prison cell, the landing or the yard; it was a place to escape to and help the day go by quicker. Those participants who stated that they were participating in education as a way to alleviate boredom were most likely to have been employed prior to coming to prison or had been predominately employed since leaving school. It may be that those prisoners who were used to having a constructive routine found it difficult to pass time on the landings and felt the need to fill their time with productive activities.

> MARK: Like I've worked all me life, it's in me and I'd go mad in me cell not doing anything and it's the same when I'm on the outside.
>
> (Mountjoy, participant)

It appears from the tone of the literature outlined earlier that participation in prison education, motivated by the alleviation of boredom or escaping prison life, is a less significant reason to undertake education than a more goal-orientated rationale such as future planning. While on the face of it, the alleviation of boredom or escaping prison life might appear to be less important reasons for participating in education, since it is ignoring education's potential benefits, this may mask other more desistance-related motives for participating, as outlined under the upcoming subheadings relating to escape.

Escaping prison and people

Participating in education allows prisoners to escape the prison environment for several hours a day. It appears for many prisoners that it is the experience of "escaping" in the school itself as distinct from education that can be beneficial. Some prisoners may be using the school to distance themselves from situations within the prison. For example, Barry was struggling with addiction when he came to prison and had managed to get clean after several attempts. On the final, successful attempt, he had used the school as part of his strategy to gain distance from other addicts and scenarios where there may be temptations to use drugs, particularly during recreational times when others would be using. He tried to access school as much as he could and reported that he tried to use the library in the evening time as a further measure to escape the landings.

> BARRY: The place is full of drugs and for an ex-addict you're going to find it hard to turn it down. So if you're not there it's not in your face, you know what I mean . . . like it's not easy to get clean in here, the more time I can spend here in the school and away from the prison the better me chances.
>
> (Mountjoy, participant)

During their school hours, participants described being removed from the prison environment, enjoying the fact that they are not surrounded by the usual prison "chatter". Prisoners' accounts indicated that they perceive themselves to be surrounded by other like-minded participants and teachers with whom they can have interesting conversations. The school provides constructive mental stimulation and a sense of calm that might not be available elsewhere in the prison. Participants often appeared to see the time in the school as time away from the prison, despite the school being physically situated in the prison. In Barry's quote earlier he mentions this, stating that the time in school is time away from the prison. Participants appear to perceive them as two distinct very separate spaces. When spending time in the school, they are mentally taken away from the prison and the associated mindset. Darren and Stephen, both participating in education in Mountjoy, gave the following quotes that really describe this element of escape that education gives them:

> STEPHEN: Here we chat about other stuff, like news stuff and that kind of thing, what's goin' on in the world outside here. Not like out there on the landing where its talkin' and moanin' about this lad or that lad, or that screw . . . just same shite talk every day . . .
>
> (Mountjoy, participant)

DARREN: The school is an oasis . . . not only an oasis in terms of the books and the literature and the knowledge but in terms of the people and the teachers and the officers who are universally supportive and encouraging. This is an oasis of civility which one doesn't always find at the end of the stairs. . . . Up here you get a real sense of calm and peace, it's a few hours where you can relax. In the prison you feel in a constant state of watchfulness . . . the school is a place where I can feel quite secure and at peace.

(Mountjoy, participant)

The European Prison Rules (1987, 2006) state that institutions should take measures to ensure that the damaging effects of incarceration are minimised (Rule 64 and Rule 102.2, respectively). These rules are in line with the Council of Europe's (1990) view that prison education is a way of addressing the harmful effects of the prison sentence by minimising the damaging effects on the person. It is also suggested that the school can provide a sanctuary or safe environment within the prison to allow space for learners to feel safe and thereby reduce the pains of imprisonment (Warner, 2007; Crewe et al., 2014). The idea of education as an escape from prison life, providing constructive mental stimulation and a distraction from the mindset of the prison, fits well with these idea of minimising the negative impact of the prison sentence or the pains of imprisonment. Therefore, escaping from prison life ought not to be seen as a less significant reason for participating in prison education, as it still leaves prisoners open to the many benefits that education can offer. It may be that it is the actual presence of a prisoner in the school, irrespective of the type of education they undertake, that has the most significant role in relation to desistance.

A theme that arose several time among participants was the use of prison education as a mean of escaping other people within the prison or criminal dissociation. In the context of desistance, dissociation from delinquent peers is argued in the desistance literature as being one of the most significant contributors to the desistance process (Graham and Bowling, 1995). Baskin and Sommers (1998) assert that the formation of a new, non-criminal identity within new peer groups is essential to the process of identity change in the offenders, which they argue is a core element in desistance. Furthermore, breaking away from anti-social peers represents a form of action that Prochaska and DiClemente (1982) argue is the fourth step of change on their five-stage continuum and represents a positive step towards modifying one's problematic behaviour. Several prisoners mentioned they were using the school to escape certain people or situations within the prison, with some prisoners using the school as a way of breaking relationships with deviant peers. Other participants highlighted the fact that being in the school allows them to keep away from criminal influences and drugs and allows them to associate with more like-minded, rehabilitation-focused people. So long as they spent their recreational time in the mainstream prison, they were expected to associate with certain people. Some had recognised the detrimental effects their friends had on their lives, and the prison school formed part of the effort to break these ties. From prisoners' own accounts, it appeared that they were taking active steps to break away from their former peer group and taking action towards desistance. Thomas gives a good account of this here. He was one of the ex-prisoners interviewed and was studying for a degree, having been released two years earlier. The ex-prisoners were asked about why they had participated in education during the sentence and were in a good position to give reflective accounts of their reasons. Here, Thomas talks about how he used education to escape the prison yard with a view to distancing himself from any trouble that may have been developing.

> THOMAS: You just need to get your head away from all that in the yard, listening to stories and lads making plans all day for what's their next job. If your down there you just end up in the middle of things, getting mixed up in things you don't want to get mixed up in again. I noticed after a while of starting up here I didn't have to worry about getting dragged into stuff, I just don't be around them no more like.
>
> (Ex-prisoner)

This is consistent with Baskin and Sommers's (1998) theory regarding the formation of a new, non-criminal identity. Prisoners wanted to break away from their old peer group, the members and membership of which possibly contributed to their identity as a "criminal". They appeared to want to get away from the war stories and the plan hatching; it no longer captured their interest because they did not want to be a "criminal" any longer. For many, this may also represent the effects of the maturational process (Hirschi and Gottfredson, 1985).

The decision to break away from these people and situations and the integration into a new peer group of like-minded people in the prison school might be seen as an effort to move away from the "criminal" identity and move towards a new, non-criminal identity in a new peer group. While the decision to break away from delinquent peers is a significant step in the desistance process, the role of prison education in this action is supportive rather than causative. The prisoner has made the decision to break ties with the peer group before coming to prison education. Prison education appears to support the process by giving the prisoner the means of breaking away from the delinquent peer group and can therefore be seen as supporting desistance-orientated action. This will be explored further in Chapter 6.

Prison education for increased education or interest in subject or module

A considerable number of the men interviewed said they were participating in prison education in order to increase their levels of education. Most of these men had a low level of education prior to commencing prison education, having left school either before or shortly after their Junior Certificate. Their lives had been characterised by low levels of educational attainment which had, according to many, stood in their way throughout their lives. Prison education gave them the opportunity to get the education that they did not get growing up. Not all prisoners had such low levels of education prior to coming to prison; some had completed their secondary education and some of these cited furthering these existing levels of education as being the reason they were participating in education. Furthermore, as they matured they realised the significance of having an education, and several raised the question of whether their lives might have turned out differently had they received more educated.

MICHAEL: When you're older, you see things better and you see what good is in school and having an education. I'd love to have had that and maybe I wouldn't be in here. But no harm in late than never.

(Mountjoy, participant)

This is representative of a deeply intrinsic reason for participating in education, which can lead to far more longevity in their attendance in the prison school (Deci et al., 1999). The number of people who cited this as the main reason they began to participate is significant, as in previous literature it has not tended to be such a prevalent reason for participating in education among samples in other studies.

A few of the prisoners stated that they had a particular interest in a subject. This was often with a view to either up skilling while in prison or developing an area that would have only previously been a hobby. Brian, for example, stated that music was a passion of his and was therefore "trying to get as much of that done as I can". This demonstrates the opportunity that a wide curriculum of prison education can provide to allow someone to explore interests that fall outside of traditional subjects or treatment-based programmes, allowing for the development of aspects of themselves that might otherwise be ignored in the narrow conceptualisation of education.

Prison education for post-release goals

Several participants (n = 8) saw education as being the way to progress in life when they were released. This was the case even for prisoners who had above-average levels of education when they came to prison. An example of this was Willy, a participant from Shelton Abbey who wanted to further his education with a view to setting up a business when he was released from prison. College was also part of his plan, and he hoped to pursue a business degree, which he felt would make him more attractive to banks when it came to financing his new business plans:

WILLY: I have two business plans drawn up from before I came in, one was to open me own fruit and veg shop, and the banks were going to give me

> money so doing the course in here will help with that. Like I've a few other ideas that if I get to college, I'll be able to get more money out of them too.
> (Shelton Abbey, participant)

This motivation is very relevant in the context of desistance where future planning, self-control and self-efficacy are all key factors in the creation of agency, a key factor in the desistance process (Maruna, 2001). While this will be examined in greater detail in Chapter 5, recognising future obstacles and planning to overcome them is representative of elements of a redemption script (Maruna, 2001). These men are clearly planning for the future, with a realistic but cautiously optimistic outlook and using education to support these plans.

Other motivations

A small number of prisoners had alternative reasons for participating in prison education. The first was in order to embellish their prison record. Stephen stated "I know I wouldn't have got out (to an open prison) if I hadn't interacted with the schools and the prison". However, when asked about the reasons that he continues to participate, he stated he now participates in order to have a better life and a career after he is released from prison. This illustrates how a seemingly "less worthy" motive can change and a "push" motivation can subsequently turn to a more intrinsic "pull" motivation (Costelloe, 2003), thus enhancing the likely success of the persons efforts in education.

Another prisoner stated that a teacher had persuaded him to come to the school. This shows the role of the teacher in encouraging people to come to education. However, it was only one prisoner who mentioned this as being his reason for getting into education in prison.

Reasons for continuing – changing motivations

In line with the literature on participation in education predicting that motives to participate can transform from push to pull factors (Costelloe, 2003; Forster, 1990), the accounts of many of the participants showed a difference between the reasons for originally getting involved in prison education and the reasons they continued to participate. Perhaps the most striking difference occurred with those prisoners who stated that they got involved in education to escape prison life, be it the boredom, the people or the routine. Despite escape being a strong original motivation of many participants, they appeared to gain far more than just distraction from their studies and continued to participate after the course had finished for a variety of reasons. Demonstrating the "hook" effect of education and the importance of providing a wide curriculum to entice participation, once the participants commenced education they begin engaging with subjects that they may not have been attracted to before and they begin to see that they can achieve positive things if they put in the effort. Craig's statement later is illustrative of many who began education for one reason and continued for another. This again echoes the earlier point that despite accessing education merely to alleviate boredom appearing to be a less worthwhile reason than perhaps engaging out of a thirst for knowledge, it shows that those who get involved out of boredom or as an escape, rather than educational gain, can experience the "hook" and find themselves enjoying education and its benefits. Giordano et al. (2002) refer to the "hook" for change in their theory of cognitive transformation, outlining what they propose are the cognitive changes that occur in the early stages of desistance. The role of prison education both in increasing a person's readiness for change and as the "hook" for change will be discussed in more depth in Chapter 5.

CRAIG: I just done the classes to break up the week. And when I got into it I really enjoyed it but firstly it was just to pass the time.

(Mountjoy, participant)

Enjoyment arose as a strong theme here, with many participants who began prison education in order to further their previous education or to alleviate boredom, such as Craig who is quoted here, saying that they continued to participate out of enjoyment of either an individual subject or the actual experience of learning itself. This sense of enjoyment often took participants by surprise since their previous experience of mainstream school was very different. The enjoyment stemmed from several things such as the subject matter they were learning, the time out from the prison and also an unexpected realisation that they were more able in their studies than they were expecting. These points are summed up well in Luke's statement that reflects his surprise at enjoying his time in the school and at being far more intelligent than he believed.

LUKE: I came up here to break up me week, like I couldn't take the same thing day in, day out anymore . . . this was the last place I thought I'd end up, even me Ma laughed when I told her cos I hated school, I had to be dragged. But I came up here and I'm lovin' it cos I'm doing so well, I'm not as stupid as I thought (laughs) . . . when you're young and feel like you're just a hassle to teachers its very hard to want to be there (in school), but here you're interacting and its stuff you are interested in and then when you do well in your work, it makes me want to do more and push meself.

(Mountjoy, participant)

Just under half stated that they were continuing with education in order to support their post-release goals. This was with a view to either a job or further education. They felt that notwithstanding the qualifications they might acquire, the fact that they participated in education would show that they used their time in prison constructively, and this might show them in a good light to potential employers. This is highlighted in Keith's quote later. He is very realistic about the challenges he will face when he is released and is hoping that education will help to show the good he has done while serving his sentence and make a difference to employers. Such awareness of their future path and the action being taken to further new goals is illustrative of a sense of agency (Maruna, 2001) and shows the signs of early-stage desistance, in particular the setting of new goals and the taking of action in fulfilment of those goals (Prochaska and DiClemente, 1982).

> KEITH: Well, I'm hoping with a bit of education I'll be able to say look what I've done with the last ten years of my life and show them. Like I know it'll be hard to get a job. I think words on a page will speak louder than my voice and see past the previous record. Like I know it'll be difficult but it gives me an extra couple of points on the board.
>
> (Mountjoy, participant)

Several of the prisoners mentioned that they had realised the value of education in terms of progression in life. They said they viewed it as a means of moving forward in life, particularly when they were released from prison.

Costelloe (2003) refers to those motivated by push factors such as avoidance or escape as simply "ending up" in the prison school. Those who are motivated by these factors are the least likely to remain in the school long term by comparison to those who are participating based on a deliberate and conscious decision. However, Costelloe (2003) also noted the way that motivations can change over time and those who are originally motivated by push factors orientate more towards pull factors such as interest in a module or post-release goals as they spend more time in the school. This can be a result of a positive experience in the prison school (Manger et al., 2013). For example, some of these participants may have had a very negative experience of mainstream education and subsequently change their views when they realise that prison education is delivered in a much different way than what they may have experienced in their youth. Furthermore, those who had negative experiences in the past may also have issues with their self-esteem and confidence, believing that they are not intelligent enough for academic work. However, when they try education they often see that they are very capable and enjoy the sense of achievement that comes from doing well. Therefore, while push factors may seem to be the least desirable motives for participation, the important thing is that prisoners are coming to the school and engaging with education; this gives the best chance of them changing their perspectives and forming motivations that will ensure that they continue with education throughout their sentence.

Previous levels of education and motivations to participation

Various pieces of literature propose that previous levels of education have a role to play in a prisoner's motivation to participate in education, arguing that those with higher levels of previous education are more likely to engage with education in prison (Forster, 1990; Manger et al., 2013). Costelloe (2003) argues that previous education is one of the primary factors in the motivation to participate. Those with less education will be motivated by push factors, while those who are more educated will tend to be more intrinsically motivated (Costelloe, 2003; Forster, 1990; Manger et al., 2013). While the sample size in the current study lacked the numbers to conduct any significant statistical analysis on this point, the qualitative findings in the current study appear to contradict previous studies. The vast majority of prisoners who were participating in prison education had not completed second-level education, with most leaving around the age of 15. Only a very small minority of participants had completed or continued beyond second-level education or had undertaken any form of trade-related education or apprenticeships. Conversely, a more significant portion of the prisoners who were not participating in education had either finished secondary school or had completed some form of further education as part of an apprenticeship. Therefore, it appears that those with higher levels of education were not more motivated to participate. In fact it appears that those with lower levels of education are more motivated to participate in prison education. There is little guidance in the findings to explain this. One explanation might be that prisoners with low levels of education would be inclined to participate in order to address their deficit in education. Yet this was only stated as a motivation to participate by a few of the participants. Alternatively, Chao (2009), referring to adult education in the mainstream sense, proposes that people access education when dispositional factors are strong enough to outweigh situational, institutional and informational barriers to participation. What this means is that while someone might want to participate in education, there are barriers to doing so such as work or finance. Many of the prisoners who were participating in education, despite not having finished secondary school, gave accounts of enjoying school but leaving in order to get a job with a view to having income for themselves and their family. This represented a situational barrier to completing their education. These barriers may be lower in the prison setting, allowing for access to education during their sentence. Furthermore, a negative experience of mainstream education in their youth was found to be a significant dispositional barrier to participation. Most of the prisoners who were participating in education had enjoyed school and therefore did not face this barrier to participation. These points will be explored further in the next section on the barriers to participation in prison education.

Summary and discussion: motivations to participate in prison education

Overall, the findings in the current study were in line with previous studies in the area. They were particularly reflective of the outcomes found in the only other Irish study, where Costelloe (2003) found that escape was the most common motivation for participation in education. In the current research, escape represented a strong push factor, with many of the participants stating that they were trying to avoid several aspects of prison life. Many mentioned boredom, but others talked about escaping situations and people. The findings show that despite escape appearing to be the least desirable reason for participation, it was often representative of deeply personal and positive motives towards change. This included such things as avoiding criminal peers or avoiding situations where drug use was a possibility. Therefore, behind these push motives lay evidence of change and perhaps the early stages of desistance.

Many participants were also motivated by pull factors and using education to address educational deficits from their youth to support their post-release goals and acquire skills or knowledge in an area that interests them. This is in line with various previous studies in this area (Diseth et al., 2008; Manger et al., 2013; Roth and Manger, 2014).

One of the most interesting findings related to the transformation of motivations that occurred for many of the participants. Costelloe (2003) and Forster (1990) stated that motivations can evolve over time, and those who are previously motivated by purely push factors can subsequently change to more pull-orientated reasons for participation. This was reflected in the finding of the current research where many of those who began taking classes as a mechanism of avoidance ended up continuing their studies out of enjoyment and in order to increase their education and support their chances on release. This reflects the evolution of motivations that can occur and shows the importance of simply getting prisoners to the prison school to give the best chance of engaging with and remaining in education throughout their sentence.

Finally, the findings in the current study tended to indicated that those who had lower levels of education are more likely to participate based on pull factors such wanting to gain an education. They also tended to be younger, wanted to plan for the future and were under taking education to support post-release goals. This is generally in line with the outcomes in previous studies (Forster, 1990; Costelloe, 2003; Manger et al., 2013; Roth and Manger, 2014), but there was little to explain the reasons for these findings. It is speculated that the younger participants are more mindful of the lifetime they have in front of them to set and achieve goals. They may be using education as part of their plan. Those who were older were less likely to be participating in education and tended to see the education levels they had as being enough for them, their lower levels of education apparently having done them no harm.

Barriers to participation in prison education

Little is known about the reasons that prisoners do not participate in prison education. Brosens et al. (2013) described the extent of the literature in relation to barriers to participation in prison education as nonexistent. While this is slowly changing and there is some empirical guidance to be found, there still remains a lack of knowledge about the reasons that prisoners decide to not participate or to leave prison education. While prison education is different from mainstream education, there is far more guidance on barriers to participation in the adult education literature than in the direct context of prison education. Given that prison education researchers usually use the same classifications as adult education (Manger et al., 2018), this broader research can also offer some clues. However, while adult education literature can be used to support the gaps in the literature on the barriers to prison education, there is also a distinct need to consider the factors that differentiate the prison setting from the community that might act as barriers to education (Brosens et al., 2015). Previous studies have given some indication of the potential barriers that exist. Overall, each of the main categories of barrier is represented in the literature, with prisoners describing a wide array of reasons for not participating in education; Manger et al. (2018) found that barriers were spread across all categories. These barriers and the inconsistencies in the findings from one study to another are likely to be founded on the fact that the prison experience differs greatly from one jurisdiction to another and from one form of education to another, for example, traditional education versus vocational training. Furthermore, the typical characteristics of those in prison differ considerably from the general population. Those in prison tend to be from marginalised backgrounds, from lower socioeconomic groups, and from communities characterised by higher than average levels of poverty, low educational attainment and early school leaving (O'Mahony, 1997; Flynn et al., 2011). It is important to bear these factors in mind when examining the previous literature on the barriers to participation in mainstream adult education as against the barriers to participation in prison education.

In terms of the adult education literature, the barriers to participation were originally divided into internal and external factors (Johnstone and Rivera, 1965). Later these were recategorised into dispositional, situational and institutional factors (Cross, 1981). Informational factors was added as a separate category by Darkenwald and Merriam (1982), though many still consider this to be a subcategory of institutional factors.

Situational barriers

Situational barriers refer to barriers that are unique to the person and their own situation, such as family or time commitments (Cross, 1981) or lack of financial support (Hardin, 2008). There is often an overlap in relation to situational and dispositional barriers since both categories refer to the individual. Cross (1981) suggests that the delineation between the two rests with the internal versus external divide. Situational, therefore, refers to the personal yet external factors experienced by the person that pose an obstacle to their participation in education. In most countries, lack of time, mostly as a result of family responsibilities, is the greatest overall barrier for those who wish to participate in education

(Rubenson and Desjardins, 2009). It is unsurprising that women experience more situational barriers than men (Johnstone and Rivera, 1965; Flynn et al., 2011) due to family responsibilities and time constraints. Situational barriers can also be linked to social class, with those from the middle class more likely to participate in adult learning. Those from the working class who participate will usually possess middle-class characteristics such as higher levels of initial schooling and active participation in community life (McGivney, 1993). Adults with low socioeconomic status experience more situational barriers (Johnstone and Rivera, 1965; Flynn et al., 2011). Those from the working class can view education as something to fill the space until real life – their working life – starts (Paldanius, 2007). While such beliefs are also attitudinal and therefore could be classified as dispositional barriers, they also relate to a person's place in life – such as working class or in prison – and are therefore also situational. Belonging to a culture that encourages education is extremely important to educational outcomes (Flynn et al., 2011). A common barrier to all forms of education including literacy, late secondary, third level and job-related training is not belonging to a culture where these forms of education are considered important. When people from such backgrounds consider pursuing adult education, they also consider the risk of isolating themselves from their families, peers and other support systems (Flynn et al., 2011). The reverse is also true, with those from the middle class more likely to participate in adult learning (McGivney, 1993). Flynn et al. (2011) found that marginalised learners experience higher situational and dispositional barriers than others and that this was caused by previous experiences and cultures relating to their background. The culture within the family of origin will have been crucial to a person's ongoing relationship with education (Flynn et al., 2011). The mindset of the previous generation of the working class was that school was unnecessary for future employment – contributing financially was important, not formal education (Flynn et al., 2011). The emotional toll of poverty also creates barriers, fostering shame in feeling different or less than despite their best efforts to change their life circumstances. Poverty, social class, racial differences and a perceived lack of ability often resulted in feelings of isolation, inferiority, hostility and poor personal relationships (Flynn et al., 2011). Where students felt they were viewed as not intelligent enough by teachers or seen as a troublemaker if they acted out, this led to frustration, lack of confidence and a reluctance to be in school and resulted in early school leaving and a reluctance to return to education later in life (Flynn et al., 2011).

In the prison context, situational factors may include an internalised narrative that education is not worth the trouble or will not be of any benefit after release (Manger et al., 2018). An important factor in relation to non-participation in vocational training is a preference for other activities in limited out-of-cell time (Brosens et al., 2015). Repeat offenders and those with longer sentences tend to access vocational education, with those who do not participate indicating that their sentence is too short or they do not need the training

(Brosens et al., 2015). Those serving short sentences (O'Keeffe et al., 2007; Alos et al., 2015) or in the early stages of imprisonment (Brosens et al., 2015) are most likely to perceive situational barriers to vocational training, rather than institutional or dispositional. Such barriers can be a result of being new to the prison environment, being on remand, uncertainty around their release date or uncertainty as to the prison where they will serve their sentence (Callan and Gardner, 2005; Brosens et al., 2015). Finally, those serving their first sentence are more likely to want to do other things such as going to work or spending time with visitors (Brosens et al., 2015). These are not necessarily bad choices since going to work will also have a positive impact on the prisoner, as will maintaining family bonds through visits.

Situational considerations can also act as turning points with education for marginalised learners. Events such as having children and wanting to be a good role model lead to a reassessment of the value of education and its role in changing future outcomes (Flynn et al., 2011). Flynn et al. (2011) also found that there were turning points and hope in the narratives of those they interviewed. They found that at various life stages, events occurred that changed expectations of education.

Institutional barriers

Institutional barriers are those policies, procedures or exclusionary criteria on the part of an institution offering adult education that preclude people from participation. Cross (1981) highlights five areas of institutional barriers as follows: (1) scheduling problems; (2) location problems; (3) shortage of interesting courses; (4) procedural or time requirements; and (5) lack of information about programmes and procedures. It appears from research that financial considerations and costly fees are the highest institutional barrier to adult education (Rubenson and Desjardins, 2009), which of course would not be relevant to the prison context. A poor curriculum, in the sense that it is irrelevant to adults' everyday lives or is uninteresting, also discourages some adult learners from enrolling in adult education (Bamber and Tett, 2010), and this might apply in the prison since the school is competing with other activities during limited out-of-cell time. Furthermore, a barrier for some adult learners is a perception that programmes use overly didactic teaching styles and inappropriate learning materials (Bamber and Tett, 2010). Both of these latter points would surely be relevant in the prison context where potential learners may expect that what they will learn will be boring and will not benefit them going forward and they will not understand a significant amount of the material, even if this is not the case in practice.

In the prison-specific context, one of the earliest studies to touch on barriers to prison education found that institutional issues were the greatest obstacles to participation, with informational factors forming a significant proportion of the barriers (Eikeland et al., 2009). For example, 20% to 25% of survey participants said that either the prison did not offer educational programmes, they were not aware of the programmes on offer, or the ones that were available were not suitable to them (Eikeland et al., 2009). This lack of information about available courses appears to be a significant institutional barrier faced by prisoners (O'Keeffe et al., 2007; Westrheim and Manger, 2014; Brosens et al., 2015; Manger et al., 2018). This is concerning. Given that education is a human right (Munoz, 2009), it is important to ensure that prisoners are provided with information in order to allow them to exercise this right. While the findings of the current study will be discussed fully later, it is interesting to note that many prisoners interviewed reported not being told about education options during their committal meeting[1] with the governor. The failure to provide prisoners with information in relation to education goes beyond being a barrier to education and could in many ways be seen to be a breach of a person's human rights.

Other institutional factors that have been found to act as barriers to prison education include inadequate practical arrangements (Manger et al., 2018), inadequate access to software and the internet (Manger et al., 2018), waiting lists for popular classes (Westrheim and Manger, 2014), not receiving any follow-up to their applications for prison education courses (Westrheim and Manger, 2014; Brosens et al., 2015) and a lack of resources and staff (O'Keeffe et al., 2007).

Dispositional barriers

Dispositional barriers, sometimes called psychosocial barriers, refer to individual beliefs, values and attitudes that obstruct organised learning. A lack of interest, feeling too old to learn, a previous negative experience with schooling or not enjoying the process of studying are common examples of dispositional barriers (Darkenwald and Merriam, 1982). Attitudes and expectations (McGivney, 1993), in addition to lack of confidence and self-esteem, (Bailey and Coleman, 1998) also act as significant barriers to educational participation. Dispositional barriers are not as consistent as situational or institutional factors and vary greatly among people and cultures (Rubenson and Desjardins, 2009). Several studies comparing education participants with non-participants indicate that negative attitudes and dispositions towards adult education are by far the most deterring factor (Rubenson, 2007). Dispositional barriers are particularly dominant among older adults, lower-educated adults and low-skill and blue-collar workers, where there has not been a prevailing culture of the value of education in their family or community as children and young adults (Flynn et al., 2011). The influence of family, past experiences with education, community perceptions, or a troubled education history and poor performance in school are significant obstacles to education (Bamber and Tett, 2010; Flynn et al., 2011). Where negative attitudes about education are held by family, friends or other significant partners, there can be a conflict in relation to participation, upward mobility or evolving social class. This can then lead to feelings of isolation and guilt that ultimately deter participation in education (Bamber and Tett, 2010). Therefore, while education is often regarded as a voluntary act, there is often a struggle among free will, self-determinism and external social factors or past personal factors that constrain the person (Rubenson and Desjardins, 2009).

In terms of prison education, dispositional barriers may relate to reading and writing difficulties, mathematical difficulties and finding it hard to concentrate in prison – however, this might also be situational as it relates to the prison itself (Manger et al., 2018). Both Manger et al. (2018) and Brosens et al. (2015) found that dispositional factors were not a significant barrier to participation in prison education. Brosens et al. (2015) found that dispositional factors were the least mentioned category in their study examining barriers to vocational training in prison. Dispositional factors may be higher than alluded to in these pieces of research, however, since it is often easier to push the reason or blame onto aspects of prison life rather than to admit or to even recognise that the true reason is related to an issue with literacy or a learning disability, for example (Manger et al., 2018). This suggestion is based on the prevalence of literacy and numeracy issues among prisoners. In a study examining educational backgrounds, 33% of prisoners self-reported reading difficulties, 25% reported writing difficulties and 25% reported mathematical difficulties (Eikeland et al., 2009). Given the extent of these highly dispositional issues, it is difficult to see how they would not be represented in a more significant way in the barriers research unless they were being hidden behind other reasons, perhaps out of a sense of shame or embarrassment. Furthermore, in society dispositional factors such as literacy or numeracy pose a more likely hindrance to men than to women. Yet this is not borne out in the prison setting, where it is women who tend to be more affected by dispositional barriers to education. Manger et al. (2018) suggest that this is because those women who are incarcerated will tend to have greater issues with such things as literacy, numeracy and addiction than is typical within the external community. Moreover, in the prison setting men are less likely to admit to such issues out of bravado, which may account for the disparity in the prison setting as against the community (Manger et al., 2018). Finally, Hawley (2011) reports that in a survey of national co-coordinators of education (or their equivalent) on a Europe-wide basis, lack of motivation and a previous negative experience of mainstream education are the most commonly cited barriers to participation in prison education. However, these results reflect the views of those responsible for prison education provision, and while this role may place them in a good position to offer an opinion, anything other than the views of prisoners themselves amounts to speculation.

Findings: barriers to participation in prison education

Given the reported value of prison education, it is important to encourage participation as much as possible. From the statistic outlined at the beginning of this chapter, it is clear that there is an enormous number of prisoners who either do not wish to participate in prison education or experience barriers to their participation. Lowering barriers to education is key to encouraging as many prisoners as possible to use the opportunity to engage with education. By understanding these barriers it will ultimately ensure that any efforts to lower them and to encourage greater participation in education can be well placed.

In the current study, both participants and non-participants were asked about the reasons for non-participation in prison education. This was done for two reasons: first, to ascertain the reasons that the actual cohort of non-participants were not participating in education and, second, to contrast the reasons given by non-participants with the reasons given by participants as to why they felt others were not participating. Many of the inmates who were now participating in education had spent periods of time when they were not participating in education and were therefore in a position to say why they felt others weren't participating. As a snapshot, motivation, illiteracy, accessibility and drugs appear to be the greatest obstacles to participation in prison education.

Lack of motivation/hopelessness

Over half of the non-participants stated that the reason they were not participating was because they had no interest in education. For many, this lack of interest in education appeared to stem from a sense of hopelessness and an inability to change their situation. They were deeply aware of the stigma they were going to face, especially in relation to employment. Fran's quote demonstrates this, where he talks about how pointless he feels it is to take any measures to change his life since society will not be forgiving of his prison sentence.

> FRAN: I don't see meself coming up here getting any benefit out of it at all . . . if I was to go out and try get a job, try change me life, I'll get asked where are ya after being, you're 45 years of age. When I say in jail for me whole life, who's going to give me a job? . . . I know for a fact if they look at me they're not going to say "well fuck it, give him a chance".
>
> (Mountjoy, non-participant)

A similar sentiment was offered by Neil, a non-participant who spoke about the role of drugs in the attitude of prisoners. Being an addict will always trump any effort to change other aspects of their life since the priority will always be drugs and drug dealing.

> NEIL: I think a lot of them don't see the point in education when they can go out and sell gear . . . they think what's the point in getting education, when I get out I'm going to be strung out again.
>
> (Mountjoy, non-participant)

It is interesting that this prisoner relayed the reasons that others were not participating in education, but not his own. He spoke in the third person despite being asked about his own reasons. It is difficult therefore to ascertain whether this is his own perception of his reasons for not accessing education or whether it is what he perceives of others and does not want to give his own personal rationale for not participating.

A small number non-participants stated that they did not see the point in participating, as they are already qualified enough for their trade or job. For example, Larry, a non-participant from Shelton Abbey, stated "*I love me trade and I have no interest in doing anything else*". This is reflective of a situational barrier where a person feels they do not need any other education since they have a trade and an education already. This attitude towards education is representative of the narrow view taken to education whereby it is only a means to an end and serves no greater purpose than ensuring a particular job. It does not recognise that participating in other courses can expand the mind and world view and can be undertaken just for the sake of it. This may be related to social class and a prevailing idea in the family of origin that education is unimportant and once employment/employability is achieved, education has no further use (Flynn et al., 2011).

Many of the participants, who often referred to the non-participant's lack of motivation as laziness, stated it as the primary reason for non-participation. The participants spoke about the other prisoners who were too lazy to do something to better themselves.

RAYMOND: They're lazy, they don't want to do anything for themselves. They're happy enough to sit down for themselves and watch telly or do whatever, they've no motivation in themselves.

(Mountjoy, participant)

These narratives are in line with the previous research by Hawley (2011), where prison educators predicted that a lack of motivation was the greatest obstacle to prison education. They also echo the findings in Manger et al. (2018), who suggested that prison education was not worth the trouble and "not worth the trouble" was a strong situational factor. Fran's quote gives a strong indication of this sense of hopelessness, with the prisoners questioning why they would bother to participate when there was nothing that could change their situation, either at present or after release. Their accounts reflected the belief that they would face insurmountable stigma and prejudice in society, with little hope of getting a job. They did not feel that education could change this. This reflects a strong sense of hopelessness and a lack of belief in their ability to overcome the various obstacles that they would face in society. The lack of motivation and the sense of hopelessness displayed represent significant situational and dispositional barriers to participation in education. The situational element arises in the sense of the situation they find themselves in – a criminal record, a prison sentence and returning to a society deeply prejudiced towards those people who have previously been to prison. The dispositional barrier arises from their sense of not being able to change their future. The sense of hopelessness is also strongly indicative of the condemnation script outlined by Maruna (2001) that will be discussed in the next chapter.

Lack of literacy

Both participants and non-participants mentioned a lack of literacy as a significant barrier to education. Many of those who were participating in prison education stated that a lack of literacy was the main reason that prisoners did not participate in prison education. They stated that it was a prevalent problem among prisoners and expected that people were too embarrassed to come to the school for literacy classes, as other prisoners would then know they were not literate. One participant from Mountjoy, Peter, who had severe literacy issues when he was committed to prison, stated that the experience of not being literate in society carried over into prison and it stopped people getting help. He explained that just because a person was in prison did not ease the feelings of shame, embarrassment and the anticipation of ridicule in not being able to read and write. There was a worry in going to the school that people would guess that there was an issue, and this caused a barrier to education.

> PETER: When I came in here (prison), I didn't feel any different, like it was the same as outside, it's not something you want people knowing wherever ya are. In me mind I knew I was no different to half of them out there (in the prison), but it's embarrassing in this day and age not being able to read or write properly. It held me back big time in me life, just not being able to do things but not being able to tell people either cos you're afraid to say it. In prison you're a tough nut, you don't go tellin' people you deepest darkest secrets or what not. For a long time I wouldn't even go to the school cos I thought the lads would see why I was going . . . and I didn't even want to say it to a teacher . . . (a) lot of lads are the same (illiterate); they won't come here out of fear or shame,. or pride.
>
> (Mountjoy, participant)

A lack of literacy was also mentioned by four non-participants from Mountjoy as being a reason for non-participation. However, none of the non-participants claimed it was the reason that they did not participate in education or that it had ever been an issue for them. Instead they mentioned it as possibly being an issue for others in accessing education in prison. Two stated that many of those who are not literate feel that they cannot participate in education as they do not know what is available for them in terms of literacy courses. Another suggested that new committals be tested and given advice on what is available to them to improve their skills. Three of the non-participants also stated that a prisoner who lacks literacy skills would be embarrassed or ashamed, and this would stand in his way.

ANDY: I think even then they might be too embarrassed to come up. It's like revealing themselves to other prisoners, like here look I can't read or write. (Mountjoy, non-participant)

Morgan and Kett (2003) highlighted the severe problem with levels of literacy among the Irish prison population. While it was not admitted to as being a problem for any of the non-participants, some prisoners participating in education speculated that literacy issues and the shame and embarrassment that surrounds them are a significant reason that prisoners are not participating. The use of Integrated Sentence Management, which was only in its infancy during the data collection phase of the research but has now been established more extensively within the prison system (Irish Prison Service, 2020), will possibly address this by assessing the needs of prisoners when they arrive in prison and using a sentence plan to address these needs. The use of peer mentoring schemes, such as Toe by Toe, where trusted and trained prisoners with good literacy skills help other prisoners on a one-to-one basis, often in their own cell so as to avoid the need to expose themselves as having literacy problems, also help to address these barriers. The prevalence of this dispositional barrier to participation in education is contrary to the findings in both Manger et al. (2018) and Brosens et al. (2015), who both found that dispositional barriers were the least significant barrier to prison education. However, they recognise that dispositional barriers may be higher than represented in their studies since it is often easier to use another factor within the prison as a reason for not participation, instead of exposing a problem with literacy on their own part (Manger et al., 2018). In the current research, either those who mentioned literacy issues tended to be talking about an issue they previously had or they were referring to the issues they thought "others" had that prevented engagement with education.

Drugs

Several non-participants reasoned that many prisoners are not participating because they are too involved in drugs to want anything more from prison life. Only one, a Mountjoy inmate, admitted that this was the reason that he was not participating in education. The others stated that prisoners used drugs to block everything out and as a result would barely realise the option for education was there and were certainly not clearheaded enough to get up and go to the school. The lives of those who were using drugs revolved around sourcing and taking drugs to the exclusion of everything else.

FRAN: There's a lot of fellas that have interests in things like drugs and they spend their days plotting and planning how to get drugs. And then when they get them they sit around and take them and smoke them. So they don't have time to go to school. And 99.9% of the lads who don't come to school, that's the reason.

(Mountjoy, non-participant)

This was echoed in many statements and opinions given by the prisoners who are participating in prison education when asked about why they believed so many other prisoners were opting to not participate in education. Those who were participating in education maintained that drugs are a significant reason that others were not participating in education. Several said that those who were using drugs had no motivation towards anything else; finding and using drugs was their focus and furthermore when using drugs they would not have the capacity to participate in education.

STEPHEN: When the drugs are involved they don't have the, em, the ability, is that the right word, to give to school, they're out of their heads and are barely able to get out of bed, not to mind coming up and working hard in the school.

(Mountjoy, participant)

Drugs did not appear to be an issue in Shelton Abbey; it was not mentioned by either participants or non-participants, most likely because it is a drug-free centre. However, some of the prisoners in Shelton Abbey did indicate that drugs were a significant obstacle for participation in education in other prisons they had been in.

Security

A significant institutional barrier in Mountjoy Prison was the security levels within the school. Half of the Mountjoy non-participants mentioned it as a reason that they were not participating in education, and most of those who had given up education cited it as one of their main reasons for giving up. There were three reasons for this. First, the location of the school was problematic from a security point of view, as it was accessible only by a single narrow stairwell which is five flights high. Second, the school itself is staffed by only two or three officers, in addition to the teachers, which is a low level of security by comparison to the rest of the prison. Third, while certain prisoners may be separated in the general prison for security, the school is not capable of enforcing this segregation and all inmates mix together in the school. Many prisoners who feel they might be a target for aggression or attacks tend to avoid the school for those reasons. Niall, a non-participant, illustrates the problem here.

NIALL: If you come up to the school there's no protection up here . . . you've two officers up here for like 20 (to) 30 prisoners, if a riot kicks off that's it. By the time they get up all them stairs. And it's not fair cos there's lads up here only in and they're only trying to pass the time and they're getting cut up. Like it's not fair on most people. Like and if they can have metal detectors for searching the people coming in for visits they could easily have them at the end of the stairs to search the people coming up to the school.

(Mountjoy, non-participant)

This represents a significant obstacle to education that does not appear to be represented in the previous literature. Security is necessarily an issue of high concern in prisons for staff and prisoners. Prison is also characterised by mistrust and watchfulness, and those within the prison are constantly vigilant of threats and aware of taking measures to protect their own safety. Any area where concerns exist is likely to be avoided by a prisoner who has reason to believe he is under any threat – which is likely to apply to a high percentage of the prison population. Taking measures to address this is difficult due to resourcing and the realities of a particular prison's physical structure. Where the prison school is seen as an "oasis" by some, it is likely to be an attractive place to spend time. However, where it is a place where prisoners perceive their fear and watchfulness must prevail it is likely to represent a significant institutional barrier to participating in education. It is unsurprising, therefore, that security, being such a strong institutional barrier, discourages many prisoners from attending the prison school.

Lack of interesting or available courses

A strong institutional barrier arising was a lack of places available in particular subjects. This mirrors the findings in Manger et al. (2018) regarding practical arrangement and that of Westrheim and Manger (2014) relating to waiting lists for popular classes. People were reluctant to attend the school due to a lack of practical or interesting subjects or having to wait for a place due to these classes being oversubscribed. In fact, some prisoners who had previously undertaken education but dropped out mentioned a lack of interesting or available courses as the main reason for leaving the school. Prisoners tended to favour the practical subjects in the school to the more academic subjects. Damien, in his quote, commented that the traditional school subjects reminded prisoners of mainstream school and this might put some people off. Subjects such as art, cookery and mosaics, for example, were extremely popular. However, those subjects tended to have waiting lists, which put prisoners off attending these classes as they did not want to wait for spaces to become available.

DAMIEN: But it is limited up here, and there's a lot of lads who don't have an interest in the stuff that's being done cos it's been done in school. And if they come in halfway through the year they have to wait, and if it's a popular subject they have to wait.

(Mountjoy, non-participant)

Andy mentioned that he wanted to do a particular subject but it was one which was limited in availability and places only seemed to go to those who were already in the school.

ANDY: And then there's the fitness instructors class that I want to get into, but the catch is you kind of have to be up in the school to get it so I'm kinda caught that way as well.

(Mountjoy, non-participant)

Andy raises an interesting issue. Where waiting lists and other requirements represent barriers to accessing education, especially in more practical and gateway modules, making an effort to lower the prerequisites may provide a route for more people to engage in education and is to be encouraged. However, where courses exist that will qualify someone for a career or profession, it seems reasonable to expect that the person would attend the school in advance of participating in that course to ensure that they not only have the capacity in terms of necessary literacy and skills but that they also have the commitment to undertake the programme. This should also be true of courses such as fitness instruction, which are ultimately quite academic with modules such anatomy and physiology inherent in their syllabi. It does not seem unfair to give preference to those who have already demonstrated a level of commitment to their education and a competence to undertake the course in advance of being allocated a place. It is interesting that the prisoner in question wished to undertake the course and understood the need to attend school in advance and yet decided this was ultimately not worth it. It is illustrative of the high dispositional barriers that exist within prisoners that even they themselves might not ultimately be aware of.

Problems in physically accessing education

An institutional factor that arose several times throughout the interviews was physical access to the school on a daily basis. In the Mountjoy sample, a small number of non-participants stated that getting to the school was an issue. One said that he tried to get to the school but was often not allowed up by prison officers as his name was not on the list of participants for that day. This is an example of the operational issues outlined by O'Gorman (2011) in his audit of prison education in Irish prisons that hinder participation in education. Christopher had formerly participated in prison education and had stopped out a sense of frustration at not being able to go to school on the days that he was scheduled for classes.

CHRISTOPHER: Cos I . . . lost motivation. I came up once or twice and just got sick of it . . . (t)here would be mornings the screws wouldn't let you up or they'd let you up too late for you to do anything.

(Mountjoy, non-participant)

This was only mentioned in the Mountjoy sample. However, this may be due to the fact that the other prison used for data collection was a low-security prison where people made their own way to the school and were not reliant on officers or unlocking of gates to access the building in Shelton Abbey. Furthermore, there was not much detail on the prevalence of this issue. While it might not have been a consistent occurrence, the nature of these learners is that they need routine and as little disruption as possible given the tentative steps they are taking towards education. Their links with the school will be fragile in the early stages, and all efforts to make access to the school as easy as possible ought to be promoted. The Joint Irish Prison Service/Education and Training Board Strategy on Education 2019–2022 indicates a commitment to ensuring specially trained officers within the school and an effort to minimise the barriers to physical access, and this is to be encouraged.

Routine and alternatives to education

An issue that does not appear to be reflected in the previous literature on the barriers to prison education and in many ways is related to the point of problems in physically accessing education is the influence of routine on participation in prison education. Some prisoners mentioned that they did not participate in prison education because when they tried to access the school and education they could not do so, either because the module they wanted was subject to a waiting list or because they tried to access the school during a holiday period. By the time they were allocated a place or the school resumed after holidays, they had established an alternative routine and were reluctant to deviate from it. This was the experience of James who is quoted here. This can also be a reason for prisoners dropping out of education as when they leave the school for a period, they lose motivation.

JAMES: I was doing grand up here I was . . . over the holidays then I kind of lost interest . . . I just couldn't be bothered coming back up. Just lost motivation basically.

(Mountjoy, non-participant)

Several prisoners mentioned they did not participate in education as they already had a set routine and/or were already engaging in alternatives such as the gym. Arriving in prison is daunting for most people; while many will have comrades in prison, others will be eager to find friends or a group where they can fit in and feel like they belong during their sentence. Along with this comes a routine that helps the days go by quicker, and once they establish this routine they are reluctant to break it. This sense of routine is outlined by Kevin.

KEVIN: I'd rather do the gym and workout all the time. Every morning I do the gym. Then I'll do me laps in the yard and then make me phone call at

> half five. Score a bit of hash and back into the cell for the night. Chill back then, have a yap on the phone.
>
> (Mountjoy, non-participant)

Routine is often dictated by the group with which they find themselves associating. This routine usually involves activities such as the school, gym or workshops or simply spending their out-of-cell time in the yard. Most of the prisoners who were participating in education had found their way to the school early in their sentence. Several of those not participating in education stated that they either arrived during the summer break or had put their name on a waiting list. When they were eventually called for the school, they had already established themselves with a group of friends and a routine and were not prepared to change this. This was the scenario faced by Damien, who arrived in prison during the summer and wanted to do a cookery class. In addition to delays due to holiday, Damien also had to go on a waiting list for this popular class. He then slipped into an easy routine and did not take up his place when it became available. This is disappointing, as subjects such as cookery can be gateway courses to other forms of education.

> DAMIEN: When I was waiting to be called, I went to the gym and a lot of lads get into the workshops so they've got their routine. So when you come into prison you're looking for your bearings, you want to find something to do, you're trying to get into a routine. As soon as you find a routine, you don't want to change so I'm happy with what I'm doing at the moment so I think that's what happens.
>
> (Mountjoy, non-participant)

However, one of the participants mentioned that they began using the gym shortly after arriving in prison and the interest in exercise led to them to enquire about the fitness instructors course in the school. Therefore, this routine, where it involves other positive activities, can be a gateway activity that might ultimately lead to the school.

On the face of it, this appears to be an issue with impeded access to the school through closures or waiting lists and is therefore institutional in nature. However, when the findings are examined further, it appears that this reluctance towards education is also quite dispositional in nature. When people were not able to access education immediately, they subsequently developed an alternative routine that they were reluctant to give up. It was apparent in the findings that routine is extremely important in prison. When people arrive in prison, they like to get into a routine as quickly as possible. It appears that if school does not form part of this original routine, they are reluctant to break their routine later in order to participate in education. Furthermore, a small number of prisoners who began participating in education but subsequently dropped out found it hard to say why they left prison education, putting it down to simply not being able to settle in the school. Perhaps this indicates again the power of habit, with those who have an established prison-orientated routine finding it difficult to switch to a school-orientated routine, thus representing a barrier to participation. If they do go to the school, they often find it difficult to settle and return to their old routine again. It appears that the barrier to participation here is dispositional and institutional in nature.

Friends and peer influence

A strong situational barrier manifest throughout the course of the interviews was being involved with a non-education-orientated peer group in prison. Showing the influence of peer group and the "birds of a feather flock together" ideology, there was an expectation that prisoners would stick with their friends, either those they knew from outside prison or friends they made since beginning their sentence. If the norm in that group did not involve the school, they were likely to stick with these friends rather than going to the school. When prisoners established themselves within a peer group, they were reluctant to leave it.

> PAUL: They have friends from the outside, already here and he sort of is pushed or expected to do the yard thing and do stuff like that. Seeing him coming up to the school, the lads would be giving him a bit of stick . . . he'd be sort of expected to join with the gang . . . and when you get into that routine out there you're not going to come up here cos if all the lads are down there no one likes being left out . . . so they all stick together and everyone heads out to the yard and basically does nothing.
>
> (Mountjoy, participant)

Again this demonstrates the importance of routine in the prison, which appears to be a priority for prisoners. It also demonstrates the strong, often negative, influence of peers in the prison setting. Perhaps a suggestion that might combat this would be to separate peers as much as possible when allocating them to a landing or cell. The use of a school buddy system may also be helpful in guiding new prisoners to the school in the early part of their sentence.

Length of sentence

Manger et al. (2018) contended that those with longer sentences faced greater institutional barriers and lower situational barriers than those serving shorter sentences. This was reflected in the current study, where prisoners mentioned being worried about the limited number of courses that were available in the prison school. An example of this is James, a non-participant, who said that he was not participating in education because he was facing a lengthy sentence and he was worried about running out of courses if he started to participate too early. Again, this represents an institutional barrier to prison education. Providing opportunities for progression such as Open University degrees and ensuring that this information was made known to all could help in lowering this barrier to education. This might help those with longer sentences engage at an early stage instead of feeling the need to pace themselves with education to make it last the entirety of their sentence.

Past experience of mainstream education

Some non-participants spoke about not enjoying mainstream school when they were younger but did not actually list it as a reason for not participating in prison education. However, it seemed that a previous negative experience can act as a subconscious barrier to education. Prisoners were asked about their reasons for leaving school in order to ascertain their past relationship with education. The reasons for leaving school fell into three distinct categories, with only one or two prisoners falling outside of this. Participants tended to report leaving school of their own accord in order to get jobs and earn money, for example. However, non-participants tended to give reasons such as expulsion, not enjoying school or various personal problems for leaving mainstream school. The accounts of Martin and Niall that follow are indicative of some of the accounts in relation to previous experiences of school.

NIALL: Like I never liked school. I went to a school where we were hit with a cane. I took the cane off the teacher and hit him with it and that was the end of me like. It just wasn't worth going.

(Mountjoy, non-participant)

MARTIN: I went to the Christian Brothers and saw terrible things happening to people. And I think a lot of times people are taking drugs to blank out a lot of things that happened to them in the past. I went to the Christian Brothers and was hit with bamboo sticks and things like that, but others had it way worse.

(Mountjoy, non-participant)

None of those who spoke negatively about their experience of mainstream education were participating in prison education. However, the analysis of the data appeared to show a strong relationship between the accounts of the non-participants and a negative past experience of education. This shows the influence that a poor experience of education in childhood can have on the life course of the individual and in particular their future educational endeavours. It appears that a past negative experience of education may have a significant influence over the life course. Educational disadvantage is widely reported as having a strong role to play in criminality (National Crime Council, 2002). Therefore, leaving school early due to a negative experience of education may have influenced the onset of offending in the first place and remains a considerable barrier as an adult to improving education and tackling the associated disadvantages. This also reflects the considerable bearing that dispositional factors can have on the life of the prisoner and their ability to access the "hooks for change" (Giordano et al., 2002) when they present themselves.

Summary and discussion: barriers to participation in prison education

The barriers to prison education faced by prisoners in the current research tends to fall into all three of the categories outline in the literature. In previous studies, institutional barriers tended to be the most common form of barrier to prison education (Eikeland et al., 2009), with informational barriers contributing significantly to these institutional obstacles. This was not reflected in the current research, with institutional issues being only a moderate contributor to the overall barriers that hindered participation. Security in the school was perhaps the greatest institutional barrier faced, with many prisoners conscious of the safety risks within the school, many mentioning the availability of knives in cooking classes as being a source of vulnerability, for example. Addressing this issue is not simple. It is unlikely that resources would allow classes to be offered on a more segregated basis. However, extra measures such as adequate staffing with extra prison officers could make a difference. Other institutional barriers, such as a lack of interesting courses, waiting lists for courses and not being able to access the school all year round were mentioned. These issues are interrelated and within the control of the prison and education service. While they are resource-dependent, there is scope to address these issues in order to promote greater participation in education. This also reinforces the need to ensure that the adult education approach, including a wide variety of subjects and courses, is offered to attract those who are considering education. Once in education, these more popular modules acted as gateways to more long-term courses of study, and therefore, addressing these issues could be an important part of increasing participation rates.

Situational and dispositional barriers were represented to a significant extent in the findings. However, there is a strong degree of overlap between the two, with many barriers having the potential to be classified as either situation or dispositional. Cross (1981) acknowledges that both are personal in nature, but situational refers to external personal barriers, while personal internal barriers are dispositional. The issue that seems to arise in the context of the current research is that the *prima facie* difficulty is situational, yet the underlying issues that are actually causing the barrier are dispositional. This can be observed in most of the points that follow. A lack of motivation to participate in prison education was the greatest barrier to participation in the current research. This was classified as a situational factor by Manger et al. (2018) due to the fact that the hopelessness relates to the situation that they find themselves in as a convicted criminal serving a sentence of imprisonment. However, it could also be argued that the sense of hopelessness is an internalised narrative and is therefore a dispositional barrier (Darkenwald and Merriam, 1982). The voices of the men were deeply negative and were characterised by a lack of confidence and a lack self-belief to see a way around the hurdles they will face upon released. Such negativity is a characteristic of the condemnation script highlighted in Chapter 5 that can undermine the desistance process (Maruna, 2001). Literacy issues and addiction are two situational hurdles that are well represented in the literature and are also reflected in the current research. Again it is difficult to classify these barriers to prison education as it is often the underlying issues, rather than the *prima facie* difficulty, that results in the barrier. In the context of low literacy, Manger et al. (2018) classify this as a dispositional barrier. While the issue is external to the person and therefore strictly situational, the low levels of self-esteem (Bailey and Coleman, 1998) in addition to the shame and fear associated with having this issue exposed are deeply internalised, and it is therefore dispositional in nature. A similar argument can be made of drug addiction. The addiction is seen to be situational, but it is the lack of interest in anything other than finding and using drugs that creates the obstacle to education, and again this is representative of a dispositional barrier. An interesting feature of the findings relating to low literacy levels was the way in which this was often hidden, mentioned only by the men who were participating in education. Those who were not participating did not mention it as a reason that they themselves were not participating. This may represent an externalising of the reasons for not participating as opposed to looking at the underlying rationale. This becomes relevant again in the context of desistance in both Chapters 5 and 6.

Finally, it appeared that a significant barrier to education in prison is a past negative experience of education. While none of the non-participants said it was a reason for not participating, their responses to other questions showed that many had been expelled or had bad memories of abuses, for example. When this is coupled with the various characteristics of marginalised learners such as a lack of educational culture growing up, it is not difficult to see why these men attach little importance to education. They do not recognise the many benefits it may hold for them. Addressing this obstacle is difficult since attendance at the school is voluntary and therefore they are unlikely to see how education in prison differs from their previous experience growing up. Encouraging prisoners to try education will be key to overcoming this.

The school space

Several of the participants and non-participants from both Mountjoy and Shelton Abbey referred to the school itself as distinct from education. This is interesting, as it denotes a difference between the actual physical space and experiences therein as distinct from the learning that takes place there. For many of those participating in prison education, the school is not experienced as part of the prison and is an escape from prison life and the prison environment. The majority of education participants experience the school as being laid back and normal by comparison to the prison landings. Participants mentioned being treated with respect and dignity and being given encouragement. This appeared to be in contrast to the way they feel they are treated in the general prison itself. This lifts their spirits and allows them to feel positive for a few hours a day. Darren succinctly summed up his experience of the school.

DARREN: The school is an oasis . . . in terms of the people and the teachers and the officers who are universally supportive and encouraging. This is an oasis of civility which one doesn't always find at the end of the stairs. . . . Up here you get a real sense of calm and peace; it's a few hours where you can relax. In the prison you feel in a constant state of watchfulness . . . the school is a place where I can feel quite secure and at peace.

(Mountjoy, participant)

This is similar to the earlier accounts in relation to the motivations to participate in prison education, where many of the men stated they originally came to the school to escape aspects of prison life. The experience of the prison can have profoundly harmful consequences for the person (Costelloe and Warner, 2014; Crewe, 2011). Time away from the carceral space in a more normalised environment can be key to ensuring the minimising of the harmful effects of the sentence. It appears that those incarcerated experience the school as providing this reprieve. Darren describes a sense of "watchfulness" that he feels he must maintain in prison. It is likely that a characteristic of prison life is a continued vigilance for one's safety which, added to the various other stresses of the prison environment, can have a strong impact on mental health. Being able to move away from this hypervigilance for even a few hours a day would be instrumental in maintaining mental health throughout the prison sentence.

Participants mentioned the teachers in the schools and made many positive comments about the role of teachers in their positive experience of education. Participants used terms such as "supporting", "encouraging", "helpful", "fantastic", "welcoming" and "down to earth" to describe the teachers. Some seemed surprised by contrast to their memories of mainstream school, where they did not experience teachers as being inclusive or attentive. Several mentioned the respect they felt from their current teachers, stating that the approach of their teachers added to their overall enjoyment of the school. Strong relationships, respect and trust are significant contributors to social capital, and thus such an approach by teachers can have a role in fostering social capital and a sense of self confidence among participants. The following quotes from Vincent, Craig and Patrick show the tone of the majority of comments made about teachers.

VINCENT: You're being encouraged and treated differently with teachers, treated with respect and with dignity. It's not as if you're a number and it's that interaction and communication.

(Shelton Abbey, participant)

CRAIG: Cos the school that I was in the teachers weren't great. If you couldn't keep up you were just left at the back so that was it. And what I've found with school in prisons if they're going too fast for you the teacher will stop or give you an extra class. They won't leave you behind.

(Mountjoy, participant)

PATRICK: I think I was lucky in that the people I met I clicked with because I used to have a problem with authority cos I hated anyone talking down to me. Like I'd be the type if they're a High Court judge or a person begging on the street, they're still a person so I find the respect approach with education really sat well with me.

(Ex-prisoner)

Among the wealth of positive comments relating to teachers in the prison school, there was also some more negative feedback. It was clear that the feedback was often dependent upon how long a person had been in education and the level they were at. Those who were new to education or who weren't engaging with education on a very regular basis seemed to maintain a degree of suspicion around the teachers and didn't seem as forthright in their praise of the teachers by comparison to those prisoners who were participating in education regularly and had been in the school for a while. Furthermore, what was seen to be a positive by one participant was mentioned in a negative way by another. In contrasting the praise of Craig in his earlier quote with the criticism by Raymond in the upcoming quote, where both are talking about a similar approach by teachers, it is clear that both construe a similar approach in quite a different manner. Raymond felt that the teachers treated him like a child when he first came to the school and he contemplated dropping out of his classes, but they eventually saw that he was capable of more and he understood that everyone needed to start somewhere and persevered.

RAYMOND: I kind of think that when you first come up the school you're kind of treated like a kid. Like and I know there are people who are like kids and can't read and write. But I think when the teachers see how far you can go, then you know there's no point in doing that (dropping out).

(Mountjoy, participant)

Another participant (Derek) also commented on how he thought the teachers were intimidated by the prisoners.

DEREK: I think a lot of teachers in here are intimidated by some prisoners . . . most of them get on well with the prisoners, but some of em ya ask them questions and it seems like they're a bit intimidated to answer ya or they're going to insult ya by answering it or something like that. In mainstream school if you're wrong you're wrong and they'll tell you you're wrong; in here they don't. They just tell you to do your best and get on with it.

(Mountjoy, participant)

It is interesting to consider the rationale of the teacher for this type of behaviour. It could be speculated that this would not come from a place of intimidation, but rather their training and a desire to explain things slowly and clearly, especially when they can afford the time with smaller class sizes than they would have if they were teaching in a mainstream school.

Criticisms of prison education

In the course of their accounts, many prisoners made negative comments about prison education. The comments focused on issues such as subject availability, time limitations, environmental obstacles and progression for participants. Criticisms were mostly made by participants, who by their presence in the school were capable of offering informed critiques of prison education. However, some comments were also made by non-participants, and these accounts at times highlighted their misconceptions about the prison school.

According to those who participated in education in prison, the greatest issue was that there was a diverse range of abilities within certain classes which hindered the progress of students. This was further compounded by the fact that prisoners often began courses midway through an academic term, slowing the progress of other participants who were frustrated by having to sit through class material they had already covered. This was mentioned only within the Mountjoy cohort, and perhaps it is the case that this is not an issue elsewhere. Here Mark talks about this problem.

MARK: That gets frustrating cos if you have a new lad coming in, you end up having to go through the last lesson that we had and it slows it down.

(Mountjoy, participant)

Another issue raised in the participants' accounts of their experience was that previous education was not always taken into account by teachers and participants found themselves in classes which they found basic before being allowed to progress. As outlined earlier, one of the most common reasons for continuing with education was enjoyment. It is imagined that a difficult part of a prison teacher's role is getting prisoners to come to the school for the first time. Once a student is in the school, the important task going forward is to keep them there and engaged with their learning. Repetitive material and material that is too basic for the prisoners will ultimately lead to boredom and frustration, the very elements of prison life they are predominantly going to the school to avoid, and this may result in prisoners deciding to leave education. Such issues should be addressed and remedies found – however, this can be difficult unless the resources exist to allow classes to be split and delivered at different levels. Of course, there is also the reality that the previous education experience of prisoners can be piecemeal in nature (O'Mahony, 1997). Prisoners may feel they have covered a certain topic in mainstream school but may not have a full knowledge of the topic. Teachers may be trying to ensure that the person has a complete foundation in the subject before advancing. In the classroom situation, it will always be necessary to go back to basics as some students may know more than others. Therefore, where resources allow it, classes should be held to allow those who are more advanced to progress quicker so as to avoid such issues undermining their attendance at the school.

While the aim in Irish prisons and in many countries around Europe is to provide a broad and wide-ranging curriculum in prisons, subject choice and availability of courses were heavily criticised by those participating and not participating in education. Participants felt that there were not enough subjects available and that the available subjects were predominantly academic; of the practical classes available, there was a high demand and limited spaces. The subjects prisoners wished to participate in were often full and required time on waiting lists. Furthermore, some students were interested in particular classes which were only available in the training unit; the example mentioned by Shane, a Mountjoy participant, was addiction studies.

SHANE: Cos there's so many people coming in and out of here, they're only short courses and then for people who are here for longer they don't really facilitate courses for them. I'm sure there's longer courses in like history and geography, but they're not something I'd be interested in so I don't really get them. Like I'd be into addiction studies but you have to go to the training unit to get it.

(Mountjoy, participant)

As mentioned earlier in relation to barriers to participation, longer-term prisoners were very aware of the limited number of courses and felt that they were running out of options in the school. The limited availability of Open University opportunities was also a source of frustration for some prisoners, and some participants questioned whether or not they would have to repeat courses within the school in order to remain in education. As with slow progress due to mixed abilities in classes, a problem that will arise here is boredom in the school. Again this is concerning, since the primary motive in attending the school for many of the prisoners was to avoid boredom. The likely outcome for many will be leaving the school to find alternatives or going back to spending their free time in the mainstream prison itself.

Warner (2018) recommends that a wide curriculum of education is available to all in line with the adult education approach to prison education. This is important in the context of the earlier comments since it appears that a varied and practical curriculum is desirable to learners. However, as always, resourcing will be an issue and staff, space and materials are considerations that constrain the school in each prison from being able to provide for the wants of every student. It is to be recommended, however, that where possible the creative and practical subjects, which are often the first to be cut back when resourcing is an issue, are well funded and resourced in order to ensure that all aspects of the person and their education is supported.

Mountjoy participants also criticised the operation of the school during prison recreational hours as hindering progress, stating that two hours was not enough time to get to the school, have classes and get back to the prison. This was of particular concern to those hoping to sit state examinations. Luke, from Mountjoy, spoke about the limited time available for education.

LUKE: Well I'm doing me leaving cert in geography, and once a week I've got an hour and a half, that's it and then I have to go sit an exam at the end of it, so it's not a lot.

(Mountjoy, participant)

A few Mountjoy prisoners also mentioned the trouble they encountered at times in getting to the school for classes due to operational issues such as failure to allow the prisoner through access gates or refusal of access because their name was not on the prison officer's list of participants for that day. This problem was also highlighted in O'Gorman's (2011) report on prison education. The Irish Prison Service has committed to training and supporting prison officers in the role of school officers, which is hoped will facilitate the efficient movement of students to and from the school with a view to ensuring that there is as little disruption as possible to the school schedule and time available for education can be maximised (Irish Prison Service, 2019).

Conclusion

This chapter has explored many issues around participation in prison education, predominantly examining the motivations to participate in prison education and the barriers to participation. The previous literature in each area was presented, followed by an exploration and discussion of the empirical findings of the current research in relation to each point. It is hoped that these findings will help to understand why prisoners are engaging with education, why they choose not to undertake education and of course what can be done in order to ensure that as many prisoners as possible engage with the education that is offered during their sentence. For policy makers and practitioners, there are two main actionable issues – getting prisoners to engage in education in the first instance and thereafter minimising attrition and optimising retention. The latter also needs to be addressed, as it appears from the narratives of prisoners that most will only give prison education one attempt; if it does not work out, they do not tend to go back to the school. Therefore, ensuring that there are various measures in place to promote participation and retention is of incredible importance. This might include widely distributed information on the courses available, increasing the number of practical courses, ensuring shorter waiting lists, promoting follow-on courses and developing year-round activities in the school to ensure continued engagement.

Note

1 In Irish prisons, each prisoner has a meeting with the governor of the prison the morning after committal to prison. At this meeting, the governor is supposed to outline various aspects of prison life, including telling the person about the educational and other opportunities available to them in that prison.

References

Alos, R., Esteban, F., Jodar, P. and Miguelez, F. (2015) Effects of Prison Work Programmes on the Employability of Ex-Prisoners. *European Journal of Criminology* 12(1), pp. 35–50. doi:10.1177/1477370814538776.

Atkins, G., Davies, N., Wilkinson, F., Pope, T., Guerin, B. and Tetlow, G. (2019) *Performance Tracker 2019: A Data-Driven Analysis of the Performance of Public Services*. London: Institute for Government.

Bailey, I. and Coleman, U. (1998) *Access and Participation in Adult Literacy Schemes*. Dublin: National Adult Literacy Agency.

Bamber, J. and Tett, L. (2010) Transforming the Learning Experiences of Non-Traditional Students: A Perspective from Higher Education. *Studies in Continuing Education* 22, pp. 57–75. doi:10.1080/713695715.

Baskin, D.R. and Sommers, I.B. (1998) *Casualties of Community Disorder: Women's Careers in Violent Crime*. Boulder: Westview Press. doi:10.1177/0093854813485412.

Behan, C. (2014) Learning to Escape: Prisoner Education, Rehabilitation and the Potential for Transformation. *Journal of Prison Education and Reentry* 1(1), pp. 20–31. doi:10.15845/jper.v1i1.594.

Boshier, R. (1983) *Education Inside: Motives for Participation in Prison Education Programmes*. Vancouver: British Columbia University.

Brosens, D. (2013) Participation in Prison Programmes: Encouraging and Discouraging Factors. In Ponsaers, P., Crawford, A., de Maillard, J., Shapland, J. and Verhage, A. (eds) *Crime, Violence, Justice and Social Order: Monitoring Contemporary Security Issues*. Antwerp: Maklu.

Brosens, D., De Donder, L., Dury, S. and Verté, D. (2015) Barriers to Participation in Vocational Orientation Programmes among Prisoners. *Journal of Prison Education and Reentry* 2(2), pp. 8–22. doi:10.1007/s10610-015-9294-6.

Broussard, S.C. and Garrison, M.E.B. (2004) The Relationship between Classroom Motivation and Academic Achievement in Elementary School-Aged Children. *Family and Consumer Sciences Research Journal* 33(2), pp. 106–120. doi:10.1177/1077727X04269573.

Callan, V. and Gardner, J. (2005) *Vocational Education and Training Provision and Recidivism in Queensland Correctional Institutions*. Adelaide: NCVER.

Chao, R. (2009) Understanding the Adult Learners' Motivation and Barriers to Learning. *Inaugural Conference of the European Society for Research on the Education of Adults*, University of Macedonia, Thessaloniki, Greece, 6–8 November 2009.

Costelloe, A. (2003) *Third Level Education in Irish Prisons: Who Participates and Why?* Unpublished Doctoral Thesis, Milton Keynes: Open University.

Costelloe, A. and Warner, K. (2014) Prison Education across Europe: Policy, Practice, Politics. *London Review of Education* 12(2), pp. 175–183. doi:10.18546/LRE.12.2.03.

Council of Europe (1987) *European Prison Rules*. Strasbourg: Council of Europe.

Council of Europe (1990) *Education in Prison: Recommendation No. R (89) 12*. 13th October 1989. Strasbourg: Council of Europe.

Council of Europe (2006) *European Prison Rules*. Strasbourg: Council of Europe.

Crewe, B. (2011) Depth, Weight, Tightness: Revisiting the Pains of Imprisonment. *Punishment & Society* 13(5), pp. 509–529. doi:10.1177/1462474511422172.

Crewe, B., Liebling, A. and Hulley, S. (2014) Heavy-Light, Absent-Present: Rethinking the 'Weight' of Imprisonment. *The British Journal of Sociology* 65(3), pp. 387–410. doi:10.1111/1468-4446.12084.

Cross, K.P. (1981) *Adults as Learners: Increasing Participation and Facilitating Learning*. San Francisco: Josey-Bass.

Darkenwald, G.G. and Merriam, S.B. (1982) *Adult Education: Foundations of Practice*. New York: Harper & Row.

Deci, E.L., Koestner, R. and Ryan, R.M. (1999) A Meta-Analytic Review of Experiments Examining the Effects of Extrinsic Rewards on Intrinsic Motivation. *Psychological Bulletin* 125(6), pp. 627–668. doi:10.1037/0033-2909.125.6.627.

Deci, E.L. and Ryan, R.M. (1985) *Intrinsic Motivation and Self-Determination in Human Behaviour*. New York: Plenum.

Diseth, Å., Eikeland, O.J., Manger, T. and Hetland, H. (2008) Education of Prison Inmates: Course Experience, Motivation, and Learning Strategies as Indicators of Evaluation. *Educational Research and Evaluation* 14, pp. 201–214. doi:10.1080/13803610801956614.

Eikeland, O.J., Manger, T. and Asbjornsen, A. (2009) *Education in Nordic Prisons: Prisoners' Educational Backgrounds, Preferences and Motivation*. Copenhagen: Norden.

Eriksson, A.-L.G. and Samuelson, S. (2007) *Kartläggning av intagnas utbildningsbakgrund – studiebehov* [Survey of Prisoners' Educational Background: Study Needs]. Norrköping: Kriminalvårdens Utvecklingsenhet.

Flynn, S., Brown, J., Johnson, A. and Rodger, S. (2011) Barriers to Education for the Marginalized Adult Learner. *Alberta Journal of Educational Research* 57(1), pp. 43–58.

Forster, W. (1981) *Prison Education in England and Wales*. Leicester: National Institute of Adult Education.

Forster, W. (1990) The Higher Education of Prisoners. In Duguid, S. (ed) *Yearbook of Correctional Education 1990*. Burnaby: Institute for the Humanities, Simon Fraser University.

Giordano, P., Cernkovich, S. and Rudolph, J. (2002) Gender, Crime and Desistance: Towards a Theory of Cognitive Transformation. *American Journal of Sociology* 107(4), pp. 990–1064. doi:10.1086/343191.

Gottfried, A.E. (1990) Academic Intrinsic Motivation in Young Elementary School Children. *Journal of Educational Psychology* 82(3), pp. 525–538. doi:10.1037/0022-0663.82.3.525.

Graham, J. and Bowling, B. (1995) *Young People and Crime, Home Office Research Study No. 145*. London: Home Office.

Hardin, C.J. (2008) Adult Students in Higher Education: A Portrait of Transitions. *New Directions for Higher Education* 2008(144), pp. 49–57. doi:10.1002/he.325.

Hawley, J. (2011) *Prison Education and Training in Europe: A Review and Commentary of Existing Literature, Analysis and Evaluation*. Birmingham: GHK.

Hirschi, T. and Gottfredson, M. (1985) Age and Crime, Logic and Scholarship. Comment on Greenberg. *American Journal of Sociology* 91(1), pp. 22–27. doi:10.1086/228243.

Irish Prison Service (2019) *Joint Irish Prison Service/Education and Training Boards Ireland Prison Education Strategy 2019–2022*. Longford: Irish Prison Service.

Irish Prison Service (2020) *Irish Prison Service Annual Report 2019*. Longford: Irish Prison Service.

Jackson, K.L. and Innes, C.A. (2000) Affective Predictors of Voluntary Inmate Program Participation. *Journal of Offender Rehabilitation* 30(3–4), pp. 1–19. doi:10.1300/J076v30n03_01.

Johnstone, J.W.C. and Rivera, R.J. (1965) *Volunteers for Learning: A Study of the Educational Pursuits of American Adults*. Chicago: Aldine Publishing Company.

Lai, E.R. (2011) *Motivation: A Literature Review*. [Online]: Pearson Research Report.

Langelid, T., Mäki, M., Raundrup, K. and Svensson, S. (eds) (2009) *Nordic Prison Education: A Lifelong Learning Perspective*. Bergen: Norden.

Manger, T., Eikeland, O.J. and Asbjørnsen, A. (2013) Effects of Educational Motives on Prisoners' Participation in Education and Educational Desires. *European Journal on Criminal Policy and Research* 19, pp. 245–257. doi:10.1007/s10610-012-9187-x.

Manger, T., Eikeland, O.J. and Asbjørnsen, A. (2018) Why Do Not More Prisoners Participate in Adult Education? An Analysis of Barriers to Education in Norwegian Prisons. *International Review of Education* 65(5), pp. 711–733. doi:10.1007/s11159-018-9724-z.

Manger, T., Eikeland, O.J., Diseth, A., Hetland, H. and Asbjørnsen, A. (2010) Prison Inmates' Educational Motives: Are They Pushed or Pulled? *Scandinavian Journal of Educational Research* 54(6), pp. 535–547. doi:10.1080/00313831.2010.522844.

Maruna, S. (2001) *Making Good: How Ex-Convicts Reform and Rebuild Their Lives*. Washington: American Psychological Association. doi:10.1037/10430-000.

Maslauskaite, K. and Mooney, C. (2018) *Doing More with Less: Prisoner Rehabilitation in Ireland*. Paris: Council of Europe Development Bank.

McGivney, V. (1993) Participation and Non-Participation: A Review of the Literature. In Edwards, R., Sieminski, S. and Zeldin, D. (eds) *Adult Learners, Education and Training*. Abingdon: Routledge.

Morgan, M. and Kett, M. (2003) *The Prison Adult Literacy Survey: Results and Implications*. Dublin: Irish Prison Service.

Munoz, V. (2009) *The Right to Education of Persons in Detention*. A/HRC/11/8, 2nd April 2009. New York: Human Rights Council.

Natale, L. (2010) *Factsheet on Education in Prisons*. London: Civitas Institute for the Study of Civil Society.

National Crime Council (2002) *Tackling the Underlying Causes of Crime: A Partnership Approach*. Dublin: The Stationary Office.

O'Gorman, T. (2011) *Audit of Education and Library Services in Irish Prisons (Draft Report)*. Longford. Irish Prison Service.

O'Keeffe, C., Senior, P. and Monti-Holland, V. (2007) Barriers to Employment, Training and Education in Prison and beyond: A Peer-Led Solution. In Sheehan, R., McIvor, G. and Trotter, C. (eds) *What Works with Women Offenders*. Portland: Willian Publishing.

O'Mahony, P. (1997) *Mountjoy Prisoners: A Sociological and Criminological Profile*. Dublin: Stationary Office.

Paldanius, S. (2007) The Rationality of Reluctance and Indifference toward Adult Education: Difficulties in Recruiting Unemployed Adults to Adult Education. In Servage, L. and Fenwick, T. (eds) *Proceedings of the Joint International Conference of the AdultEducation Research Conference (AERC) (48th National Conference) and the Canadian Association for the Study of Adult Education (CASAE) (26th National Conference)*. Ottawa: CASAE.

Parsons, M. and Langenbach, M. (1993) The Reasons Inmates Indicate They Participate in Prison Education Programs: Another Look at Boshier's PEPS. *Journal of Correctional Education* 44(1), pp. 38–41.

Prochaska, J.O. and DiClemente, C.C. (1982) Stages and Processes of Self-Change of Smoking: Towards an Integrative Model of Change. *Journal of Consulting and Clinical Psychology* 51(3), pp. 90–395. doi:10.1037/0022-006X.51.3.390.

Roth, B.B. and Manger, T. (2014) The Relationship between Prisoners' Educational Motives and Previous Incarceration, Sentence Length, and Sentence Served. *London Review of Education* 12, pp. 209–220. doi:10.1007/s10610-012-9187-x.

Rubenson, K. (2007) *Determinants of Formal and Informal Canadian Adult Learning: Insights from the Adult Education and Training Surveys*. Ottawa: Learning Policy Directorate.

Rubenson, K. and Desjardins, R. (2009) The Impact of Welfare State Regimes on Barriers to Participation in Adult Education: A Bounded Agency Model. *Adult Education Quarterly* 59(3), pp. 187–207. doi:10.1177/0741713609331548.

Skaalvik, E.M., Finbak, L. and Pettersen, T. (2003) *Undervisning i fengsel. På rett kjøl?* [Education in Prison: On an Even Keel?]. Bergen: Fylkesmannen i Hordaland, Utdanningsavdelinga.

Stana, R.M., Trisler, C., Haskins, M.G., Hall, M., Seltser, B., Schauer, M. and Brock, J. (1993) *Federal Prisons: Inmate and Staff Views on Education and Work Training Programs*. Washington: U.S. General Accountability Office.

Warner, K. (2007) Against the Narrowing of Perspectives: How Do We See Learning, Prisons and Prisoners? *Journal of Correctional Education* 58(2), pp. 170–183.

Warner, K. (2018) Every Possible Learning Opportunity: The Capacity of Education in Prison to Challenge Dehumanisation and Liberate 'the Whole Person'. *Advancing Corrections, Journal of the International Corrections and Prisons Association* 6, pp. 32–45.

Westrheim, K. and Manger, T. (2014) Iraqi Prisoners in Norway: Educational Background, Participation, Preferences and Barriers to Education. *Journal of Prison Education and Reentry* 1(1), pp. 6–19. doi:10.15845/jper.v1i1.

Wolf Harlow, C.W. (2003) *Education and Correctional Populations*. Washington: Department of Justice.

Chapter 5

Personal change, desistance and prison education

The current book draws upon research that was carried out with the view to exploring two significant criminological concepts and their relationship to each other. The previous chapters have focused on the concept of prison education, exploring the various theories relating to the concept and subsequently examining several elements of the findings on prisoners' experience of education. The current chapter will turn the focus to desistance from crime, particularly the narrative theories of desistance. The accounts of those interviewed will be explored with a view to connecting the various themes that emerged to the desistance framework. Both participants and the group of former prisoners spoke about their experience of prison education and in particular the benefits they have experienced through participation in education. These accounts provide valuable data, showing many links between prison education and the desistance process. This differs from the traditional measure of prison education that is quantitative in nature, focused only on a lack of recidivism and revealing little about how education supports the person or their move away from criminality. This chapter, along with Chapter 6, which looks at the more structural elements of desistance, hopes to illuminate the journey or process behind the move towards desistance by looking at the ways in which prison education can impact and enhance the life of the person and potentially support their journey towards desistance. It is acknowledged at the outset that desistance is not generally seen to occur in prison, since this is a time of enforced incapacitation. However, it is possible that the seeds of desistance can be sown at this point and that education can reinforce efforts to promote and support desistant goals. This chapter will look at how this happens and essentially conceptualise prison education as a form of pre-desistance, forming the foundation of the structural changes in the upcoming chapters. The literature explored will be limited to that relevant to the themes emerging in the study, rather than serving as a systematic list of all desistance literature – which would simply be too broad for the parameters of the current book. The literature and findings from the current study will be outlined and discussed under three headings later on agency, cognitive changes and hope and expectations.

Desistance

Within both society and criminology, there is a vested interest in the drive to lower crime rates. A significant amount of crime is the result of recidivism. Hence, finding ways of reducing reoffending through a variety of efforts including probationary work, correctional interventions or post-prison programmes is desirable. A wealth of attention is paid to examining "what works" and with good reason. Rehabilitative efforts are evident throughout the criminal justice system. Each arm of the justice system is trying to ascertain why people offend and develop interventions that help people achieve more stable and law-abiding lives. The growth of desistance research has been fuelled by the desire to inform these efforts. Desistance research explores the journey a person goes through to find their way out of crime and offending. However, the answers produced have not been simple. Desistance is a deeply personal journey, and studies have found a variety of competing factors. Various schools of thought have developed, and there are many conflicting views on the processes that occur during the various stages of desistance.

The conflict surrounding desistance can be found in as minor a matter as its definition. Academics have proposed various definitions of the concept, yet succinctly summing up all that is meant by this broad concept has proven difficult. Farrall and Bowling's (1999: 258) definition, while technically accurate, has been criticised as overly simplistic in many ways, describing desistance as "the moment that a criminal career ends". It can be argued that such a thing as desistance does not occur in any one moment. Shover (1996: 121) states that desistance is "the voluntary termination of serious criminal participation". Both definitions appear to refer to a place in time, a moment of termination, rather than an ongoing process. Shover (1996) refers to the termination of "serious offending", and it must be questioned whether desistance can be said to have occurred if the offender is still offending, despite the fact that those in the early stages of desistance tend to oscillate between periods of conformity and deviance (Burnett, 2004). However, in line with Shover's (1996) wording, the word "termination" has also been proposed by others as an appropriate phrase by which to characterise desistance (Laub and Sampson, 2001; Bottoms et al., 2004), as it is when the criminal career terminates fully, as opposed to partially, that is the relevant matter. Again, even this terminology can be criticised. For instance, "termination" can only be truly measured upon the death of a person (Maruna, 2001); at any time until that point, the person may begin offending again (Bottoms et al., 2004). This would suggest that desistance is a process, a continuing commitment to stay straight, rather than one momentary decision to go straight. In light of these critiques, Maruna's (2001: 26) definition of desistance is proposed as "the long term abstinence from crime among individuals who had previously engaged in persistent patterns of criminal offending". This definition reflects desistance as a process; it does not rule out reoffending in the future but also reflects that there must be some chronological distance between the last episode of offending and being said to have desisted. Yet this also seems to refer to someone who is crime-free for a long period of time and is in the secondary stage of desistance.

Maintaining desistance long term is the difficulty, particularly in the face of frustrating times and temptation (Maruna, 2001). Crime-free gaps are normal, particularly after release from prison. There is widespread recognition that the process is not clear-cut, with progression and regression characterising the journey for most as opposed to a resounding cessation (Healy, 2010). Burnett (2004: 169) stated that "rather than a steady progression, we suspect that, whilst moving generally in a conformist direction, people oscillate on what we might visualise as a dimension or continuum, between criminality and conformity. On such a continuum, complete criminality and complete conformity are for the vast majority, points never likely to be reached". It is important to remember this when researching desistance.

It should also be noted that what is described in these definitions are the various stages of desistance, namely primary and secondary desistance (Maruna and Farrall, 2004). Primary desistance is characterised by an oscillation between crime and conformity, with crime-free gaps between the two states. What is described in the definitions of Maruna (2001), Shover (1996) and Farrall and Bowling (1999) earlier is secondary desistance. Secondary desistance is a more long-term process, with the person no longer seeing crime as an option and adopting a new, non-criminal identity (Maruna and Farrall, 2004). The early stages of desistance have not received as much attention in terms of research as secondary desistance, which in many ways is seen as true desistance. However, this is changing and several studies have examined this important stage that must be passed through by each person who wishes to reach secondary desistance. Given the number of times a person may enter and relapse from this stage of desistance, it is an important area to study with a view to ascertaining what best can be done to move offenders into primary desistance and help them progress to secondary desistance. Many offenders do achieve secondary and complete desistance and the factors that play a role in that process will be discussed later.

Several of these definitions also pose a difficulty when examining prison education in the context of desistance, especially when considering whether desistance can be said to take place in prison or whether this period of time is discounted when considering desistance. Taking Maruna's (2001) study as an example, anyone serving a long sentence could be said to be abstinent from crime for a long period. Yet this is an enforced abstinence since the person is incapacitated by the prison sentence. Furthermore, to take Farrall and Bowling's (1999) definition, the moment a criminal career ends, if a person is serving a sentence and does not reoffend after release, is the "moment" measured from the date of release from prison or their last episode of offending? Or is it the moment when the person made the decision that they will not offend again? We can look at this in the context of someone who is an addict, for example.

There is always a chance that they will relapse, yet from shortly after their detox they will be referred to as "sober", despite the strong chance they might relapse, with that chance decreasing the longer a period of time they remain in sobriety. Moreover, they will most likely celebrate their one-year "anniversary" on the date after they had their last drink. Therefore, the issue is complex, with sobriety being judged from several key times: from a moment or date in time; from shortly after declaring an intention to quit; and only being viewed as truly sober after a long-term abstinence. This is an important consideration in the current study. There is a general consensus that those who are in prison cannot be said to be desisting. Yet this is perhaps dependent upon which definition is ascribed to. Those who committed a crime and were apprehended may have remained in the community awaiting trial for an excess of six months. If they made a conscious decision to go straight after they were charged and remained crime-free during that time and anticipate doing the same after prison, can this intervening period of imprisonment not also be seen as desistance? It can be argued that classifying imprisonment as a period of desistance is misguided since a person does not have the chance to offend during their sentence. However, evidence suggests that there is ample opportunity for criminality in prison (Threadwell et al., 2019). While this is a debatable topic, it is most likely dependent upon each person and case. For the most part, this book will align with the view that desistance has not officially occurred and any evidence of pro-desistance characteristics or intentions are merely indicators of desistance being possible or likely in the future. This debate will also be relevant later when exploring the idea of participation in prison education as a form of pre-desistance.

The criminal trajectory: predisposing factors

At this stage it is purported to give a short contextual overview of the various pieces of desistance literature that will become relevant to the discussions at certain points in both this chapter and Chapter 6. While desistance is a complex process, there is now general agreement that the journey is usually gradual and influenced by various intrinsic and extrinsic factors in an "interplay between individual choices and a range of wider social forces, institutional and societal practices" (Farrall and Bowling, 1999: 261). Laub and Sampson (2001) also note that any comprehensive discussion of desistance would need to include both internal and external factors. However, while both are seen to have a role in desistance, the focus has been on the structural factors that contribute to desistance.

When examining factors that impact desistance, it is important to understand the predisposing factors in the hope that focus on these areas that cause criminality can in turn foster desistance. Many life course studies of the criminal career have young juvenile offenders in order to determine the risk factors and predict criminal career trajectories. The Cambridge study (Farrington, 1997, Farrington et al., 2006) is perhaps the best known of these studies, and it showed clear differences, most of a structural nature, between individuals who did and did not offend. Those who offended were impulsive, lacked good parental supervision, experienced social deprivation, had low educational performance and had family member(s) engaged in crime. These characteristics such low educational attainment, social deprivation and a family history of criminality are mirrored in the Irish prison population (O'Mahony, 1997). Those who did not offend had more stable upbringings, came from law-abiding families and, of particular relevance to the current study, had good education records (Farrington, 1997). Therefore, it appears that levels of education are one of the differentiating factors between criminality and conformity. Gottfredson and Hirschi (1990) suggest that the life course is predetermined, and those who are delinquent in their early years will go on to choose delinquent friends and a delinquent spouse and will carry on with their criminal ways right into adulthood. Peer group can be highly influential, with Glueck and Glueck (1950) putting forth the idea that "birds of a feather stick together", and youngsters tend to associate and seek out people who are like-minded and from similar backgrounds. This is often the reason they end up associating with people from their disadvantaged area, thus contributing to offending. Having a juvenile record is a strong predictor of later offending (Blumstein et al., 1986). In adult males, Farrington (1986) found a strong correlation between unemployment and higher crime rates. Drug use, problems at school and the lack of social bonds have also been identified as among the most important risk factors for offending among males (Flood-Page et al., 2000). There is a cumulative effect, and 50% of those who were considered highly vulnerable (four risk factors or more) were offending at a higher rate. However, this also meant that 50% of those who were highly vulnerable were either offending at low rates or not offending at all, showing that criminal careers and pathways are not inevitable and trajectories can be altered (Flood-Page et al., 2000). Other longitudinal research on criminal careers has also revealed that changes in offending trajectories are possible and frequently occur. Rutter et al. (1990) found that at-risk children often circumvented criminal trajectories if certain factors were present, shielding them from particular difficulties. Education, for example, can be a significant factor. Children who liked school, for instance, often tended to plan proactively for better futures and had better outcomes in later life such as strong marriages and stable employment (Rutter et al., 1990). Furthermore, Graham and Bowling (1995) found that those children who perceived their own school work to be above average were more likely to desist. These studies are encouraging from the perspective of prison education. Those who are younger are more likely to participate in prison education (Manger et al., 2013). Given the malleable nature of the life course, interventions such as education at an early point in the criminal or prison life course may be a potential turning point in these trajectories.

While childhood risk factors show a strong and consistent relationship with crime, adult life events often exert a more important influence on behaviour

(Laub and Sampson, 2001). Despite there being differing chronologies and circumstances to desistance, almost all offenders cease to offend. Laub and Sampson (1993) suggest that irrespective of the time of onset of offending, the adult life course matters regardless of how one gets there. Therefore, while characteristics and circumstances in childhood may be predictors of delinquency and criminality, they do not operate as indicators of ability or inability to desist from crime. Despite the trajectories that one is set on in early childhood, life events and social ties in adulthood can counteract these trajectories and encourage desistance (Laub and Sampson, 1993). The effect of early experiences on offending begins to diminish after the age of 30 and recent experiences become more significant (Cline, 1980). Given the influence that education can have in helping to overcome risk factors in order to circumvent criminal trajectories in juveniles and young adults, perhaps it is possible that it can have a role in influencing the trajectories later in life as well through the mechanisms outlined later in this chapter. While the behaviour of persistent offenders will have been influenced by various factors throughout the life course, perhaps education can help to provide a new meaning structure that can be a more prominent influence than past experiences, in line with Cline's (1980) theory.

These studies tend to focus predominantly on the structural factors as being indicators of criminal careers, yet it is possible to see the influence of individual and dispositional factors in these studies. This is reflected in the desistance literature, where there appears to be a greater focus on structural theories, over and above narrative and agentic theories that focus on the role of intrinsic factors particular to the offender such as education or agency (Healy, 2010). Chapter 6 will focus on the structural theories to a greater extent than the current chapter, which will predominantly explore the findings in relation to the narrative theories and the effects of prison education on the individual through the sections that follow.

Cognitive and personal changes in desistance

There are now many theories about how and why people decide to "go straight". This is in contrast to the old view that once a person begins offending, they are entering a vicious cycle leading to increasingly serious and more frequent reoffending. However, recent research shows that people, despite the social exclusion and labelling that go with being an offender, manage to break away from crime. Desistance is an extremely subjective and personal process. For that reason, there is a vast framework of literature surrounding the concept. Significant space within the framework of criminological research is given to studies examining the elements that give structure in the life of the offender, including social bonds such as relationships and employment. However, Healy (2010) asserts that cognitive factors are also highly significant in the desistance process. Narrative theories take a more inward view, attributing desistance to subjective changes within the person such as the reevaluation of life choices following a negative experience with the life of crime, for example (Cusson and Pinsonneault, 1986), or the experience of becoming a parent (Burnett, 1992). Laub and Sampson (2001: 55) outline the importance of research into the role of the individual in desistance, proposing that "given the role of human agency in the desistance process, we need to find a way to measure individual motivation, free will and ultimately the decision to initiate and embrace the process of change". Despite many such endorsements of the value of narrative theories, the role of the individual and subjective factors is under-researched (Healy, 2010). The following section will give an overview of the narrative theories of change that are most relevant to the findings in the current research. Therefore, this not an exhaustive account of the theories; rather, it is an overview of some of the most important elements that arose as themes in the accounts of the men in the current study. As mentioned earlier, given the broad findings of this research the findings and discussion will be presented under each heading, rather than forming a stand-alone section in this chapter, in order to explicitly show the links that exist between the prison education findings and the desistance literature. A summary will then be provided at the end of the chapter to draw this together and make any final points.

Agency, desistance and prison education

Agency is seen to be a significant contributor to the desistance process (Maruna, 2001; Healy, 2010; King, 2013), with Maguire and Raynor (2006) suggesting that it is as important as, if not more important than, structural factors such as social bonds in the desistance process. Agency relates to a reliance on one's own inner resources to achieve change in their life or life goals (Maruna, 2001). Healy (2014: 874), while referring to agency is "ineffable" defines it as "a dynamic interaction between the person and their social world that is directed towards the achievement of a meaningful and credible new self". It may also refer to things such as successfully rising to challenges, achieving peer recognition, developing an increased insight into oneself or empowerment (McAdams, 2001). Self-esteem, a sense of purpose and strong self-control are also argued as being composite elements of agency (Cote, 1997). Agency forms the basis of a range of cognitive and emotional resources that support effective interaction and navigation of the social world (Giordano et al., 2002; Healy, 2014). It provides the foundation for self-will and the ability to exercise that will in order to resist the influence of others (Farrall and Bowling, 1999). In this manner, it is key to supporting efforts to desist from crime in the early stages of desistance, as one is reliant on their own resources of self and coping strategies in order to support their goals such as identity change, structural attainments and overcoming the various barriers to reintegration in the face of the pull of anti-social temptations.

One of the most extensive and well-known studies to contribute to the literature in this area was carried out by Maruna (2001). He compared the narratives of both persisters and desisters and found significant differences between the two in several areas. Maruna's (2001) study found evidence of a narrative he called the "redemption script" that characterised the identity of those who had desisted from crime. A redemption script is composed of two elements, namely agency and generativity, and is an ethos that desisters live by where they view their past mistakes as lessons which structure their current lives as they try to "make good" (Maruna, 2001). Desisters believed in their ability to change and have good lives, to face the challenges of reintegration and to foster new pro-social identities. Conversely, the identities of those who continued to offend were dominated by a "condemnation script" which is characterised by a fatalistic outlook on life, whereby offenders perceive that there is little point in trying to desist as the walls to be faced on release are insurmountable (Maruna, 2001). Hart and Healy (2018) argue that the delineation between desisters and persisters in terms of agency may be overly simplistic. She claims that both may possess a form of agency, since each are rational actors, yet they may exercise it in different ways and to achieve different goals, in furtherance of their new (or old) identity. A key aspect of successful agentic action in the desistance process is the imagination of a new, meaning and credible identity (Healy, 2014) that exercises pro-social choices within specific social contexts (Bottoms et al., 2004).

While there is a lack of clarity and consensus on the true conceptualisation of agency, the earlier outline offers a good starting point for the exploration of the concept through the prism of its potential links with prison education. Throughout the interviews, there was significant evidence of agency in the accounts of those who were participating in education. This evidence was represented in several themes, such as self-awareness and self-control, which will be outlined under the elements that follow.

Self-awareness

McAdams (2001) cites an increased insight into oneself as an indicator of agency. It is proposed here that McAdams's (2001) indicator of agency, an increased insight into oneself, is represented in the concept of "self-awareness". In terms of the theoretical relationship between self-awareness and prison education, Morris (1962) proposes that prison education leads to an increased awareness of feelings and thoughts, fostering a degree of self-awareness. A strong theme among the participants was an increased degree of self-awareness, particularly an awareness of their own behaviours, and was manifest in several different ways throughout the data.

Reflecting the literature relating to prison education, in particular social psychological development theory, several of the participants gave accounts of feeling more in control and had more awareness of their situation, in that they as an individual could choose to live a certain way, that their actions have consequences and they could control their actions and outcomes. An illustration of this is mentioned by Keith, a Mountjoy participant, as follows:

KEITH: Like coming to prison has made me think and doing the education has made me realise I am an individual, separate to anyone else. Like the school has given me more information, not just about learning from books but also about meself and how to deal with situations. Like I'm not wearing the blinkers or as one-tracked as I usually was. There's always two points to everything.

(Mountjoy, participant)

A strong degree of self-awareness was also evident in the account of participants where they acknowledged their own role in their criminality, rather than placing the blame externally. This demonstrates an increased focus on and awareness of their own actions. It also shows an inclination to look inward, rather than externally for sources of blame. They appeared to be accepting responsibility for their own situation in life.

MICHAEL: Like with me a lot was greed and scamming and I wanted more money the more I got, I had to keep up with x and y down the road. Most crimes are down to greed and when you in here and ya have nothing it shows you that money counts for so little and it's other things that are important.

(Mountjoy, participant)

EOIN: Stupidity is the main reason. Not being able to say no. That's basically it. Greed for easy money.

(Shelton Abbey, participant)

This acceptance of responsibility is also important in the context of cognitive change and a shift towards a less anti-criminal mind set. Persistent offenders showed evidence of mollification, or a tendency towards externalising blame rather than taking responsibility (Walters, 1995). Those who were more accepting of their own role in their offending had a greater chance of not recidivating upon release (Walters, 1995). This will be discussed in more detail in the following section on cognitive changes.

Participants were very aware of how their actions had caused hurt to others, be it their family or the victims of the crime, and were able to express their sorrow for that. For example, some participants said that prison education had helped them see that they had hurt their family by prioritising friends and now they were in prison as a result. Their children were now missing their father, and they were sorry for that. They also resolved to change things by making better decisions when they were released. Furthermore, showing an awareness of his own traits, feelings and behaviours, one of the ex-prisoners (Thomas, quoted here) reported that a major benefit of prison education was that it helped him to become aware of quite a few personal issues that were holding him back in life and were likely to be contributing to his offending.

THOMAS: She's a very important person. And I did a lot of work on my own self-awareness in prison to get a hold on myself so that when I got I out I'd be in a good place for her. I kind of had blinkered vision for a long time; I only really saw myself, but I knew I needed to start looking at the people I cared about and what I was doing and what I had done and how it impacted on them. Without that I wouldn't have been able to build the bridges I have done with her. And education was a big part of that too.

(Ex-prisoner)

Conversely, there was little evidence of this among non-participants, who were inclined to place the blame for their offending externally, such as on friends who had led them into delinquency, as was the case for Kevin. Another common source of blame for offending was the level of social welfare payment provided by the government, which is summed up in Fran's quote. It ought to be noted that under Irish Social Welfare schemes, if Fran was a custodian of these four children, he would be entitled to various other payments in respect of these children, in addition to rent/housing supplementary payments. In fact, for some, such as Kevin, they did not view their crime as wrong, as was often the cases where the crime committed did not have a discernible victim or where force or violence was not involved.

FRAN: Money. That's it. Nobody does it for any other reason, no matter what they tell you, it's about money. It's about survival. Like I said, I don't have a job. And the government expect(s) me to survive on €190 a week. Me with four kids.

(Mountjoy, non-participant)

KEVIN: Like me mates would be getting on to me that they were going doing this or doing that and I wasn't going to be left out, it was just what we did. Most of the time we were just havin' a laugh and I suppose it snowballed from there. And most of the stuff we do it wasn't causin' any harm really like, any gear we sold was to people who wanted it, we never had to force anyone to buy smack.

(Mountjoy, non-participant)

While some of these points are also representative of themes such as responsibility and empathy, they show how participants have carried out some degree of self-examination and are aware of their own behaviours and feelings. The points also indicate the significant extent to which they attribute this increase in self-awareness to prison education. These examples from the accounts of participants and ex-prisoners demonstrate an increased insight into one's self, consistent with McAdams's (2001) indictor of agency. Furthermore, the prisoners credit these attributes to having participated in education, which confirms Morris's (1962) finding that participation in prison education can promote a sense of self awareness. This shows how prison education, through its role in promoting self-awareness in prisoners, can contribute to an increased sense of agency in the prisoner. When contrasted with the attitudes of those who are not participating in education, the contrast is even more stark and it shows that those who are not participating retain a strong lack of awareness of their own role in both their criminality and their own power to overcome their issues and change their lives going forward.

Opens their minds/changes perspective

Similar to the idea of self-awareness is the degree of insight and reflective ability that is a composite element of agency (McAdams, 2001). Drawing on the prison education literature, prison education and adult education have been shown to transform the way people view the world. Mezirow (2000) refers to the role education can play in enabling people to challenge their view of the world and change mindsets and frames of reference and encouraging them to be more inclusive and reflective of their beliefs and opinions. Moral development and conscious strengthening is also a purported benefit of participating in prison education (Duguid, 1998). Participants considered these to be significant benefits of participating in education. For instance, many of those interviewed claimed that prison education changed their outlook and perspective, which in turn had an effect on many other areas of their life. A strong example of this is given by Eoin, whose quote demonstrates significant moral development in terms of a changed outlook. It also shows self-awareness and also awareness of others, with the recognition of the selfish and detrimental decisions of the past and a shift towards making decisions that are right for him and his family. There appeared to be a shift in perceptions about options in life, with participants realising that crime was not the only option available to them but that there were other ways and opportunities to earn a living. Participants, such as Vincent, mentioned subjects such as crime awareness and sociology as being particularly important for their changing perspectives on how they viewed their life and their offending behaviour. This is illustrative of some of the statements showing new perspectives in those who participate in prison education, which is in line with both the education and desistance literature.

EOIN: I'm starting to see things in a whole different light. This course here has just opened my eyes about the decisions I made in the past and the fact that I've never really planned for anything, so it's got my mind thinking differently. Like from now on I want to set out a life plan. I want to start making decisions and the right decisions at that. A lot of my decisions have been more based on me, selfish decisions. But I mean I'm a father so I need to make better decisions than the ones I made in the past.

(Shelton Abbey, participant)

VINCENT: Well, I like to think I look at life in a different perspective, especially doing that crime awareness course in Mountjoy. You have a one-track mind and then you start looking at it from other peoples' perspectives; it kind of gives you a broader sense of things. It just opens your mind like.

(Shelton Abbey, participant)

Compared to the community, the prison world is limited and living life in such an closed environment can cause a perspective to become quite narrow and restricted. It is easy to imagine that in prison it would be easy to become very insular and focused on one's own situation. One could quickly become absorbed into the mundane nature of life in prison, resulting in a very inward and narrowed perspective. Several participants also spoke of how prison education went against the narrowing of perspectives in prison, a key purpose of prison education (Council of Europe, 1990), and allowed them to expand their mind and perspective.

DARREN: It is very easy, particularly in an environment like this for perspective to be narrowed, narrowed, narrowed right down to . . . its 2.15 pm (and) the cell door is unlocked. And it is only by being in a place like this that you can learn all sorts of things. I'm doing political studies, and at the moment we are doing the Israel/Palestine conflict, you know something that I would've known something about but I didn't know anything about it in its great detail and it's wonderful. That's a simple example and that broadens one's whole perspective.

(Mountjoy, participant)

Darren describes this diminishing perspective that can occur in prison and the manner in which education acts to counteract this by exposing the person to new experiences and new perspectives and allows the persons world view to expand, rather than contract, during their sentence. This is also likely to have a generative impact since the person will be less likely to focus entirely on themselves but maintain an outward view that considers others. This could help by making reintegration with family and others less problematic on release due to an ability to be able to relate to and have empathy for others, rather than focusing entirely on their own world view.

Confidence, self-esteem and empowerment

A strong theme to emerge through the interviews was the sense among participants that prison education was increasing their confidence and self-esteem, which gave them a feeling of empowerment in relation to their situation and their future. These elements are directly related to a person's sense of agency (Cote, 1997; McAdams, 2001), which is key to the redemption script and desistance (Maruna, 2001). In the prison education literature, education is proposed as building a prisoner's self-esteem (Ubah and Robinson, 2003), demonstrating an overlap between the benefits of prison education and the indicators of agency. A particularly prominent theme among those participating in education was the manner in which education increased their self-esteem and belief in their own efficacy. Participants mentioned that they felt much more confident in their own abilities to succeed and achieve their goals. In several cases, the sense of confidence and self-esteem expressed by participants appeared to be a type of social confidence, which they would have previously lacked when dealing with people outside of their immediate social group. This is typical of those who would have previously been deemed marginalised learners, having a sense of being "less than" and lacking the ability to interact with those from social classes (Flynn et al., 2011). Those participating in prison education, such as Craig, gave accounts of how they now felt capable of holding conversations about a wide range of issues having increased their levels of education, stating that prior to getting involved in education they did not feel that they knew enough to engage with other people.

CRAIG: We were watching a history programme and a discussion started up . . . we had a great discussion just from what we watched and what we'd learned. Now that's not something I'd have ever done before like. Like I've got more confidence in my own opinion and me own voice now that I never had before.

(Shelton Abbey, participant)

ANTHONY: When I was taking drugs, I got confidence from that, but when I stopped taking them my level of confidence dropped and the education has given me that same sense of confidence, to be able to engage with people and not feel inferior to them. Like I can engage with people in any situation and I can hold a conversation with people about politics and what's going on in the world and not feel stupid, which I would've done before so that's the big difference.

(Ex-prisoner)

In many ways, this feeling of being inferior may have left these men feeling like they were reliant on their own social group and peers with little ability to break free of peers or to stand up to peers due to a lack of confidence in themselves. Not having enough confidence to assert their own voice in certain situations may have been a cause of criminality for some. Keith touches on this and it was echoed by others, stating that education created the confidence to feel they could think for themselves and they felt confident that they were capable of making their own way and choices rather than following the crowd. This also represents a strong level of independence, awareness and maturity on the part of the participant.

KEITH: (I)t's given me a lot of confidence. Like before I would've just went with the crowd whereas now I'll go "stop and think".

(Mountjoy, participant)

Some also mentioned that their increased self-esteem as a result of education made them feel more capable of participating in society and having a voice. Mark gives the example here of feeling like he had a much greater understanding of society and politics to the extent that he now felt he could use his right to vote. In the context of the current study, this is particularly relevant to the idea of social bonds and social capital, which places a strong emphasis on civic participation (Forrest and Kearns, 2001). Furthermore, this sense of self-esteem was also manifest in the self-belief shown by prisoners who were resolute in their ability to achieve their goals such as securing employment and succeeding on release from prison.

MARK: (Education) gives ya a better understanding of things, what people are talking about, you know what they're on about, you understand how the country works. Like I'm going to vote and I feel I can do that now cos I can understand what I'm voting for.

(Mountjoy, participant)

Finally, confidence did not always come directly from the education itself, but some mentioned that they got a lot of confidence from the teachers and the experience of the school as opposed to the actual education. This seemed to stem from participants having to take active responsibility for their own education. Participants felt that they had committed to bettering themselves, and this promotes many positive feelings such as confidence, esteem and a consideration of their own self-worth. This appeared to be reinforced by teachers entrusting them with certain levels of responsibility, as prisoners appreciated gestures as simple as being trusted to borrow and return a book to a teacher. Participants felt that their educational efforts were met with trust and respect from those in authority. To an even greater extent, certain initiatives that train participants to help other prisoners, such as AVP (Alternatives to Violence Programme) or Toe by Toe (prisoners teaching other prisoners literacy skills), have a massive impact on the prisoner. These programmes are a great source of confidence for the facilitators, who feel they have earned the trust and respect of those who selected them for the roles and they feel that they are capable of helping those in difficulty. Stephen's and Vincent's accounts both show the sense of pride they have in taking control of their education. They also show the influence of the role of the teacher in their journey. Being treated with respect and with dignity and being seen as a person, not just a number, fosters a degree of self-worth that these men may not have experienced before in their lives:

STEPHEN: I'm a facilitator for the AVP, and that's great for like your confidence and all. Like up here they put their trust in you to facilitate that and its shows ya that someone sees some good in ya. I never really had much confidence in myself but I feel it building with the AVP and stuff. Like it shows me too that you're not a lost cause.

(Mountjoy, participant)

VINCENT: You're doing something for yourself . . . you're being encouraged and treated differently with teachers, treated with respect and with dignity. It's not as if you're a number and it's that interaction and communication . . . it's good for your confidence and self-esteem too. And the knowledge that you learn will carry on through after prison.

(Shelton Abbey, participant)

All of these benefits were mentioned as being attributable to participation in prison education, which confirms Ubah and Robinson's (2003) assertion that prison education increases self-esteem. Furthermore, it also shows a degree of overlap with the desistance literature, where self-esteem, self-worth and self-belief are argued to be a composite element of agency (Cote and Levine, 2014). It appears on this basis that prison education, through its role in building self-esteem, which is evidenced in accounts of the participants, can contribute to an overall sense of agency in the prisoner. Therefore, it could be argued that in relation to agency and desistance, self-esteem provides the confidence to face the challenges of release and helps prisoners believe that they have the ability to overcome barriers. The elements of self-belief and self-worth are also important. It appeared that many of the participants did not see that they were worthy of a good life or had the capacity to change their situations. Participation in education seemed to change that. They believed in their own power to achieve their goals and to change their path in life. They could also see good in themselves that was reflected through the positive interactions of their teachers. Such positive reinforcements are important, especially in terms of agency and in contributing to a future pro-social identity.

Self-control

Strong self-control was highlighted by Cote and Levine (2014) as being another indicator of agency, an important factor for desistance (Maruna, 2001). Again, there is overlap here between the prison education and desistance theory, with Callan and Gardner (2005) finding that prison education gave prisoners increased self-control. Self-control was a significant theme throughout the interviews, with participants in prison education expressing a strong sense of control over their own emotions, their lives and their outcomes, consistent with Callan and Gardner (2005). Participants explained that prison education showed them that they were autonomous people who could think for themselves and gave them the confidence to do that. According to those who participated in prison education, it helped them feel a greater sense of control over their own lives and outcomes. They also felt that education was showing them that if they worked hard they could achieve their goals and that this was within their own power and control. Vincent's account reflects these things, as he describes feeling a sense of self determinism, rather than allowing others and their opinions to dictate his course in life.

VINCENT: I've learned things about meself. Coming from where I come from, you're taught that you're no good, you're useless, even from being in school as a kid. Today I can realise that if I put my mind down to anything that it's achievable. And I realise me alone can only do that. It's up to you at the end of the day . . . I have control over what way my life goes. I can choose to go back to "Smack Cul de sac", I call it that cos its dead end, or live a life on "Quality Street". Like it's up to me I make them decisions at the end of the day, and for years I was a victim and blamed everyone else so today I'm more about taking responsibility for where my life goes.

(Shelton Abbey, participant)

It appeared from the accounts of various prisoners that they had found a sense of personal autonomy. Their sense of autonomy and control was particularly prevalent in the accounts when considering release. Participants were much more confident in the levels of control that they would have over their life when they were released (this will also be explored further in Chapter 6). They accredited this to their increased ability to make the right decisions, to take different paths than they had previously and to rely on themselves instead of following the crowd, among other things. The prisoners attributed all of this to their participation in prison education. Again, this confirms Callan and Gardner's (2005) finding that prison education can increase self-control.

Moreover, highlighting the difference that prison education can make, such an expectation of control was not very evident among the non-participants. Instead, they expressed a sense of powerlessness over certain situations and over the actions of other people, rather than highlighting the degree of control they had within themselves. Such hopelessness, as can be observed in Andy's quote is also representative of the condemnation script whereby people view their outcomes as being outside of their control (Maruna, 2001).

ANDY: No, because I already know there's nothing for me. Nothing's going to help me, I'm in here for a long time and I don't have to worry about being rehabilitated.

(Mountjoy, non-participant)

In terms of self-control there is a significant difference between the accounts of both participants and non-participants. Control is a significant factor in the makeup of agency (Cote, 1997) and consequently has a strong role to play in the desistance process. Control over one's outcomes is also relevant to the redemption script narrative highlighted in the work of Maruna (2001). This demonstrates again the possible role that prison education may play in the desistance process. By increasing self-control, which in turn contributes to a sense of agency (Cote, 1997) and a "can do" attitude, prison education may be seen to have an indirect role to play in the desistance process.

Overall, agency is posited as having a significant part to play in the desistance process (Maguire and Raynor, 2006). The discussion under each of the headings earlier demonstrated the manner in which education, through the workings of moral development and social psychological development, can bring about significant changes in those who participate, which in turn can contribute to an increased sense of agency. The simple definition of agency which was outlined earlier was the "reliance on one's own inner resources to achieve change or life goals" (Maruna, 2001). The findings of this study appear to show that prisoners feel education can enhance and help mobilise the inner resources of the person, appearing to facilitate change in prisoners' lives. On this basis, it appears that prison education has a role to play in increasing agency. Furthermore, by understanding the ways in which education promotes agency, it is also possible to find ways to support its development. For example, Ubah and Robinson (2003) argue that moral development is maximised through the prisoner's participation in social and cultural subjects such as history, philosophy, literature and sociology. Perhaps by focusing on subjects such as these, which would be in line with the broad, adult education approach, it might encourage the development of agency. By knowing these things, we can optimise prison education provision to ensure that it has the maximum benefit for the person in the various aspects of their life. These changes, such as a new perspective, more positive outlook and increased awareness, are also representative of early desistance narratives as outlined by King (2013) and again show the capacity of education to support desistance efforts. Narrative and identity change is explored in greater detail in the next section.

Identity change, desistance and prison education

The creation or adoption of a new social identity is also suggested as playing a significant role in the desistance process (Maruna, 2001; Giordano et al., 2002). Maruna et al. (2004) stated that as a person goes through the desistance process, identity change is almost an inevitable outcome due to the cognitive transformations that take place. Baskin and Sommers (1998) also refer to identity, stating that a vital part of the desistance process is "discontinuance", which involves both objective and subjective change, encompassing new social networks and the formation of a new social identity as a non-offender. The new social networks are such that they support the new, non-criminal identity of the person (Baskin and Sommers, 1998).

It appears that identity is part of a wider system of reform on the part of the offender. Graham and Bowling (1995), for instance, found that changes in identity, maturity, a sense of direction and the recognition of the consequences and cost of crime are significant factors in the desistance process. New stakes in conformity need to be developed, and the process of reforming identity in turn strengthens these stakes in conformity (Laub and Sampson, 2001). Supporting this notion, LeBel et al. (2008) found that men who took on the identity of father or family man, facilitated by the social bonds within their family, were much more successful in desisting than those who remained self-characterised as criminals. All of these points illustrate the symbiotic and reciprocal nature of both individual and structural factors in the desistance process. The mindset and inner resources of the person facilitate change in the structural elements of their life. In turn, stronger structural supports facilitate increased mobilisation of the inner resources. Identity change has been predominantly associated with secondary desistance (Maruna, 2001; Giordano et al., 2002). Moreover, high levels of personal agency, as outlined earlier, are also argued as being relatively absent in early desistance, growing and strengthening over time as the person moves towards complete desistance. However, King (2013) argues that studies stating that narrative and identity change do not materialise until secondary desistance may be misguided. There is a potential that the processes of identity change and narrative change begin at a much earlier stage than the research on secondary desistance suggests, finding a strong degree of overlap in the narratives of early desisters in his own study when compared to the narratives of secondary desisters in the previous literature (King, 2013). Early desistance narratives were characterised by several key themes including a greater understanding of past offending such as the impact of those behaviours on their own life, their family and the victim. This helps to consider and conceptualise a new present or future identity, removed from their previous, deviant self. Such a view is also reinforced by a strengthening sense of moral agency to support the evolving identity of the person. This point relating to early desistance narratives and identity change is interesting in terms of prison education. The findings outlined earlier in relation to agentic changes on the part of participants show evidence of a renewed outlook and awareness of the impact of their offending, all of which related to King's (2013) suggested early desistance narratives. It will be argued later in this chapter that despite the fact that desistance cannot strictly be said to occur in prison – as it will only ever be an enforced desistance – that a form of pre-desistance can begin through the narrative, cognitive and identity change fostered through education.

Generativity and identity

The evolution of agency, awareness and empathy can culminate in a new identity strongly characterised by a desire to make amends for their hurts and past failings through generative goals and commitment to a good life going forward. An element of the redemption script (Maruna, 2001), generativity is a commitment to the promotion of the well-being and welfare of others and the next generation in particular. Evidence of such a script is indicative of a move on the person's part towards desistance and the creation of a new pro-social identity (Maruna, 2001). In Maruna's (2001) study, the desisters showed a strong desire to give back and make amends to those close to them and to society for the wrongs they had committed. Many of them wished to become counsellors, for instance. These generative desires usually establish themselves when the desister has developed a strong sense of self and has created social bonds with family and society. Maruna referred to those people as "wounded healers". In terms of the prison education literature, this is similar to the idea of moral development theory. Hobler (1999) found that education allows people to see the hurts they have caused and fosters a new, less selfish approach to life. They become less self-satisfying and more concerned with altruistic aims (Hobler, 1999).

In the current study, generativity arose as a theme several times, particularly among those who were participating in prison education. In general, evidence of generativity arose in relation to career goals, making amends to family and helping other prisoners. In terms of career goals, several participants mentioned that prison education gave them a taste for further study, either in prison or on release, with a view to entering professions which would be deemed generative. The most common of these was as an addiction counsellor, particularly among those men who were recovering addicts. Here Thomas talks about how education began with him having to make a choice between the school or workshops in prison. He was glad he had chosen education since it led him a path that culminated in him getting a college place when he left prison, and he was now on his way to becoming a counsellor:

THOMAS: It was a blessing in disguise that I went with education over workshops. And it was coming towards the end that I really started considering college when I got out. I always thought in my head it would be nice to do something with young people, the homeless, ex-prisoners but I didn't know which way to go about it . . . I just always liked helping people . . . even during prison steering people, especially the younger ones, and maybe trying to get them up to the school or the workshops.

(Ex-prisoner)

One man also wanted to get some coaching qualifications in order to coach children's soccer. He had previously been involved in soccer coaching and felt he had let his family down by becoming involved criminality and getting a jail sentence. When released, he wanted to gain formal qualifications in juvenile coaching as a way to make amends to his own children and be more involved in their lives. Both of these examples indicated a desire to give back and a concern for the welfare of the next generation.

Remaining with the idea of the welfare of the next generation, the theme of generativity was also observed among the men who wished to make amends for the hurt they had caused their family, particularly their children. In the first instance, they stated that prison education had helped them see the hurt they had caused their family, especially their children. Thomas, who was also quoted earlier, had very little contact with his daughter while she was growing up due criminality during her early years, followed by a long prison sentence. She was in her teenage years when he got out of prison, and a priority of his was to build a relationship with her. He credited education with giving him the awareness and insight to realise the hurt he had caused. This was also the case for Gary, who is using education to be the best version of himself for his daughter. Both examples show the participants' strong desire to make up for lost time, to make amends and to build strong relationships for the future.

THOMAS: I did a lot of work on my own self-awareness in prison to get a hold on myself so that when I got I out I'd be in a good place for her. I kind of had blinkered vision for a long time; I only really saw myself, but I knew I needed to start looking at the people I cared about and what I was doing and what I had done and how it impacted on them. Without that, I wouldn't have been able to build the bridges I have done with her. And education was a big part of that.

(Ex-prisoner)

GARY: I'm doing the education for myself but also for her. Like if I didn't have my daughter, I'd probably still be doing it and I wouldn't be still in crime but she's my motivator as well . . . I want to do what I can now to make up for being away, being right myself is the best thing I can do for her. That means I can be there and try (to) undo for when I wasn't.

(Ex-prisoner)

As a result, many were now participating in education with a view to supporting their families when they were released, and several of the participants said an advantage of their increased levels of education was that they would be able to help their children with homework and would have a better understanding of what their children were going through at school. While this will be explored in much greater detail in Chapter 6 under the structural discussions, these quotes from Mark and Daniel show how education can help participants to become more aware of the hurt they caused and also help to put it right. It helps parents reestablish a connection with their children, and it is also important to them to now feel that they can help their children with their homework. Besides being a potential catalyst for their offending, their own previous lack of education may have created barriers to strong relationships with their children where they felt that they could not do the small things such as help with homework, for example. By removing these obstacles, it allows them to engage with children and to make up for the hurt they caused and their absence.

MARK: Like I find with the education, when I go talk to the kids, like I have a lad that's 11 and you can ask him how's school and what are you doing. Like he went to see the Jeannie Johnson, is that the boat? Well it just means I can interact with them.

(Mountjoy, participant)

DANIEL: Well there's a few in the English class who aren't very good, and I think it's an issue. I can read and write but I can't spell too well, and that's why I'm doing English. And even though my job has nothing to do with writing, I want to be able to help my son with his homework and things.

(Shelton Abbey, participant)

Evidence of generativity was not confined to post-release goals or scenarios. It was also possible to observe this within the prison itself. Several of the prisoners interviewed were facilitators of the AVP or Toe by Toe. Both of these are initiatives that utilise the skills of participants who receive special training in order to help other prisoners. These programmes are a great source of confidence for the facilitators who feel they have earned the trust and respect of those who selected them for the roles and they feel that they are capable of helping those in difficulty. One of the facilitators, Stephen, mentioned that this was a complete turnaround for him, as he would previously have been the one encouraging the fight.

STEPHEN: I'm a facilitator for the AVP (Alternatives to Violence Programme) and that's great for like your confidence and all. Like up here they put their trust in you to facilitate that, and (it) shows ya that someone sees some good in ya. I never really had much confidence in myself, but I feel it building with the AVP and stuff. Like it shows me too that you're not a lost cause. My temper got me into a lot of trouble over the years and so did me fists and then I'm in here for murder. But now I'm a facilitator for AVP . . . I can try help people through that programme to not make the same mistakes as me.

(Mountjoy, participant)

These points, relating to prisoners' career goals, family goals and their desire to help others, both in prison and after release, are consistent with Maruna's (2001) concept of generativity. These points also illustrate the role that education can play in increasing generativity. It also shows the way in which these participants started to see themselves in a new way, no longer a lost cause as Stephen says, but as someone who is capable of being a role model and a support for others. Furthermore, the redemption script was outlined earlier as embodying the concepts of both agency and generativity (Maruna, 2001). Considering these concepts together, namely the strong generative goals, when reinforced by the self-awareness, self-esteem and self-control, which are embodied in the concept of agency, it is possible to see how the presence of such a script can have a powerful impact on the desistance process, contributing in particular to the process of imagining a new law-abiding self-identity. These are powerful changes in the outlook of these men. The potential of education in the development of these changes, which has been evidenced through the accounts of prisoners and outlined earlier, is a strong endorsement of the capacity of prison education to foster desistance or support the process.

Cognitive transformations in identity change

Many theories of prison education relate to the changes that prison education can facilitate in the offender. These were outlined in Chapter 3 as being increased awareness (Morris, 1962), developing cognitive processes and fostering new behavioural patterns (Ubah and Robinson, 2003), among many other things. In relation to adult education, Mezirow's (1991) theory of transformational learning proposes that adult educators should guide adult learners to transform. He proposed that every person's outlook and perspective is defined by their meaning structure which encompasses a person's knowledge, values, beliefs, morality and understanding of social structures (Mezirow, 1991) and, through learning, these meaning structures can be transformed. The benefits of enhanced meaning structures are growth, intellectual maturity and critical reflection on one's own beliefs and values. Though this model is directed more at self-directed than directed learning, it is still possible to see such benefits of education in the accounts of the participants and ex-prisoners.

Stages of cognitive and behavioural change

In terms of the desistance rather than educational literature, several studies have linked cognitive change to desistance and early-stage desistance in particular. Giordano et al. (2002) propose that cognitive change is an important factor in desistance, with structural factors playing a lesser role. They contend that the offender's own mindset and cognitive changes are important in the early stages of desistance (Giordano et al., 2002). In order to fully capitalise on cognitive change, to transform it into structural and personal advantages that support desistance, the individual needs to (1) be open to the possibility of change; (2) be able to recognise viable hooks for change; (3) envisage a replacement self; and (4) develop a changed outlook on criminal behaviour that does not encourage a continuing criminal lifestyle (Giordano et al., 2002). Agency and how it is exercised by the person will also have a strong role to play in supporting these cognitive changes (Giordano et al., 2002). Vaughan (2007) and Prochaska and DiClemente (1982) also propose models of cognitive change that closely mirror the steps given here. Vaughan (2007) proposes three key stages to desistance that are similar to the steps outlined by Giordano et al. (2002). Here the first stage is discernment, where the offender reviews their possible choices, contemplating whether they are open to considering a new kind of life. The question being weighed up by the person is whether they are ready to consider other options (Vaughan, 2007). This is similar to the first step in Giordano et al.'s (2002) steps to cognitive transformation, where the possibility of change is being considered. The second stage is deliberation, where the offender weighs up the pros and cons of the various options and looks at the possible versions of themselves that may emerge (Vaughan, 2007). Giordano et al. (2002) refer to this as the development of a conventional replacement self. However, this can be made difficult by the underlying fear for the level of acceptance there will be for this new self, as the person risks alienating themselves from previous peers and also risks not being accepted by society and achieving civic integration because of their criminal past (Aresti et al., 2010). Finally, in line with steps 3 and 4 of Giordano et al.'s (2002) stages of cognitive transformation, the third stage is dedication. Dedication is characterised by a commitment to a new self that no longer considers criminality as an option (Vaughan, 2007).

Prochaska and DiClemente (1982) propose six stages of change in their transtheoretical model (TTM), which has been viewed as perhaps the most influential theory of behavioural change. While this model was originally developed in relation to addiction and behavioural issues such as alcohol use (Davidson et al., 1991) and intimate partner violence (Easton et al., 2000), it has also been endorsed in the criminological literature in relation to offender rehabilitation (McMurran et al., 1998; Hemphill and Howell, 2000; Williamson et al., 2003) and in the desistance literature as possible indicators of early-stage change (Casey et al., 2010). The model proposes that change in problematic behaviour is characterised by a set progression through a sequence of changes or stages (Prochaska and Diclemente, 1984) that result in changed beliefs, values, attitudes and behaviours and the subsequent development of strategies to change behaviour (Begun et al., 2011). The first stage is pre-contemplation, where the actor is unaware that their behaviour is problematic and has no intention to change (Prochaska and DiClemente, 1982). Second is contemplation, where an awareness develops of the problem and the actor considers a way to overcome it and address the behaviour within the near future (Prochaska and DiClemente, 1982). The third stage of Prochaska and DiClemente's (1982) model is preparation, where the person has not taken action but is planning on or is committed to doing so within the next month. They might begin telling people of their intention to take action, for example. The fourth stage is the action stage, where the person takes specific action to modify their behaviour or circumstance in order to overcome their problem. The fifth stage is maintenance, where the person must work to maintain the changes that have been brought about by the action phase and in order to prevent relapse (Prochaska and DiClemente, 1982).

There are several commonalities among these three theories and when the accounts of those men interviewed were reviewed, there were strong links among the theories and the findings. In order to discuss the links with prison education, these theories will be categorised based on their commonalities and the corresponding links with prison education explored.

The first category is represented by Prochaska and DiClemente's (1982) notion of pre-contemplation. This is essentially sub-change, where there is no recognition of the need to change, and is often characterised by pro-criminal attitudes (Gendreau et al., 1996). This was a strong theme in the accounts of those who were not participating in prison education, with little evidence of this among those participating in education. Those who were not participating did not see the problem with their behaviour, and many did not anticipate any changes to how they lived their life after release. This was very clear in the some of the accounts given by those not participating in prison education, such as Richie and David, who are both talking about release here. It is clear from their statements that they do not perceive any problems with how things are or see a need for change.

RICHIE: Everyone looks forward to getting out, but the thing is when you're in here everyone does be screaming to get out and then when you get out like what's out there, there's nothing really out there. More charge sheets. . . . When I get back out, I'll be honest, I'm a robber miss. I'm a robber, ya know what I mean. so that's all I know, that's all I'm gonna do.

(Mountjoy, non-participant)

DAVID: I don't see the point of it, working 40 hours a week for €500 or €600. Like I'd make double that in twenty minutes . . . I don't care about coming back; I've a lot of mates in here.

(Mountjoy, non-participant)

The second categorisation would include the elements of contemplation (Prochaska and DiClemente, 1982; Vaughan, 2007), deliberation (Vaughan, 2007), considering the replacement self (Giordano et al., 2002) and being open to change (Giordano et al., 2002). Each of these represent the internal processes that are set in motion when someone recognises that change is needed and is considering what might be done in order to address the problematic actions or behaviours. Shane is a participant in prison education, and his account is representative of many who had found education valuable in giving the time and space to contemplate life, mistakes made and the future they wanted. This quote was also chosen as it shows the desire to be more of a family man, and this may perhaps represent part of Shane's reformulated identity from criminal to good father and husband. Such features were not represented in the accounts given by those who were not participating in education, which again shows the potential link between prison education and the early cognitive changes that lead to desistance.

SHANE: I think when you come into prison it gives you an awful lot of time to think about what's maybe important. Before you come in here, if you're into drugs you don't have time to think or you don't put them first like. But when you come in here and you see that they're making the effort to come in here to see you every week and they're missing you, you realise what you have outside and I think then you make your choices based on that you know . . . (t)he time it gives you to think in here, it gives you choices about what you want to put first in your life, like to put my family first, and if I come back in here I wouldn't be putting them first. It's hard enough being in here away from them.

(Mountjoy, participant)

A third category that can be taken from the combination of the earlier theories relates to moving forward with change such as recognising hooks and opportunities (Giordano et al., 2002), preparing to take imminent action and subsequently taking action (Prochaska and DiClemente, 1984) and being committed or dedicated to change (Vaughan, 2007). According to Giordano et al. (2002), cognitive changes influence a person's receptiveness to opportunities or "hooks" for change, and availing of these hooks for change can have a significant impact on whether or not an offender can desist successfully. Prison-based interventions such as education have the capacity to act as "hooks" (Giordano et al., 2002). This was represented in the statements of those participating in education who saw it as a way to better their position and progress in life. It is encouraging that they were thinking along these lines and clearly had the desire or plan to desist upon release.

RAYMOND: Well, I just wanted to better meself for when I got out. As I said, I was hoping to go to college so if I can do education . . . I know then whether I can go further and better meself.

(Mountjoy, participant)

VINCENT: I suppose as you get older you come to realise the significance of education and you know it's a necessity in life if you want to progress in that that life. So, for my future I suppose, I'd be thinking down the road.

(Shelton Abbey, participant)

Finally, the fourth category evident in the earlier theories is where the person has moved through the process and can be seen to have a renewed anti-criminal outlook (Giordano et al., 2002) and is in a maintenance phase (Prochaska and DiClemente, 1984) whereby they now have a set identity as an ex-offender and this this new non-criminal lifestyle is an established state of mind. Noel is an ex-prisoner who spoke about desistance and how there is a degree of effort in ensuring that he did not fall back into old ways or even risk exposing himself to that possibility. It shows that desistance is indeed a process and that it requires work and maintenance. Noel also mentions the influence of school in a humorous way, but he alludes to the idea that some of the skills he used such as planning ahead, consideration and awareness came from time in the school, perhaps planning time and approaches to academic work, and this followed through on release to support behaviours and thoughts.

> NOEL: I don't know, in the early days it was tough, you're kinda watchin' yourself cos you know there's a lot at stake. I was on probation, and if I was even seen with the wrong lads I knew I could just be done and end up back inside. I tried to be organised so I was leaving as little to chance as possible, watching me money so I didn't end up needing cash, making sure I stayed sober, I even planned the routes I'd walk home and the times to stop me bumping into people. As time goes on you relax, but you have to go at it seriously to give it a shot . . . I used to laugh at myself thinking me old teacher in the 'joy would be slappin' me on the back for using me soft skills to plan ahead.
>
> (Ex-prisoner)

Overall, prison education may be relevant to early desistance in supporting the offender to move from the pre-contemplation stage to the subsequent stages that allow more focused and rehabilitation-orientated work to be undertaken by the individual. Based on the accounts here, it appears that education is already facilitating prisoners to work through these stages of change. When comparing statements from non-participants to those who were participating in education, it is clear that the non-participants remain vastly in the pre-contemplation stage. They do not identify any problematic behaviour on their part, their offending seems normalised such as in the case of Richie and David who are quoted earlier, and they are happy to live the criminal lifestyle. Conversely, those who are participating in education tend to be far more aware of how problematic their previous behaviour was; they show empathy for the hurt to victims and family, they actively take responsibility for it and acknowledge their own power in decision making. Many participants appear to be contemplating renewed efforts at desistance when released with plans for work and family. The next chapter will also show the extent to which some have plans to overcome past hurdles and mistakes such as distancing themselves from problematic peer groups. They were able to see the obstacles they would face on release and plan to overcome them and not make the same mistakes. Shane's quote earlier is a good example of this. As mentioned earlier, it may be that education is the action that facilitates a change in thinking and behaviour or that prompts the early realisation that change is required to avoid imprisonment again. This ability to plan for the future is very positive and is also reflective of the redemption script among participants (Maruna, 2001)

Criminal thinking styles

Changes in criminal thinking patterns were examined by Healy (2010), who found that those who were in the primary stages of desistance had far lower levels of criminal thinking styles than those who continued to offend. This was measured using the Psychological Inventory of Criminal Thinking Styles (PICTS) (Walters, 1995) that measures eight elements of cognitive thinking styles which support or characterise criminal behaviour. The elements are (1) mollification; (2) cutoff; (3) entitlement; (4) power orientation; (5) cognitive indolence; (6) discontinuity; (7) sentimentality; and (8) superoptimism (Walters, 1995). While this is a quantitative measure of criminal thinking patterns, it was possible to qualitatively observe several differences between participants and non-participants across some of these categories. It is possible that this may indicate a lowering of criminal thinking levels on the part of participants. While there were small degrees of each element within the various accounts, there were only four that were represented to any reportable extent. Where these links were found, the significance is evident in the differing accounts of the participants and non-participants.

Mollification is the externalisation of blame for past criminality using excuses, rationalisation and blame (Walters, 1995). This appeared to be far less of a theme among the prisoners who were participating in education by comparison to those who were not participating. Those who were not participating in education were quick to point to external sources of blame that took responsibility out of their hands and put it on another person or factor. Jason, a non-participant, put his offending down to low levels of social welfare. Friends (Kevin's quote) and intoxicants (Christopher's quote) also featured as common rationalisations for offending:

JASON: Money . . . (i)t's about survival. Like I said, I don't have a job. And the government expect(s) me to survive on €190 a week. Me with four kids.
(Mountjoy, non-participant)

CHRISTOPHER: I can't remember one time that I got a charge that it was when I was straight, when I was sober. But when I have drink in me I just don't give a fuck like.
(Mountjoy, non-participant)

KEVIN: Well see I'm easily led I am, very easily led on. I hate letting people down and I was doing things for mates.
(Mountjoy, non-participant)

Conversely, those who were participating in education were likely to accept blame themselves. They gave more intrinsic and self-responsible reasons for offending, demonstrating an awareness of their own actions. By accepting responsibility, they also accept a degree of control: since they are the cause of the offending, they are also the ones in control of their future actions, which is important in terms of agency (Cote and Levine, 2014).

MICHAEL: (A) lot was greed and scamming, and I wanted more money; the more I got, I had to keep up with x and y down the road. Most crimes are down to greed.

(Mountjoy, participant)

The second element of criminal thinking that was evident through the interviews was entitlement. Entitlement is a person's belief in their own right to commit crime out of necessity, privilege or justifications (Walters and Lowenkamp, 2016). Again, this was an element that was notable in the accounts of the non-participants. The earlier quote from Jason illustrates the extent to which this element of entitlement to money and support is used as a rationalisation for committing crime. This is contrasted to the account of Eoin, where the core factor behind offending is the same. However, rather than justifying it, the blame is internalised and he does not seem to use an excuse of entitlement to this money to justify his actions. Many of the participants expressed concerns about how they would survive financially when they got out of prison, but all planned to moderate their lifestyles or get jobs to support themselves. An example of this is this quote from Shane where he talks about cutting back on luxuries and potentially having to live on welfare benefits.

SHANE: I won't be back here. Like no matter what, there's always other options and work and I realise that. And if the worst came to the worst, there's benefits there. Alright we might have to cut back on things, like we can't go out for meals or can't bring the kids to the zoo, but you can live on the benefits that are there. You don't have to go out and do things like that.

(Mountjoy, participant)

Sentimentality is an attempt to atone for previous criminal acts through good deeds (Walters, 1995) This is similar to the idea of generativity described earlier in relation to identity change whereby those who have committed crimes see the hurt they have caused and wish to make amends. This more caring, empathetic person is often represented in the new replacement self through their dedication to steering others onto the right path, making up for their previous failings to family and children and even choosing career paths in professions related to their own previous wrongdoings, such as addiction counsellors. This was a prevalent theme among those participating in education, with many aspiring to become the "wounded healers". There were several relevant quotes outlined earlier under the generativity heading. Thomas and Gary were ex prisoners who spoke of repairing relationships and making amends to their children for the time they had missed with them, in addition to aspiring to help young offenders by steering them towards the right track. There were also accounts from those in prison such as Mark and Daniel, who were representative of the many prisoners who were hoping education would allow them to help their own children when they got out. Stephen and John were already putting their generative aspirations to good use within the prison by becoming facilitators for AVP and Toe by Toe. These elements of sentimentality were not represented to any extent among the accounts of non-participants. They were generally not sorry for what they had done and showed little remorse, as can be seen in the quote from Christopher. Observing the differing tone between participants and non-participants would appear to suggest that education is helping to encourage such behavioural change.

CHRISTOPHER: I'm genuinely sorry that a mother is missing her son. Other than that, not really. I'd have very little remorse. Like I do feel sorry for his mother cos I think if that was me how me own mother would feel, but that's empathy. That's the only thing that separates us from animals like. Other than that I don't feel that sorry for him. Like I found a 30-year-old in bed with my kid brother's 15-year-old girlfriend, didn't end well for him.

(Mountjoy, non-participant)

Finally, discontinuity is an inability to remain focused on and follow through on goals, intentions, promises or commitments. Clearly those who were participating in education were able to set and maintain goals, as was evidenced through their participation over time. However, some of those prisoners who were not participating in education had previously participated and had left, their accounts showing evidence of not being able to stay focused on their goals, such as finishing secondary school, as was the case for Larry. Larry seemed to be unable to follow through on goals in two respects: first, his initial goal of desisting from crime and, second, finishing his studies.

LARRY: Yea, look, last time I got out I had big ideas of seeing the kids, getting a job, or doing a business plan and being legit. But then you're going out to the same people and the same places and I tried hard at the start but then you just think why the fuck would ya bother. . . . And this time I did come to the school cos I had a longer stretch and maybe I'd get me Leaving (Certificate) done, but I don't know it just wasn't for me really, I don't know why, I just couldn't settle.

(Shelton Abbey, non-participant)

Across these four categories, the accounts suggest that those men participating in education show less evidence of criminal thinking styles than those who are not participating in education. Mollification, entitlement, lack of sentimentality and discontinuity were featured greatly in the accounts of those who were not participating in prison education, showing that they are likely to have maintained their previous levels of criminal thinking and have experienced little cognitive change in this area. While this is a qualitative analysis of only four of the elements of the quantitative scale, it is impossible to quantify exactly the extent to which education may impact the criminal thinking styles of participants, and the accounts of the participants tend to show that comparatively speaking participation in education can possibly result in lower levels of criminal thinking and thus may help facilitate early-stage desistance.

Hope, expectations and prison education

Several studies have found that hope and expectations can play a positive role in desistance, particularly in the early stages. Burnett (1994) looked at the role of "hope" in the desistance process and stated that the definition of hope, in the criminological context, is "the perceived availability of successful pathways to related goals". Expectations and beliefs are important aspects of desistance, with those offenders who believe they will return to criminality at higher risk of criminal activity on their return to society (Burnett, 1994; Lloyd and Serin, 2012). Hope and agency are heavily linked, with hope contributing to agentic factors such as confidence, motivation and self-belief that lend support in overcoming challenges after release (Farrall and Calverley, 2006). Higher levels of agentic beliefs, such as a belief in one's ability to financially support themselves after prison (Shover and Thompson, 1992), or to be in control of one's own life, for example, were also related to lower reoffending risks (Lloyd and Serin, 2012). Where a person has strong levels of hope, they are more likely to recognise and seize pro-social opportunities and make them more resilient in the face of setbacks (Burnett and Maruna, 2004; LeBel et al., 2008). Research on hope's role in the desistance process suggests that a person's ability to remain crime-free can be enhanced by focusing on their ability to visualise a positive desistance outcome and their ability to attain these outcomes (Lloyd and Serin, 2012). Therefore, any measures that contribute to a person's sense of self-belief can be seen as enhancing the chances of a successful outcome on release. Lloyd and Serin (2012) found that participation in institutional rehabilitation programmes, such as prison education, was related to greater levels of negative expectations about the consequences of crime, which in turn can be indicative of a likelihood of more successful outcomes on release (Lloyd and Serin, 2012).

Perhaps the best-known study relating to hope in the desistance process was carried out by Burnett (1994): she conducted interviews with offenders just before release from prison, and she asked them about their hopes of desisting, with follow-up interviews two years later. To a large extent, their predictions were accurate. Of those who stated that they were definitely going to desist, only 30% returned to offending within the two-year study period. This was over half the rate of those who were pessimistic (over 60% reoffended) and one third of the rate at which the sceptics were reoffending (over 95% of the sceptics reoffended) (Burnett, 1994). This shows two things. First, prisoners are quite accurate in predicting their own paths. Second, optimism, hope and self-belief play a large part in the prisoner's chances of desisting. In a follow-up study ten years later, Burnett and Maruna (2004) found that 47 members of the sample (37%) had been successful in avoiding a further sentence of imprisonment. In terms of the "hope scale", those who were definite about their chances of desisting were those who faired best over the ten years, with only 40% reimprisoned compared with 70% of sceptics. Those who were definite about their chances of desisting were the most likely to remain out of jail over that ten-year period (Burnett and Maruna, 2004). Furthermore, prisoners who had high levels of hope were better able to cope with social problems, where they arose, such as relationship breakdowns or the loss of a job (Burnett and Maruna, 2004). Therefore, measures that facilitate the generation of hope, motivation and agency will be crucial in building the confidence and self-belief to successfully navigate the challenges upon release from prison.

In the current study, a notable theme differentiating prison education participants from non-participants is the element of hope throughout the narratives. While this is also related to the idea of agency as outlined earlier, where participants and non-participants were shown as being of a more redemption or condemnation orientation, the concept of hope in a successful outcome after release was very prevalent among those who were participating in prison education. This was in marked contrast to those who were not participating in prison education, who had little hope that anything would change in their life in the near future. Comparing the quotes from both a participant and a non-participant, Shane, a prison education participant, speaks very definitely about how hopeful he is that he will not be back in prison, whereas Richie, who was not participating in prison education, is very adamant about it being a foregone conclusion that he will return to prison.

SHANE: I won't be back here. Like no matter what, there's always other options and work and I realise that. And if the worst came to the worst, there's benefits there. Alright we might have to cut back on things, like we can't go out for meals or can't bring the kids to the zoo, but you can live on the benefits that are there. You don't have to go out and do things like that.

(Mountjoy, participant)

RICHIE: When I get back out, I'll be honest, I'm a robber miss. I'm a robber, ya know what I mean. so that's all I know, that's all I'm gonna do . . . the way I see it that (being clean) just cuts out the desperation, I'll have a clear head doing it, so I'll probably be a better robber.

(Mountjoy, non-participant)

As outlined earlier, self-predicted outcomes are significant in relation to post-release outcomes (Burnett, 1994; Lloyd and Serin, 2012), tending to be accurate, with a strong, positive correlation between those who estimated they would desist from offending and those who did not return to prison in the study period (Burnett, 1994; Burnett and Maruna, 2004). Those prisoners who were participating in prison education, such as Shane, tended to hold a strong belief in their ability to exercise control over their own direction, with those prisoners who were participating in education appearing to be much more resolute in their belief that they would be successful on release and would not return to prison again. While the current study did not have the scope to follow up on post-release outcomes, the significance of Burnett's (1994) study is the idea that those who predict desistance are most likely to actually achieve it. In many ways, it reflects the power of self-esteem and confidence in one's own abilities. In the current study, half of the prisoners were adamant they would not return to prison, consistent with Burnett's (1994) idea of "definites", who subsequently showed much lower levels of offending than those who were less resolute. The vast majority of these "definites" in the current study were participating in prison education. It is noteworthy that a number of these participants came to education in order to alleviate boredom but explained that they continued to participate with a view to supporting post-release goals. It may also be, as suggested by Lloyd and Serin (2012), that participating in institutional programmes can lead to greater negative expectations towards the outcomes of crime, which creates a belief and intention around future behaviour. It might be surmised here that education, through the various cognitive changes that were highlighted in the findings, created or strengthened the resolve of these prisoners to desist and that they were consequently using education as a means of attaining this.

Summary and additional discussion

Throughout this chapter, the elements of desistance relating to individual change have been examined through the lens of prison education, using the accounts of those men interviewed to illuminate the links between their experiences of education and the desistance process. The presence of various factors that link education to the desistance process can be observed among the participants, particularly by contrast to the narratives of the non-participants, who were far less likely to reflect desistance-related themes in their interviews. Following is a summary of the links between prison education and desistance outlined in this chapter, along with the contrasting lack of any such evidence in the statements of the non-participants.

Agency relates to the capability of a person to act as their own "agent", to be their own person and to be in control of their own life and destiny. This involves growing the "self" and the aspects associated with being an effective citizen. Elements of agency, therefore, include self-esteem, self-confidence, self-efficacy, self-control, self-awareness and self-responsibility (Cote, 1997; McAdams, 2001). There were previous links between prison education and agency established in the literature, with Morris (1962) finding that prison education promotes self-awareness and an increased insight into one's self. Mezirow's theory of transformative learning (2000) suggests that education opens the mind, changes perspectives and encourages self-reflection. Prison education is also associated with conscious strengthening (Duguids, 1998), greater levels of empathy (Duguids, 1998), greater self-esteem (Ubah and Robinson, 2003) and increased self-control (Callan and Gardner, 2005), and it helps to prevent the damaging impact of imprisonment on the person (Council of Europe, 1990; Warner, 2007). There was significant evidence of each of these themes in the accounts of those participating in education. Participants reported greater levels of self-awareness, realising how their own actions had led to their current situation. They could see how it had impacted others, such as their family and the victims of their crimes, and were aware of the actions needed on their part to put things rights. This was in direct contrast to the non-participants, who were more likely to place the blame elsewhere than to realise their own role in their situation. Participants also reported that education had opened their minds to other ways of looking at situations and their life. They were more reflective and empathetic and could see other ways of living that did not involve criminality. They felt more confident and empowered to have a voice in both their own personal life and in society, reflecting a desire to be more civically engaged. They also reported that because they could see things more clearly and had greater confidence, they would be more in control of their own life and outcomes going forward. All of this showed strong evidence of links to the constituent elements of agency and the way in which prison education can support its development. This is even more acute by contrast to the accounts of the non-participants, who showed very little evidence of agency. Many continued to assert their lack of personal responsibility for their criminality, tending to place the blame on external sources. This demonstrates the strong contrast in attitudes between participants and non-participants, and of great concern was the blatant and unapologetic pronouncement by several of the non-participants that they would continue offending when released.

Several themes that arose which were pertinent to identity and cognitive change were also explored. Overall, there were strong links shown between the accounts of the non-participants and desistance theory, relating in particular to generativity, cognitive transformations and criminal thinking styles. In relation to generativity, it was shown earlier that many of the participants had a desire to make amends for their past mistakes and to help others going forward. In numerous cases, the participants were using prison education to further this goal, such as helping with homework, coaching, undertaking addiction studies or hoping that prison education would be a stepping stone to a career that involved helping others when they were released. Cognitive change was a prominent theme among participants and was similar to the points outlined under agency earlier, such as increased self-awareness and changed outlook. Moreover, the participants showed a strong desire to change. Many appeared to already be considering replacement selves and were using education to take action. There was clear evidence that some participants were at various stages of change, with non-participants generally not reflecting any desire or actions towards change and ex-prisoners maintaining a crime-free lifestyle which they attribute to prison education. This is indicative of the role that prison can play in supporting the desistance process: by supporting aspirations of change, it can provide a hook for change or indeed promote the recognition of other hooks when they present themselves. Exploring several characteristics of criminal thinking styles, Walters (1995) also showed strong differences between participants and non-participants. Those who were not participating in education showed far higher levels of criminal thinking such as externalising and rationalising blame for crime, showing evidence of feeling entitled to commit crime to support themselves and a general inability to stay focused on and follow through with their goals. The participants showed far less evidence of these elements and were more likely to take personal responsibility for their past and future actions. Again this shows how education can encourage reflection, awareness and responsibility.

Finally, the hope of desistance was prevalent among the accounts of participants, yet was sorely lacking among non-participants. Many participants were adamant they would not return to prison. Several studies have linked such expectations with lower levels of reoffending (Burnett, 1994; Lloyd and Serin, 2012). While there are distinct differences in the accounts of both groups, there is also evidence that participation in institutional programmes such as education can impact expectations. Education appears to increase the expectation of negative outcomes from crime, and this can lead to a higher likelihood of success upon release (Lloyd and Serin, 2012).

It is acknowledged throughout this book that while the aim is to link prison education to the desistance framework in order to begin to unpack the ways in which education can support a person in their life after release, it is not possible to state that any of the men interviewed were currently desisting from crime, with the exception of the ex-prisoners. However, that is not to say that the early precursors of desistance cannot be observed or promoted within the prison setting. The findings presented in the current chapter are very strongly linked to various aspects of desistance success. The participants show very strong evidence of many elements of both early and later stages of desistance, most of which can be associated with cognitive change, which were not observed among those who were not participating in education. Therefore, while prison education cannot be said to definitively cause desistance (for several reasons), it may be that prison education can act to encourage and support a form of pre desistance. It is not primary or second desistance *per se*. Rather it is a period before these two phases where the decisions, reflection and supporting groundwork is laid so as to put the person in the best position, or even ahead of the curve, when they are released.

In terms of how education achieves these things, drawing on findings from both this chapter and Chapter 4, there are several points to be made. Prison education removes prisoners from the prison setting for several hours a day and provides the opportunity to engage in education, which has an impact on both cognitive change and skills development. As participants progress with education, it promotes critical and analytical skills which when applied to their own scenario will often allow a greater deal of introspection than was previously possible. This is manifest in greater self-awareness, a more open mind and empathy, for example. However, the prison school, as opposed to prison education, also allows a space for relaxation, reflection and positive interactions. During this time, participants are given an external focus and must put their mind to matters outside of themselves for that period. Having this mental space, away from anti-social influences and negative attitudes, on a consistent basis can have a strong cumulative impact over time. Moreover, many of those who undertake education in prison will have very negative self-perceptions from experiences such as societal labelling and low levels of achievement. The confidence gained from pro-social interactions with teachers and others in the school environment can be crucial in reforming their identity as someone who is a good person and capable of achieving their goals. Therefore, in many ways it may be the prison space, along with education, that is significantly beneficial.

Conclusion

This chapter has explored the narrative theories of desistance, focusing on the ways in which prison education can support internal changes that are important in the desistance process. It was broadly argued that prison education can support desistance through the formation of agentic factors, supporting cognitive changes, promoting consideration of a replacement identity, reducing criminal thinking and fostering generativity and hope. The theories related to both early- and later-stage desistance, but the myriad of personal changes that were fostered through prison education allowed for a general conceptualisation of prison education as a form of pre-desistance. The upcoming chapter will explore structural theories of desistance. This will build on the work presented in this chapter and continue to explore the ways in which prison education can support the efforts to strengthen relationships, gain employment and build social bonds.

References

Aresti, A., Eatough, V. and Brooks-Gordon, B. (2010) Doing Time after Time: An Interpretative Phenomenological Analysis of Reformed Ex-Prisoners' Experiences of Self-Change, Identity and Career Opportunities. *Psychology, Crime & Law* 16(3), pp. 169–190. doi:10.1080/10683160802516273.

Baskin, D.R. and Sommers, I.B. (1998) *Casualties of Community Disorder: Women's Careers in Violent Crime*, Boulder: Westview Press.

Begun, A.L., Rose, S.J. and LeBel, T.P. (2011) Intervening with Women in Jail around Alcohol and Substance Abuse during Preparation for Community Reentry. *Alcoholism Treatment Quarterly* 29(4), pp. 453–478. doi:10.1080/07347324.2011.608333.

Blumstein, A., Cohen, J., Roth, J. and Visher, C. (eds) (1986) *Criminal Careers and "Career Criminals."* Washington, DC: National Academy Press.

Bottoms, A., Shapland, J., Costello, A., Holmes, D. and Muir, G. (2004) Towards Desistance: Theoretical Underpinnings for an Empirical Study. *Howard Journal of Criminal Justice* 43(4), pp. 368–389.

Burnett, R. (1992) *The Dynamics of Recidivism: Summary Report*. Oxford: Centre for Criminological Research, University of Oxford.

Burnett, R. (1994) Recidivism and Imprisonment. *Home Office Research Bulletin* 36, pp. 19–22. London: Home Office.

Burnett, R. (2004) To Reoffend or Not to Reoffend? The Ambivalence of Convicted Property Offenders. In Maruna, S. and Immarigeon, R. (eds) *After Crime and Punishment: Pathways to Offender Reintegration*. Devon: Willan.

Burnett, R. and Maruna, S. (2004) So 'Prison Works' Does It? The Criminal Careers of 130 Men Released from Prison under Home Secretary, Michael Howard. *Howard Journal of Criminal Justice* 43(4), pp. 390–405.

Callan, V. and Gardner, J. (2005) *Vocational Education and Training Provision and Recidivism in Queensland Correctional Institutions*. Adelaide: NCVER.

Casey, S., Day, A. and Howells, A. (2010) The Application of the Transtheoretical Model to Offender Populations: Some Critical Issues. *Legal and Criminological Psychology* 10, pp. 157–171. doi:10.1348/135532505X36714.

Cline, H.F. (1980) Criminal Behaviour over the Life Span. In Orville, G., Brim, Jr. and Kagan, J. (eds) *Constancy and Change in Human Development*. Cambridge: Harvard University Press.

Cote, J.E. (1997) An Empirical Test of the Identity Capital Model. *Journal of Adolescence* 20(5), pp. 367–394.

Cote, J.E. and Levine, C.G. (2014) *Identity, Formation, Agency and Culture: A Social Psychological Synthesis*. Mahwah, NJ: Lawrence Erlbaum Associates.

Council of Europe (1990) *Education in Prison: Recommendation No. R (89) 12*. 13th October 1989. Strasbourg: Council of Europe.

Cusson, M. and Pinsonneault, P. (1986) The Decision to Give Up Crime. In Clarke, R. and Cornish, D. (eds) *The Reasoning Criminal*. New York: Springer-Verlag.

Davidson, R., Rollnick, S. and MacEwan, I. (eds) (1991) *Counselling Problem Drinkers*. London: Routledge.

Duguid, S. (1998) Policy, Praxis and Rehabilitation: Prison Education in Canada 1945–1995. In Forster, W. (ed) *Education behind Bars: International Comparisons*. Leicester: National Institute of Adult Continuing Education.

Easton, C., Swan, S. and Sinha, R. (2000) Motivation to Change Substance Use among Offenders of Domestic Violence. *Journal of Substance Abuse Treatment* 19(1), pp. 1–5.

Farrall, S. and Bowling, B. (1999) Structuration, Human Development and Desistance from Crime. *British Journal of Criminology* 39, pp. 253–268.

Farrall, S. and Calverley, A. (2006) *Understanding Desistance from Crime: Theoretical Directions in Resettlement and Rehabilitation*. Maidenhead: Open University Press.

Farrington, D.P. (1986) Age and Crime. In Tonry, M. and Morris, N. (eds) *Crime and Justice: An Annual Review of Research*. Vol. 7. Chicago: Chicago University Press.

Farrington, D.P. (1997) Human Development and Criminal Careers. In Maguire, M., Morgan, R. and Reiner, R. (eds) *Oxford Handbook of Criminology*. 2nd ed. Oxford: Oxford University Press.

Farrington, D.P., Coid, J., Harnett, L., Jolliffe, D., Soteriou, N., Turner, R. and West, D. (2006) *Criminal Careers Up to Age 50 and Life Success Up to Age 48: New Findings from the Cambridge Study of Delinquent Development*. London: Home Office.

Flood-Page, C., Campbell, S., Harrington, V. and Miller, J. (2000) *Youth Crime: Findings for the 1998/99 Youth Lifestyles Survey: Home Office Research Study 209*. London: Home Office.

Flynn, S., Brown. J., Johnson. A. and Rodger, S. (2011) Barriers to Education for the Marginalized Adult Learner. *Alberta Journal of Educational Research* 57(1), pp. 43–58.

Forrest, R. and Kearns, A. (2001) Social Cohesion, Social Capital and the Neighborhood. *Urban Studies* 38(12), pp. 2125–2143.

Gendreau, P., Little, T. and Goggin, C. (1996) A Meta-Analysis of the Predictors of Adult Offender Recidivism: What Work! *Criminology* 34(4), pp. 575–607.

Giordano, P., Cernkovich, S. and Rudolph, J. (2002) Gender, Crime and Desistance: Towards a Theory of Cognitive Transformation. *American Journal of Sociology* 107(4), pp. 990–1064. doi:10.1086/343191.

Glueck, S. and Glueck, E. (1950) *Unravelling Juvenile Delinquency*. New York: Commonwealth Fund.

Gottfredson, M. and Hirschi, T. (1990) *A General Theory of Crime*. Stanford: Stanford University Press.

Graham, J. and Bowling, B. (1995) *Young People and Crime: Home Office Research Study No. 145*. London: Home Office.

Healy, D. (2010) *The Dynamics of Desistance: Charting Pathways through Change*. Cullompton: Willan Publishing.

Healy, D. (2014) Becoming a Desister. *British Journal of Criminology* 54, pp. 873–891.

Hart, W. and Healy, D. (2018) 'An Inside Job': An Autobiographical Account of Desistance. *European Journal of Probation* 10(2), pp. 103–119. doi:10.1177/2066220318783426.

Hemphill, J. and Howell, A. (2000) Adolescent Offenders and Stages of Change. *Psychological Assessment* 12, pp. 371–381. doi:10.1037/1040-3590.12.4.371.

Hobler, B. (1999) Correctional Education: Now and in the Future. *Journal of Correctional Education* 50, pp. 102–105.

King, S. (2013) Assisted Desistance and Experiences of Probation Supervision. *Probation Journal* 60(2), pp. 136–151. doi:10.1177/0264550513478320.

Laub, J.H. and Sampson, R.J. (1993) Turning Points in the Life Course: Why Change Matters to the Study of Crime. *Criminology* 31(3), pp. 301–332.

Laub, J.H. and Sampson, R.J. (2001) Understanding Desistance from Crime. *Crime and Justice* 28, pp. 1–69.

LeBel, T., Burnett, R., Maruna, S. and Bushway, S. (2008) The 'Chicken and Egg' of Subjective and Social Factors in Desistance from Crime. *European Journal of Criminology* 5(2), pp. 131–159.

Lloyd, C.D. and Serin, R.C. (2012) Agency and Outcome Expectancies for Crime Desistance: Measuring Offenders' Personal Beliefs about Change. *Psychology, Crime & Law* 6, pp. 543–565. doi:10.1080/1068316X.2010.511221.

Maguire, M. and Raynor, P. (2006) How the Resettlement of Prisoners Promotes Desistance from Crime: Or Does It? *Criminology and Criminal Justice* 6(1), pp. 19–38.

Manger, T., Eikeland, O.J. and Asbjørnsen, A. (2013) Effects of Educational Motives on Prisoners' Participation in Education and Educational Desires. *European Journal on Criminal Policy and Research* 19, pp. 245–257. doi:10.1007/s10610-012-9187-x.

Maruna, S. (2001) *Making Good: How Ex-Convicts Reform and Rebuild Their Lives*. Washington: American Psychological Association. doi:10.1037/10430-000.

Maruna, S. and Farrall, S. (2004) Desistance from Crime: A Theoretical Reformulation. *Kolner Zeitschrift fur Soziologie und Sozialpsychologie* 43, pp. 171–194. doi:10.1007/978-3-322-80474-7_7.

Maruna, S., Immarigeon, S. and LeBel, T. (2004) Prisoner Reintegration: Theory and Practice. In Maruna, S. and Immarigeon, R. (eds) *After Crime and Punishment: Pathways to Prisoner Reintegration*. Cullomton: Willan Publishing.

McAdams, D.P. (2001) *Coding Autobiographical Episodes for Themes of Agency and Communion*. Unpublished Manuscript. Evanston, IL: Northwestern University.

McMurran, M., Tyler, P., Hogue, T., Cooper, K., Dunseath, W. and McDaid, D. (1998) Measuring Motivation to Change in Offenders. *Psychology, Crime and Law*, pp. 43–50. doi:10.1080/10683169808401746.

Mezirow, J. (1991) *Transformative Dimensions of Adult Learning*. San Francisco: Jossey-Bass.

Mezirow, J. (2000) Learning to Think Like an Adult: Core Concepts of Transformation Theory. In Mezirow, J. (ed) *Learning as Transformation: Critical Perspectives on a Theory in Progress*. San Francisco: Jossey-Bass.

Morris, C.W. (1962) *Mind, Self and Society: From the Standpoint of Social Behaviourist*. Chicago: University Press of Chicago.

O'Mahony, P. (1997) *Mountjoy Prisoners: A Sociological and Criminological Profile*. Dublin: Stationary Office.

Prochaska, J.O. and DiClemente, C.C. (1982) Stages and Processes of Self-Change of Smoking: Towards an Integrative Model of Change. *Journal of Consulting and Clinical Psychology* 51(3), pp. 390–395. doi:10.1037/0022-006X.51.3.390.

Prochaska, J.O. and DiClemente, C.C. (1984) *The Transtheoretical Approach: Crossing Traditional Boundaries of Therapy*. Homewood, IL: Dow Jones Irwin.

Rutter, M., Quinton, D. and Hill, J. (1990) Longitudinal Data in the Study of Causal Processes: Some Uses and Some Pitfalls. In Rutter, M. (ed) *Studies of Psychological Risk: The Power of Longitudinal Data*. Cambridge: Cambridge University Press.

Shover, N. (1996) *Great Pretenders: Pursuits and Careers of Persistent Thieves*. Boulder: Westview Press.

Shover, N. and Thompson, C.Y. (1992) Age, Differential Expectations, and Crime Desistance. *Criminology* 30, pp. 89–104. doi:10.1111/j.1745-9125.1992.tb01094.

Threadwell, J., Gooch, K. and Barkham, G. (2019) *Crime in Prisons: Where Now and Where Next?* Staffordshire: Staffordshire Police Commission.

Ubah, C.B.A. and Robinson, R.L. (2003) A Grounded Look at the Debate over Prison-Based Education: Optimistic Theory versus Pessimistic Worldview. *The Prison Journal* 83, pp. 115–129.

Vaughan, B. (2007) The Internal Narrative of Desistance. *The British Journal of Criminology* 47(3), pp. 390–404.

Walters, G.D. (1995) The Psychological Inventory of Criminal Thinking Styles: Part I: Reliability and Preliminary Validity. *Criminal Justice and Behavior* 22(3), pp. 307–325. doi: 10.1177/0093854895022003008.

Walters, G.D. and Lowenkamp, C.T. (2016) Predicting Recidivism with the Psychological Inventory of Criminal Thinking Styles (PICTS) in Community-Supervised Male and Female Federal Offenders. *Psychological Assessment* 28(6), pp. 652–659. doi:10.1037/pas0000210.

Warner, K. (2007) Against the Narrowing of Perspectives: How Do We See Learning, Prisons and Prisoners? *Journal of Correctional Education* 58(2), pp. 170–183.

Williamson, P., Day, A., Howells, K., Bubner, S. and Jauncey, S. (2003) Assessing Offender Readiness to Change Problems with Anger. *Psychology Crime & Law* 9, pp. 295–307. doi:10.1080/1068316031000073371.

Chapter 6

Structural theories, social bonds and prison education

Desistance is a complex process involving a dynamic interaction among a variety of factors that ultimately facilitate a person's move away from criminality. The degree to which various factors impact this journey is the subject of significant debate. Desistance will ultimately require a culmination of various intrinsic and extrinsic resources available to the individual. Chapter 5 focused on the intrinsic elements, exploring the more narrative and cognitive theories of desistance that relate to the findings of this research. That chapter also examined the ways in which the benefits of prison education related to the literature on desistance. It was argued that prison education can support desistance by contributing to various aspects of agency, cognitive transformation, identity change and acts as a form of pre-desistance. This chapter will review the external and structural aspects of desistance with a view to building on the material presented in the previous chapters to continue examining the role of prison education in enhancing the life of the person and supporting the desistance process. However, given the broad span of the findings, this material will go beyond the traditional structural mechanisms of building social bonds, such as employment and relationships, and will also explore the structural aspects of the early release phase as the person begins to try to establish themselves as a citizen again. This will look at aspects of reintegration such as accommodation, finance, addiction and overcoming institutionalisation and the role that education can play in supporting this early phase of desistance.

Structural theories of desistance relate to extrinsic factors such as social, institutional, situational, historical and cultural aspects of a person's experience that contextualise and inform their choices and actions (Bersani and Doherty, 2018). Structural theories focus on the personal and social relationships in a person's life from which they can draw support when moving towards desistance and which will often act as a counterbalance to the struggles they face when released from prison. The barriers to reintegration are significant. A failure to successfully navigate these obstacles will often lead to a return to criminality and to prison. In many ways, these barriers to reintegration mirror the very structures that are necessary to promote desistance. The released offender faces a multitude of issues as they try to put in place the various structures that will allow them to meet their basic needs and participate in society (Martynowicz and Quigley, 2010). The manner in which the offender deals with or overcomes these barriers will have a strong impact on their chances of desistance (Martynowicz and Quigley, 2010). Among the most significant of these barriers are employment and finance, reestablishing and maintaining positive relationships, finding stable accommodation, managing addictions and having low educational levels and low social bonds/social capital. These same issues such as employment, family relationships and peer relations are a significant focus of the structural theories of desistance since these are the key sources of positive social bonds that will tie a person to conformity. Yet many states reduce the efforts to promote rehabilitation and desistance to an impossibly simplistic goal, providing prison education as a mechanism of rehabilitation in the hope of increasing the employability of the person. While education can increase employment skills (Porporino and Robinson, 1992; Tewksbury and Stengel, 2006), the person is often coming from a background characterised by very low levels of education, a poor employment history and socioeconomic deprivation. They will also return to a society steeped in stigma and prejudice towards ex-prisoners. All of these factors create obstacles to the employment market. It is important therefore that other structural elements are strong in order to ensure that where employment is not possible, there are other stabilising factors to ground the person in society. By understanding the manner in which prison education can contribute to the various structural elements, instead of employment alone, it may be possible to ensure that prison education is meeting the actual needs of prisoners and not simply being treated as a mechanism of employment preparation. Moreover, perpetuation of structural elements such as social bonds takes time; it is a gradual investment, and therefore the development of internal mechanisms of self-support will also be important in providing foundational stability to the efforts to construct a new crime-free identity and life.

The key structural elements found in the accounts of those interviewed will be outlined later in addition to an overview of the relevant literature and theories. As with the previous chapters, the findings of the current research study will be added throughout in order to contribute to the overall discussion of each issue and to highlight the impact that education can have in terms of enhancing the ability of the prisoners and ex-prisoners to put in place the necessary structures and social bonds to allow them to live a life of conformity and leave their criminality behind.

Overview of structural factors

There are a variety of socio-structural factors proposed in the literature as having a role in the desistance process, with a volume of empirical studies to support these relationships. The focus with such theories is the impact of social bonds or ties on the process of desistance. One of the earliest studies relevant to this area by Glueck and Glueck (1940, 1974) claimed that as people mature, they begin to gain stakes in conformity, such as employment and a family, and this moves them away from crime and towards conformity. However, maturational theories do not recognise individual pathways in the desistance process and the individual experiences of various social and structural factors (Maruna, 1997). As research progressed, the focus shifted away from who desists and when to why they desist and how. Laub and Sampson (2001) stated that despite the fact that there are many studies that link adult offending to childhood anti-social behaviour, changes in offending patterns and desistance can happen spontaneously and are often structured by changes in adult social bonds. As a person goes through life, they acquire bonds such as a significant partner or a spouse, children, a home and perhaps a job that are each legitimate sources of achievement and pride (Trasler, 1980; Gottfredson and Hirschi, 1990), and this can facilitate desistance. Shover and Thompson (1992) found that the development of conventional social bonds has a strong role to play in the process of desistance. This impact arises in several ways. People are inhibited from committing crime as they increase their social bonds and ties to conformity (Meisenhelder, 1977). Such ties create interdependence, obligations and restraint that increase the opportunity cost of crime (Meisenhelder, 1977). As offenders began to feel accepted and trusted in social circles, it increases their ties to conformity and strengthens their resolve to desist (Meisenhelder, 1977). Sampson and Laub (1993) found that social bonds are instrumental in the creation and maintenance of social capital. Furthermore, social bonds provide a sense of normality and stability which act as a shield to the negativity and labelling that they will be subjected to upon release. However, the strength and quality of these bonds, including the level of connection and interdependence a person has with the various structures in their network, are crucial (Sampson and Laub, 2003).

The two strongest factors in life course transitions (Sampson and Laub, 1993) or in the formation of bonds to society/conformity (Meisenhelder, 1977; Shover, 1996) are said to be employment and marriage. The social stakes that offenders acquire through work and family are capable of adding structure and support to their lives, thus facilitating desistance. The existence of familial ties served as a reinforcement of their resolve to continue with their desistance (Meisenhelder, 1977). It also provides a sense of belonging and a source of emotional support. Other non-familial ties, such as employment and pro-social peers, provide the offender with additional resources and investment in society (Meisenhelder, 1977).

Social bonds can also work in the opposite direction if they are anti-social in nature or if they begin to unwind. Identities can be shaped by the sets of relationships in which they participate and the social rules they internalise and prioritise (Weaver, 2016). Therefore, where relationships are of an anti-social nature, such as bonding with anti-social and delinquent peer groups, these can have a criminogenic impact on the life of the person. Furthermore, as bonds destabilising in pro-social relationships, such as people being laid off from work, their levels of formal social control and social ties weaken and this can lead to a return to offending or late-onset offending (Laub and Sampson, 1993). Therefore, turning points and social bonds can be either positive or negative. Vaughan (2007) echoes this and notes that despite the fact that the prisoner depends on social ties such as employment and relationships, where these social ties are broken it is very difficult to maintain desistance. He suggests that desisters carry out "moral conversations" with themselves where they weigh up the options available to them going forward that may result in them deciding to "go straight". However, this does not mean that they will succeed; there may be setbacks along the way, which is to be expected especially since for many potential desisters the life of crime is all they have known since their teenage years or even before, particularly if parents or siblings have also been offenders (Vaughan, 2007). Therefore, it is the simple things such as bonds to family, relationships and employment that will be most important while the person establishes their new crime-free life (Vaughan, 2007).

Several elements imperative to the discussion of social bonds and desistance, including marriage, parenthood, employment, peer relations and social capital, will be examined in more detail later, particularly those structural factors that were prominent themes in the interviews and surveys that were carried out for the current study.

Family relationships: marriage, parenthood and desistance

Pro-social supports and relationships play a key role in the reintegration and desistance process (Weaver, 2016). Family ties have been shown to be a major influence in the desistance process. For instance, living at home with parents and having a positive relationship with parents helped facilitate desistance in young people (Graham and Bowling, 1995). A lack of social support has been linked to psychological distress (Biggam and Power, 1997). However, despite the fact that a large number of prisoners reside with their families upon release (LaVigne et al., 2004), many prisoners are released to unstable or unsuitable accommodation that can result in them feeling isolated, slipping into a transitory lifestyle, returning to problematic drug use and ultimately recidivism (Baldry et al., 2003). While numerous reports have shown the benefits of stable and supportive family and social relationships in the reintegration and desistance process, research has also shown that negative social connections such as delinquent friends (Graham and Bowling, 1995) or relationships formed with acquaintances met during incarceration (Moore, 1996) will often encourage the ex-prisoner to resume criminal activity. Therefore, in terms of relationships, it is the quality and not the quantity that will prove most important. The most common relationships represented in the desistance literature are marriage and peer relations. Both of these will be explored later, in addition to the data from the interviews carried out in the current research, to continue drawing out the links between desistance and prison education. Another strong theme arising in the current study was parenthood, which, despite its prevalence among the prison population and the capacity for it to be a transformatory experience, is quite underrepresented in the literature. The following section will also examine the literature that does exist on parenthood and explore any links that exist with prison education.

Marriage

Many theorists have asserted the value of marriage in the process of "going straight" (Glueck and Glueck, 1940; Cusson and Pinsonneault, 1986; Sampson et al., 2006; Craig et al., 2014). For example, Sampson et al. (2006) found that marriage resulted in a 35% decrease in offending compared to those who were unmarried. More recently, Kendler et al. (2017) found marriage to be associated with a 47% reduction in offending in men and a 67% reduction in offending among women. Sampson and Laub (2003) stated that the impact of marriage on the life course of offenders is one of strongest influences in the desistance process. This effect of the marital bond on desistance is gradual (Laub et al., 1998), with the strength and degree of emotional investment in the marriage being instrumental (Sampson and Laub, 2003). The link between marriage and desistance appears to be "robust", yet what is less clear is the manner through which marriage interferes with criminality and facilitates desistance (Bersani and Doherty, 2013: 400). There are several perspectives evident in the literature. Marriage can be viewed as a turning point (Sampson and Laub, 1993; Sampson and Laub, 2003). The social stakes acquired through marriage are capable of adding structure and support to offenders lives, thus facilitating desistance (Laub and Sampson, 1993). Sampson and Laub (1993) also examined the process of change within the life course. They believe that it is not marriage itself that has the desistant effect but it is the emotional ties, interdependence and bond between the two people that will lead to a reduction in offending. Moreover, the control exerted by a spouse over contact and time with peers will also have an impact (Sampson and Laub, 1993). Laub et al. (1998), analysing the criminal histories of 500 delinquent boys who were followed into adulthood by Glueck and Glueck (1950, 1968), demonstrated the influence of marriage as a turning point in the life course and the effects of marriage on the desistance process. Using yearly longitudinal data, the research showed that increases in levels of desistance were seen from three years post-marriage. Therefore, it appears that while good marriages have an effect on desistance, this only occurs after the bond has had time to mature and grow (Laub et al., 1998). This may explain Horney et al.'s (1995) suggestion that living with a girlfriend actually increased the chances of offending, since this early stage of the relationship may not remain the *status quo* for a sufficiently long period to show benefits in terms of desistance.

The earlier in life an offender enters into a good marriage, the earlier into the marriage the benefits were seen in terms of reduced offending (Laub et al.,

1998). This could be explained by the solidifying of habits as time goes on. Those who marry earlier are not as entrenched in the habits of the criminal lifestyle or may not have fully formed a criminal identity yet. This lifestyle is easier to overcome the earlier the intervening element occurs; those who marry later are further immersed in the criminal mindset and lifestyle and may take somewhat longer to reverse these habits and behaviours as a result.

It is proposed that the bonds created by marriage are important in strengthening resolve and determination to desist (Shover, 1996). Marriage also assists in developing a more conventional lifestyle to frame the new identity as a non-offender (Mischkowitz, 1994). Furthermore, it is argued that marriage provides a sense of normality and stability that offenders feel acts as a shield to the negativity and effects of labelling to which they are subjected (Meisenhelder, 1977). The existence of familial ties served as a reinforcement of their resolve to continue with their desistance (Meisenhelder, 1977; Shover, 1996). It also provides a sense of belonging and a source of emotional support. Other non-familial ties provide the offender with additional resources and investment in society and desistance. As former prisoners began to feel accepted and trusted in social circles, it increased their ties to conformity and strengthened their resolve to desist (Meisenhelder, 1977). It might be pointed out here that many of the beneficial aspects of marriage are similar to the impacts of both mainstream and prison education on individuals. The sense of normalisation, the shielding from negativity and the emotional support and stabilising effect of both marriage and education may indicate the mechanism by which prison education can have similar impacts in the lives of offenders to other structural factors which have been shown to have a role in the desistance process.

The relationship must be strong (Skardhamar et al., 2015) and the spouse must be of a pro-social, anti-criminal disposition in order for the impact of the marriage to be influential (Cusson and Pinsonneault, 1986). The anti-criminal aspect is important here as a criminal spouse has been associated with much higher risks of offending on the part of both spouses (Kendler et al., 2017). Living with a spouse has a strong impact on desistance, but being married and living separate from a spouse does not have such a positive impact (Horney et al., 1995; Farrington and West, 1995). Those living separate to their wife had much higher rates of offending than those who lived together (Farrington and West, 1995), with Horney et al. (1995) finding that such a situation doubled the chances of reoffending. This confirms Sampson and Laub's (2003) theory that it is the strength of the bonds, as opposed to the rite of marriage itself, that is important. These findings were echoed in part by Savolainen (2009), who contends that both marriage and cohabitation decrease offending.

Several studies suggest that the impact of marriage on desistance is not direct. Rather, marriage interferes with other aspects of the offender's life, which in turn has an impact on offending. Marriage interferes with the time and opportunity to access peers, which in turn has an impact on desistance. (Osgood and Lee, 1993; Warr, 1998, 2002). In terms of criminal trajectories, Warr (1998) found that marriage has two important effects. Marriage significantly reduces the time available to spend with friends, and furthermore marriage alters the type of friends a person spends time with. In particular, it reduces the number of delinquent friends a person associates with. In terms of maintaining peer relationships, rates remain stable for those who did not marry but showed a decrease of up to 80% for those respondents who married (Warr, 1998). The study showed that it is not just the marriage itself that has an effect on the life course of the offender, but that marriage has an impact on other structures within the life of the offender such as peer relations, interference with which can have a significant impact on desistance. Similarly, Knight et al. (1977) state that although marriage does not decrease criminality, it decreases anti-social behaviour such as drinking and drug use and this results in decreased offending and desistance. Moreover, marriage decreases the opportunity to associate with delinquent peers. In a similar way to the earlier point regarding education's potential to have similar effects on the desistance process as marriage, it is speculated that perhaps an offender's participation in prison education could interfere with peer relations and other anti-social behaviour. Within the prison, the use of leisure time to participate in education, rather than spending time in the general prison population with other gang members or delinquent peers, would constitute a move away from these people and fracturing of relations. This will be explored in more detail under the heading of peer relations later.

Parenthood

A key source of social bonds that has been quite overlooked in the desistance research to date is parenthood. This is surprising given that the lifestyles of those who are involved in delinquency tend to result in lower rates of marriage and lower levels of employment, yet they are more likely to have children from a younger age. It would seem that parenthood is the most likely structural factor common to offenders, yet marriage and employment are far more represented in the desistance literature. Of the little research that exists, the evidence in relation to the role of parenthood in desistance is highly conflicting. Morgan and Waite (1987) found that fatherhood had no impact on desistance. However, Sampson and Laub (1993) in their age-graded theory of informal social control argued that a commitment to being a parent fosters a shift in identity. They found that, in much the same way as marriage, parenting results in less unstructured time with peers and more time participating in family activities and responsibilities. However, later quantitative analysis did not corroborate this and showed that parenthood had no significant effect of desistance (Sampson and Laub, 2003). Nonetheless, other studies have since reinforced the earlier finding by Sampson et al. (2006) (Kerr et al., 2011; Boonstoppel, 2019).

Studies relating to subjective factors in desistence suggest that parenthood can provide the mould for a new replacement self (Giordano et al., 2002).

However, any changes from parenthood are also likely to result from structural factors, in addition to or instead of cognitive or identity change alone. Increased social support (Knoester and Eggebeen, 2006), increased interactions with others (Knoester and Eggebeen, 2006) based on fatherhood and not criminality, role expectations (Knoester et al., 2007), expectations around income generation (Abell, 2018) and less unstructured leisure time to spend with peers (Sampson et al., 2006) are potential structural mechanisms that may reduce the criminality of the parent. However, those studies that have found an effect of parenthood on desistance showed several contingent factors for that desistance effect to occur. Recent research found that residing with the child or co-parent is more likely to result in reduced offending (Boonstoppel, 2019). In this study, desisting fathers reported that they moved away from crime as their priorities shifted away from themselves and towards their concern and responsibilities for others. This resulted in a consideration of the impact of their offending on their children before making the decision to commit a crime. By co-residing with children and possibly with a romantic partner, the daily routine now revolved around childcare and duties to their children. This in turn leaves little time for crime but also reinforces the identity as a full-time father, which is incompatible with offending (Boonstoppel, 2019). Conversely, those fathers who did not reside with their children often viewed their childcare responsibilities as babysitting (Boonstoppel, 2019). This was often insufficient to foster cognitive shifts that would manifest in changes to routine or lifestyle, showing that regular interaction with children can have a desistant effect (Boonstoppel, 2019). Those fathers who committed to their parenting role and chose to fulfil the expectation of a father experienced changes in social networks and routine that in turn decreased offending (Abell, 2018). Those who were unwilling to commit to their parental role, regardless of whether they were co-resident or non-co-resident did not experience parenthood as a turning point (Boonstoppel, 2019).

Some studies have also focused on the timing of parenthood, with those who were married when having children experiencing a greater reduction in offending than unmarried parents (Farrington and West, 1995; Savolainen, 2009). This may be due to the combined impact of both marriage and parenthood, and thus the "full respectability package" is often argued as contributing more to desistance than either event in isolation (Sampson et al., 2006: 468). However, an unpacking of the individual contribution of each is far beyond the scope of this chapter.

Research also found that parenthood can exacerbate offending. While parenthood is conceptualised as being a joyful and happy time, it is also one of the most stressful, with strain being put on resources such as time and money. The gendered expectations of men as breadwinners and providers can promote men to resort to criminality in order to ensure that they provide for their family. This often results in a decrease in aggressive crime and an increase in income-driven crimes such as property crime or drug dealing (Abell, 2018). Where the person is not in stable and well-paid employment, it can result in a return to criminality in order to support their role as breadwinner or good father, even on the part of men who were generally committed to their parenting role (Edin et al., 2004).

While the research is quite sparse, it appears that parenthood can have some effect on desistance. The degree of impact will be contingent on several factors including the level of involvement of the father in the life of the child, assumption of childcare responsibilities, legitimate opportunities to support their child, a reduction in unstructured socialising with peers and a cohabitation with the child and partner if possible. Much like marriage, it is the strength of the relationship and degree of investment in it that will determine the extent to which it has an impact on criminality.

Family relationships, desistance and prison education – findings

Marriage did not emerge as a particularly important theme in accounts of prisoners and ex-prisoners interviewed. It is not that marriage was not mentioned at all, but it was not mentioned often. It might have been that some of those interviewed were simply too young to be married, with an average age of marriage for Irish men being 36.4 years (Central Statistics Office, 2019). While there was a good range of ages among those interviewed, particularly given that those participating in education tended to be slightly older, the average age of the Irish prisoner is far younger than 36 years of age. In some cases, spouses and marriage did come up, just not as a prevalent theme. However, children and family of origin appeared to be more significant themes. The statements relevant to prison education and desistance fell broadly into two categories: (1) what they could, would or hoped to do for their families and (2) the way in which their families had or would help and support their reintegration and desistance from crime.

Prison education: renewed priorities and parental engagement

The bonds between prisoners and their families are often broken or strained by both the offending behaviour and the process of imprisonment. Schuller et al. (2002) referred to the power of education to extend, enrich, repair and dismantle relationships. It appears from the accounts of the participants that they were relying on education to help enrich and repair their relationships with family following their incarceration, and education was supporting that in many ways. For example, Mark and Michael both spoke about the way in which education was helping them engage with their children while still in prison. They both refer to their ability to engage with their children about the topics they are learning in school. Michael is happy to encourage his children to make the most of their opportunity to go to school and is proud to show his children what he is achieving in his educational journey.

MARK: Like I find with the education, when I go talk to the kids, like I have a lad that's 11 and you can ask him how's school and what are you doing. Like he went to see the Jeannie Johnson, is that the boat? Well it just means I can interact with them.

(Mountjoy, participant)

MICHAEL: Like now that they're getting older (and) it's good that I can talk to them about what they're doing in school, the stuff that I never learned there, so that's a good thing with the kids but I always tell them to go to school and they're lucky that they love it and never miss a day unless they're sick. I tell them about school and show them me certs and they're interested in that too.

(Mountjoy, participant)

In both a motivating and generative sense, participants stated that they were aware of the hurt they had caused their children, and they wanted to be able to support their families on release. Based on the accounts of those participating or who had participated in prison education, the cognitive changes fostered through participation in education and the workings of moral development theory (Morris, 1962) appeared to facilitate their awareness of the pain and harm their criminality had caused their family and which in turn was associated with a desire to make amends. The extent to which education could actually achieve the creation or repair of family bonds could not be ascertained in the accounts of the current prisoners; their statements were aspirational in nature. However, the ex-prisoner narratives were very insightful in terms of showing how education could help promote stronger family relations and bonds. For example, Thomas credited the impact of prison education on his mentality as being the most significant factor in repairing his relationship with his daughter. This demonstrates the "repairing" function of education (Schuller et al., 2002).

THOMAS: She's a very important person. And I did a lot of work on my own self-awareness in prison to get a hold on myself so that when I got I out I'd be in a good place for her. I kind of had blinkered vision for a long time; I only really saw myself, but I knew I needed to start looking at the people I cared about and what I was doing and what I had done and how it impacted on them. Without that, I wouldn't have been able to build the bridges I have done with her. And education was a big part of that.

(Ex-prisoner)

Several participants also said that they had reassessed their priorities. Prior to coming to prison, they spent little time with their family and instead prioritised their peer group. These participants stated that prison education had helped them see the hurt that they were causing their family and their priorities would be different when they were released. This demonstrates a degree of awareness for the feelings of others, as outlined in moral development theory (Morris, 1962), as being a benefit of prison education. Shane, who is quoted here, has two children and a partner and makes a very relevant statement relating to how education gave him time and space to consider the choices he had made and what he might do differently in future:

SHANE: Your friends are the ones who seem to matter, and I put them first. I had a family at home but as soon as the phone rang I'd be gone. And because they're you're friends you want to keep in them, don't want them slagging ya. And that's what got me in trouble. If I'd stayed home with my family, I wouldn't be in this mess. It was me own fault at the end of the day, that's the choice I made but it took ending up in here to see that . . . the time (prison education) gives you to think in here, it gives you choices about what you want to put first in your life, like to put my family first and if I come back in here I wouldn't be putting them first. It's hard enough being in here away from them.

(Mountjoy, participant)

This point is further reinforced by Jason, who in a similar way credits education with giving him the opportunity to consider what is important in life and to reevaluate past decisions and choices:

JASON: I think when you come into prison and especially with education it gives you an awful lot of time to think about what's maybe important. Before you come in here, if you're into drugs you don't have time to think or you don't put them first like. But when you come in here and you see that they're making the effort to come in here to see you every week and they're missing you, you realise what you have outside and I think then you make your choices based on that you know and have a better way of seeing things.

(Mountjoy, participant)

Family as motivation and support in education and desistance

Indicating the reciprocal nature of familial relationships, prisoners were also aware of the importance of relationship and family support on their own life, both past and future. Patrick, an ex-prisoner, who began a degree in social science after his release, speaks about the support of his parents in the period after he was released from prison. The quote highlights how important family support is in navigating the various obstacles that arise in the early stages of reintegration.

PATRICK: Yeah, they were brilliant. And my mother was very good, she knew exactly what I needed to fill out and what I needed for college and everything. And even though my dad was a bit sceptical in the beginning cos I was going to do social science and he didn't see that as a qualification for an actual particular job, I think he sees the good in it now and say's "you're going to college, good man, good man". Like they knew nothing until the day I was arrested, they thought maybe I smoked a bit of hash and then they realised what it turned out to be. But they were really supportive, and I couldn't stress how important it is to have some support. You couldn't do it by yourself.

(Ex-prisoner)

JOSEPH: I have a lot of support off me family and all that; they will support me 100% when I get out.

(Mountjoy, participant)

For some prisoners, their family acted as a motivating factor to carry on with prison education and to "go straight" after release. Gary, one of the ex-prisoners who took part in the study, talks about how his daughter was part of his motivation for education both in prison and in his studies after release. Sean also talks about release and how he is looking forward to family events such as his daughter's confirmation and how he expects these things will contribute to his desistance.

GARY: It's hard to say. I think my daughter being honest because she always came first, I'm doing the education for myself but also for her. Like if I didn't have my daughter, I'd probably still be doing it and I wouldn't be still in crime but she's my motivator as well.

(Ex-prisoner)

SEAN: Well I'm off drugs now altogether and I'm off it a year. Like I have a 12-year-old daughter who's making her confirmation in May so I have a lot to look forward (to). All of that will keep me straight.

(Mountjoy, participant)

Finally, Kevin, a non-participant, said that when he got out this time his priority was to settle down with his girlfriend and try to have a family. He felt his girlfriend would be able to talk him out of committing crime and this would help him settle down. He stated the following:

KEVIN: When I get out, I'm going to settle down, with me girlfriend and I'm going to try get a baby with her, try (to) get a job. Do something with me life instead of doing crime all the time. . . . You need a girlfriend like to walk around with, and if you're going off to do something she'll say don't do it. You need someone to pull you back from it . . . I want a missus that if I say I'm going to do this or that that she'll start fighting with me. You need someone like that. So that's what I'm going to try do, I'm going to settle down.

(Mountjoy, non-participant)

This raises two points. First, there is an awareness of the importance of family as a stabilising factor after release from prison and in the effort to desist from crime. However, in a less positive way, Kevin is placing the responsibility for his desistance in someone else's hands. It could be questioned that should he reoffend, is it then his girlfriend's fault for not holding the reigns tighter? The previous chapter explored the idea of cognitive change and noted the differences in the accounts of participants and non-participants; those who were participating in education showed greater evidence of self-responsibility and were less likely to blame external sources for their criminality. This account by Kevin, a non-participant, is very external in nature, and while the intention is good, he is not taking personal responsibility for choices and their consequences.

Discussing the role of prison education in family relationships and desistance

It appears from the accounts of prisoners and ex-prisoners that family and relationships are both a source of motivation to desist and a support to the process of community reintegration. Prison education can also play a role in the process by facilitating engagement with children, helping moral development, developing an insight into life choices and priorities and supporting the other structures (such as employment) that will allow the person to remain within the community where they can have a relationship with their family members. Prison education also has an effect on the enrichment and repair of relationships with family. The literature discussed earlier shows the extent to which marriage and parenthood can have an impact on reduced offending. Those prisoners who emerge from prison to broken relationships and to children who are hurt and estranged will find it difficult to assume a role or identity as a committed husband or father or to become integrated into the life of his children as an established caregiver, seen as essential to the operation of marriage and parenthood as contributors to desistance (Boonstoppel, 2019). Many of the men show evidence of wanting to make amends for the hurt they have caused and create stronger relationships with their children.

From the perspective of familial relationships, prison education can support reintegration in several ways. First, as evidenced in the accounts of the participants, it can create an awareness of the hurt they have caused by giving the person time and space to reflect on their previous choices and helping them to clarify the important things in their life. This is related to the theme of generativity that was discussed in the previous chapter, and it also appears to be very relevant here in terms of the desire to make amends for past mistakes (Maruna, 2001). Furthermore, the desire to engage with their children shows evidence of identity change from criminal to father, which has been shown by LeBel et al. (2008) to result in higher levels of desistance. Both of these are indicative of identity change linked to early-stage desistance (King, 2013).

It can also help build bridges with family by providing the skills and confidence to parents who may have previously struggled with literacy to interact with their children's education and promoting active engagement, for example. The participants also spoke about having increased confidence, self-efficacy, self-awareness and empathy, which are important attributes when trying to repair relationships and make amends. These processes take time and patience, and it is important that the men here were aware of that in order to be resilient to early obstacles and rejections. Third, education allows the time and space to reflect on how to go about building bridges with family in a more level-headed way. Finally, family relationships are reciprocal in nature. By healing these relationships they not only become a father or husband again, to the advantage of both themselves and their children, but they also gain the support of their family who can be strong sources of emotional support and social bonds in the journey towards desistance. Patrick earlier talked about the support he received from his parents when he came out of prison. They were instrumental in ensuring that he navigated the various obstacles after release in order to realise his goal of going to college. These barriers and prerequisites to support services can prove overwhelming following release, since so much needs to be put in place at one time. Having sources of support to help navigate these issues can be a significant help in the period of reintegration. It appears that education can promote reconnection with family, repairing and enriching relationships and thereby facilitating access to the many pro-desistance effects of strong family bonds.

Peer relations and desistance

Criminologists have long recognised the impact of delinquent peers on criminality (Gottfredson and Hirschi, 1990; Warr, 1993; Giordano et al., 2003). Association with deviant peers is a strong indicator of criminal behaviour. Unstructured social time with friends and the delinquency of those friends is a strong indicator of likely involvement in criminality (Giordano et al., 2003), with the onset of offending usually occurring after the integration into a delinquent peer group (Elliott and Menard, 1996). Sutherland (1947) attributed intimate social networks as being the source of crime and delinquency in his differential association theory, stating that delinquency is a learned behaviour when associating with others in intimate groups and referring to the process of becoming deviant as attitude transference (Sutherland, 1947), with those that are exposed to criminal associates likely to become criminal too. A sense of belonging is of critical importance to the members of a group (Weaver, 2016). Therefore, members of the peer group collectively participate in group behaviours that they might not otherwise engage in alone to ensure acceptance and a sense of belonging. Motivation to engage in the delinquent activities is underpinned by fear of losing their place in the peer group because they failed to act in line with the relational norms and rules of the group (Weaver, 2016). In fact, the pain of isolation from their peer group is a significant fear and an obstacle to desistance for many (Nugent and Schinkel, 2016). Individuals who associate with criminal peers, either new or old, experience much higher rates of recidivism (Visher and Travis, 2011). Furthermore, returning to the age crime curve described earlier, offending was said to peak in mid to late teens. This is also the age at which commitment to peers in terms of time and strength of the relationship is at its strongest, again indicating the causal impact of peer group on offending (Warr, 1993).

It is asserted that those factors that cause offending are usually those whose absence contributes to desistance. With that in mind, Graham and Bowling (1995) found that breaking away from delinquent peers is an important part of the desistance process. One of the earliest studies in the area found that of the offenders who desisted from crime, half had dissociated from their delinquent peers (Knight and West, 1975). Life course transitions, particularly marriage, affect criminality because they interfere with peer relationships which may otherwise be harmful to the desistance process (Warr, 1998; Laub and Sampson, 2001). There are varying rationales put forward for why certain social institutions may interfere with peer relations. One explanation put forward is that competing demands on a person's time results in less unstructured time being available for friends (Horney et al., 1995; Warr, 1998). Warr found that 57% of married respondents spent no more than one evening a week with their friends compared to unmarried respondents, 35% of whom spent at least four evenings a week with their friends. Laub and Sampson (2001) subsequently refuted this based on their theory of social control, hypothesising that marriage facilitated reduced peer contact through the control exerted by a spouse over their partner's availability to friends. However, these perspectives have also been criticised as not fully explaining the dynamics of moving away from criminal peers or being less susceptible to their influence, especially since not everyone has experienced a social catalyst such as marriage to initiate this distancing from the influence of the peer group (Giordano et al., 2003). It is therefore reasonable to assume that some of these changes are developmental and agentic in nature, stemming from cognitive shifts. Such shifts can of course be the precursors to structural transitions such as marriage, but they can also occur independently (Giordano et al., 2003). Giordano et al. (2003) argue that some of these changes may arise from a broader frame of reference for life experience that is a result of getting older and wiser. As people mature, fitting in and being liked become less important and this can cause people to become less susceptible to peer pressure and influence, thus helping desistance (Giordano et al., 2003).

While Baskin and Sommers (1998) focused on the role of identity change in the desistance process, their work also touched on the detrimental effects of delinquent peers to the formation and maintenance of a new, non-criminal identity. They argue that an offender must create a network of relationships which support the new, non-criminal identity. They also illustrate the active role the person must play in the process and the move away from their old identity and their old peers and towards a new, non-delinquent identity (Baskin and Sommers, 1998). Maruna and Roy (2007) refer to a process of "knifing off" from crime, whereby individuals distance themselves from their ties to criminality, be it social network, particular environments or patterns of behaviour. The knifing off of associates is proposed as being part of this process of leaving their delinquent past behind (Maruna and Roy, 2007). However, Maruna and Roy (2007) also acknowledge that knifing off by itself is probably not sufficient to facilitate desistance and must be supported by a future life script. Similarly, where people choose to avoid the situations and people that contribute to offending, this is referred to as "diachronic self-control" (Shapland and Bottoms, 2011: 274).

Spending time with friends is not a bad thing in itself; rather it is the type of friends whom an offender associates with that is the issue (Sutherland, 1947). Peers can be either coercive or supportive (Colvin, 2000), and where they fall into the latter category they can be a significant source of support on reentry to the community (Visher and Travis, 2003; Weaver, 2016). Indeed where people need to create distance between themselves and others in order to avoid offending, it can lead to a "restricted and impoverished existence" (Nugent and Schinkel, 2016: 569) Furthermore, where behavioural change was observed in significant others, it had the effect of triggering a process of reflection, where a person reviews their own behaviour by comparison to that of their peers, which can motivate individuals to make changes in their own lifestyles (Weaver, 2016). This may partly explain the influence of maturational theory on desistance. As people grow older they mature, but so too do friends, and witnessing the changes in their lives and the desire to continue to belong may prompt the reflection and identity change necessary to remain part of the group, which may no longer include criminality. Seeing friends with whom they share a similar life course move away from crime to a more conventional lifestyle also gives a sense of hope that this is an achievable goal despite the perceived obstacles (Weaver, 2016).

Peer relationships, prison education and desistance – findings

The findings of the current study align quite closely with the aforementioned literature in relation to the impact of peers on delinquency and desistance. In terms of the direct links between prison education and social bonds with peers, there were several significant observations in the findings which will be outlined under the relevant headings.

Peer group's role in criminality

A significant theme among prisoners was the weight they attribute to the influence of others in their offending. Most of the non-participants blamed their criminal behaviour on their peer group and wanting to belong, fit in with and impress their friends. Martin and Kevin describe this here as follows:

MARTIN: Like you want to impress your mates and you want the stuff they have and once you start doing stuff and they know you'll do it you can't really say no then. Even when you go back out, you just end up doing the same all over again. I think that's why lads are coming back in all the time.

(Mountjoy, non-participant)

KEVIN: Well see I'm easily led I am, very easily led on. I hate letting people down and I was doing things for mates.

(Mountjoy, non-participant)

When asked about reoffending and returning to prison, Martin and Nigel gave the following reasons for not being successful in their efforts to desist:

MARTIN: Probably not changing me mates and listening to me da when I got out the last time . . . I don't know, it's hard though when you're hanging around with people for so long to try make new friends.

(Mountjoy non-participant)

NIGEL: Most of my mates when I left prison the first time around were on drugs, and if someone asked me if they could get a hold of drugs I just made a call to one of me mates and I got it for them. And on the day in question I just happened to be getting an ounce and half of cocaine for someone and the guards just happened to come across it.

(Shelton Abbey, non-participant)

These quotes and the other similar quotes that came up during the interviews have significance in two ways. First, they demonstrate the impact of delinquent peers on the criminal trajectory of an individual and show the negative impact that peers can have on the desistance process. In the first instance, prisoners felt they had fallen in with the wrong crowd; once they started offending they could not say no to doing favours for their friends and wanted to have the things their friends had. In relation to desistance or reintegration after a prison sentence, a number of them stated that after their last release from prison they went back to their old neighbourhoods with the same people and inevitably ended up making the same mistakes, similar to Martin's second quote earlier. Many of the men did not know how to move away from friends when they were released, as they were present within their communities and they needed friends – this demonstrates the same desire for belonging (Weaver, 2016) that led to offending in the first place. It is interesting that they seemed reliant on their friends. They did not have another peer group and therefore believed they had no option but to engage with these particular friends. They appeared to be as important and integral a structure as family. The word structure is used deliberately here. There did not actually appear to be an affection on the part of these men for their friends; they were not spoken about in fond terms throughout the interviews. In fact, the tone tended to illustrate at times that these were merely acquaintances or people in their life, only due to geography, circumstance and shared (illicit) experiences similar to that spoken about by Weaver (2016).

Moreover, these accounts also were from non-participants and show an unwillingness to take personal responsibility for their own actions. Instead the blame for their offending is being placed externally, unlike those who were participating in prison education who were more likely to show self-responsibility (see the concept of mollification by Walters [1995] in Chapter 5 for greater discussion). This tendency to not take personal responsibility is indicative of greater levels of criminal thinking than those who accept that they made their own decision, even if it was on foot of a plan made by a peer group. This indicates again the positive impact of prison education on the moral development of the person.

Prison education and peer relations

There appeared to be a desire among participants to use education to escape certain delinquent peers within the prison. This was with a view either to desistance, to control addictions or simply because they did not like to be around a particular person. Being in the school allowed them to distance themselves from criminal peers and drugs and allows them to associate with more like-minded, rehabilitation-focused prisoners. Darren illustrates this when he speaks about how after being in the school for a little while, he began to realise the distance this was creating between him and his previous associates:

> DARREN: You just need to get your head away from all that in the yard, listen to stories and lads making plans all day for what's their next job. If you're down there, you just end up in the middle of things, getting mixed up in things you don't want to get mixed up in again. I noticed after a while of starting up here I didn't have to worry about getting dragged into stuff, I just don't be around them no more like.
>
> (Mountjoy, participant)

It is encouraging that prison education can provide this form of distance between people. The recognition of a need to do this is indicative of a desire to change, which may be showing both the power of education to change perspectives and also to facilitate the necessary processes for optimal distancing and desistance.

Participants referred to how education had given them confidence in their own abilities to make decisions for themselves, rather than following the crowd. It appeared that they were referring to friends and how going along with the plans and decisions of others had gotten them into trouble, such as in the quote from Keith. Moreover, the participants also said that education had given them the space and clarity to realise how they were wrong to prioritise friends over their children and family and they would work to change this (quotes relating to this theme are given earlier in the section on family). All of these participants put these realisations down to the influence of prison education.

KEITH: Like I know this might sound silly, like I can make an individual decision and think for meself now rather than following the crowd.

(Mountjoy, participant)

The accounts of some of the ex-prisoners indicated that interference with peer relations was the most significant influence of education in relation to their desistance. The main influence of education in terms of social bonds appeared to be a change in the prisoner's circle of friends. All of the ex-prisoners stated that being more educated when they came out of prison resulted in their circle of friends changing, either intentionally or as an indirect result of their increased levels of education. An example of a deliberate change of friends was given by Thomas, who stated that he "just gave up on the friends that were bad for (him)". Some ex-prisoners, such as Anthony and Patrick, said they simply drifted away from their old friends. They spoke about education creating distance with their old peers. Coming out of prison with a new set of friends, a better education, a new outlook and different interests meant the men had far less in common with their old friends. Instead they began bonding with other, more like-minded people. The quotations here illustrate this point made by them:

ANTHONY: My interests have totally changed, and I find now that I don't really go to the pub with them. All they talk about is football and my interests have totally changed. I used to be into football, but now I'm more interested in politics and that kind of thing and I spend more time with the people from college and that kind of thing. I'm still friendly with them but not as close as before.

(Ex-prisoner)

PATRICK: I started to have less and less in common with my mates. Like they're still reading the *Sun* newspaper and I find myself looking through the *Independent*. Then I was a lot more confident, my friends changed and I'd be hanging out with people from college . . . and while I'll talk to anyone, I just found I had more in common with those people (from college).

(Ex-prisoner)

Both of these accounts illustrate the indirect role that education can have in creating distance between the offender and their peer group or delinquent friends. This is a strong affirmation by the ex-prisoners of the power of prison education in the creation of pro-social bonds and the severing of ties with the delinquent peer group. It also indicates the way in which cognitive changes can operate to underpin future structural changes in desistance.

The participants and non-participants who were interviewed appeared to be very aware of the impact that their peer group had on their offending, and many were aware of how to go about remedying this. In terms of relocation, a small number of prisoners who wished to desist from crime after release that relocation was the ideal way of doing so, recognising the impact moving away from their peers could have on the process. Andy, a non-participant stated:

ANDY: I'd probably like to get out of me old area . . . cos if I start bumping into me old friends again, like they haven't changed. And it'd only be a matter of time before I was in here again.

(Mountjoy, non-participant)

Prisoners were aware that education and in turn employment could be a means of creating a new peer group and allow them to move away from those who were a negative influence on their lives. While this theory was much clearer in the ex-prisoner interviews, there was evidence that those who were still in prison understood or expected that this is how education would operate upon release. Martin, a non-participant, spoke about the trouble he was having breaking away from old friends who he had met during employment, stating that he would need to change jobs and possibly careers to distance himself from them. He was also aware of the fact that prison education would be the pathway in respect of a new career and break from those who were influencing his offending, though there did not appear to be any intention to do this.

MARTIN: If I wanted to change my job, I'd have to do more education. And I suppose then I'd be able to make some more mates there and get away from the others.

(Mountjoy, non-participant)

This demonstrates that Martin is aware that jobs, career and future prospects are often rooted in a foundation of education. It shows too that non-participants are also aware of the benefits of education.

Finally, in some cases prisoners were angry about the way their friends had treated them and had decided that those friendships had ended. This often stemmed from the hurt that is often experienced by prisoners when they are forgotten about by friends after they were sentenced to prison. There was a difference observed in the tone of the participants and non-participants. Non-participants, such as Andy, were still very caught up in anger at their friends for abandoning them. However, participants such as Craig seemed to be more calm and rational, realising their friends had perhaps done them a favour in acting the way they had.

ANDY: I won't be with all me mates anymore. And they're like backstabbing cunts they are, yeah? I mean when you're locked up, out of sight, out of

mind. When they're meant to be doing things for ya, they don't do anything for ya. Then when they're locked up, they do be relying on you and asking you to do this and that and you're not letting them down. You learn from that as well. You just say they did nothing for me when I was locked up so when I get out I'll do jack shit for them. I'll just look after meself.
(Mountjoy, non-participant)

CRAIG: (W)hen I got arrested, they all legged it and I never heard from them again. The fellas I was knocking around with were all taxi drivers and when they heard I got arrested they just didn't want to know, which suited me fine.
(Shelton Abbey, participant)

Discussing prison educations role in peer relationships

The earlier points provide strong evidence of the influence that prison education can have in the disruption of peer relationships. Prison education does this in a number of ways, most of which are rooted in the cognitive and subjective changes that occur through participation. The previous chapter outlined the reported benefits of education in terms of increased agency, an altered outlook on life, a sense of being able to see what is important in life and changed interests, for example. These have arisen as key themes again here. They are mentioned as providing the foundation for changes in relation to peer group and friends. There is a realisation on the part of participants and non-participants about the negative role that these people have played in their life course to date. Many recognise what they should do about this in order to have a more positive outcome when released this time. However, the participants seemed to be aware of "why" they should do this – they realised what they were missing out on or the mistakes they had made personally to a far greater extent than the non-participants. They were also more likely to have either dissociated from these peers or had a plan to do so – and in some cases were able to use the prison school to facilitate this. Finally, the accounts of ex-prisoners gave the greatest evidence in support of prison educations role in their desistance. Several of the ex-prisoners believed that because prison education had changed their outlook and interests to such a great extent, it had the simple effect of creating an incompatibility between the person and their former group in terms of interests, outlook and identity. These are strong ratifications for the power of prison education and are invaluable in demonstrating the way in which prison education can support desistance. However, some of the accounts also raise questions around what has the biggest impact on desistance – is it the education itself or the school? It appears that both have a strong role in relation to peer group distancing. Prison education underlies the cognitive changes that facilitates change, but the school can also provide the space for "time out", to be away from the negative prison mindset and away from the chatter, both of which have a role in interfering with peer relationships.

Employment, financial stability and desistance

Finance is a significant obstacle for prisoners on their release. They are usually released with little or no money and often with unpaid debts accrued that need to be met (Shinkfield and Graffam, 2009). There is a substantive link between debt and substance abuse, with those who are in debt at least twice as likely to abuse drugs or alcohol than those with no debt, which will likely cause either reoffending, a relapse into addiction or both (LaVigne et al., 2004). Without money, one cannot secure accommodation or healthcare; they may even be or become indebted, which can in turn lead to increased substance abuse and eventual recidivism (LaVigne et al., 2004). Without legitimate funds, a person will most likely return to illegitimate sources of income (Shinkfield and Graffam, 2009). While money can be gained through social welfare systems or through employment, employment is a preferable source of legitimate finances for several of reasons.

Studies have shown the power of employment in reducing reoffending, with unemployed ex-prisoners twice as likely to reoffend as those in either full- or part-time employment (Law Reform Commission, 2007). Employment has the power to reduce reoffending by between 30% and 50% (Home Office, 2002). It is important then that offenders find employment as soon as possible after release. However, discrimination in the employment market is one of the greatest barriers faced by ex-offenders (Skardhamar and Savolainen, 2012). The National Economic and Social Forum (2001) stated that only 52% of Irish employers would consider employing someone who had a previous conviction. Other studies have shown that percentage to be lower. Sherlock (2007), in a study carried out by the Small Firms Association, stated that on average 76% of companies would be unwilling to employ ex-offenders. This percentage was higher depending on the sector in question, the highest being the distribution sector with 87% of employers stating that they would not employ an ex-offender (Sherlock, 2007). This discrimination can often amount to a life sentence by preventing the offender from earning a living that is commensurate with his or her skills, leading in turn to a greater tendency to reoffend (MacKinnon and Wells, 2001). Failing to find a job on release can therefore be a criminogenic force in itself (Louks et al., 1998).

In addition to the stigma that comes with being an ex-prisoner, lack of education and skills often poses a significant obstacle to securing stable employment and also in gaining access to vital services on release. Prisoners tend to come from the most educationally disadvantaged groups in society. O'Mahony (1997) reported that 29% of prisoners surveyed had significant problems with literacy. Morgan and Kett (2003) found that 53% of Irish prisoners surveyed had literacy levels in the two lowest categories, compared to 22.6% of the general public. Almost 7% of prisoners claimed to have never had any formal education (O'Mahony, 1997). Thirty-nine percent had not progressed to secondary school, and 57% of the offenders had received some second-level education (complete or incomplete) but had never progressed to the third level. The average age for leaving education was 14.7 years. Fifty-seven percent had left school by the age of 15 years (O'Mahony, 1997). These statistics highlight the problems that prisoners face upon release. Literacy is a general prerequisite to entering the workforce. Having a low level of education or literacy will prove to be a severely limiting factor when trying to secure employment in an increasingly educated workforce (Martynowicz and Quigley, 2010). A lack of literacy may not in itself be a cause of crime but is a significant contributing factor by limiting employment opportunities and contributing to social exclusion (Morgan and Kett, 2003).

A number of studies have found that stable employment has a significant impact on the desistance process (Meisenhelder, 1977; Sampson and Laub, 1993, 2003; Pezzin, 1995). Many studies have shown that employment is perhaps the strongest factor in reduced reoffending (Lipsey, 1995; Savolainen, 2009). Moreover, Laub and Sampson (1993) attribute employment and marriage with being the most important factors in life course transitions. Employment creates social and economic resources, structure and routine (Sampson and Laub, 1993, 2003). Laub and Sampson's (2001) belief that employment and marriage are the two strongest factors in life course transitions is based on the degree of structure, support and social bonds these institutions add to the lives of offenders. The creation and maintenance of social capital is an important aspect of the desistance process (Laub and Sampson, 1993). Employment can be viewed as a turning point because of the social ties and bonds it creates, thus contributing to social capital (Laub and Sampson, 1993). However, there are others schools of thought in explaining the role of employment in the desistance process. Employment can also be viewed as a hook for change or as a consequence of maturational theory. In both cases, employment will be a result of desistance as opposed to a cause of desistance (Skardhamar and Savolainen, 2012). It appeared that the majority of those who found employment had desisted prior to this transition, and becoming employed did not cause a further reduction in offending (Skardhamar and Savolainen, 2014). However, their study also identified a small group (less than 2%) that experienced substantial reductions in their offending, having taken up employment during a period of active offending. This small subset is more consistent with the turning point hypothesis, whereby their employment is the cause of the desistance. However, regardless of which comes first, desistance or employment, securing employment will either result in desistance or will provide significant support to preconceived desistance efforts in several ways.

First, the mutual trust and respect that exists between an employer and employee creates obligations and bonds (Laub and Sampson, 1993). The decision of an employer to give a previous offender a chance is often reciprocally met with a desire on the part of the offender to honour the faith that has been put in them. This creates trust within the employment and, depending upon the nature of the work, the trust and bonds can also be created with other employees (Laub and Sampson, 1993). The creation of bonds with other employees can create further pro-social relationships which can help in the development of a new non-criminal identity and peer group (Wright and Cullen, 2004). Other valuable aspects of a job, such as the instilling of self-worth, the provision of social and economic resources and structured everyday routine activities are often associated with criminal desistance (Sampson and Laub, 1993, 2003). Finally, arguably one of the strongest impacts of employment appears to be in its ability to fracture relations with anti-social peers and promote new social bonds with law-abiding co-workers (Wright and Cullen, 2004). Much like Warr's (1998) argument in relation to decreased recreational time available to a person when they get married, it may be the case that the more time a person spends in work, the less time they have to spend with friends. This can in turn decrease the likelihood of offending, particularly where their peer group is implicit in their previous offending. Wright and Cullen (2004) claim that by developing bonds with co-workers, bonds with anti-social peers can weaken, decreasing reoffending. With more time being spent among workmates, there is often an unconscious shift in peer group from old, delinquent friends to new friends created through employment. Sampson and Laub (2003) warn that it must be stable employment and the offender must be emotionally invested in the work in order for the job to have an appreciable benefit. Co-workers will also recognise the new, non-criminal identity of the offender, reinforcing the new replacement self of the person (Baskin and Sommers, 1998). Finally, investigating the influence of current and future earnings on desistance, Pezzin (1995) found that those who have higher earnings from legitimate sources were more likely to desist as they have more to lose if they decide to reoffend. Therefore, those who are in stable employment with sufficient salaries are more likely to consider the loss of earnings from this employment should they receive a custodial sentence, which makes them think twice before committing a crime.

Employment, prison education and desistance: findings

In terms of the role that education and prison education can play in the process of securing employment after release, Chapter 3 outlined various benefits of prison education that are relevant here. Porporino and Robinson (1992) found that of those prisoners who had participated in prison education during their sentence, 79% had secured full-time employment within the study period of one year, with most having found a job within a month of release. Academic and vocational training programmes have also been associated with providing more marketable job skills, and the belief among participants is that participation in these programmes will help them secure employment when they are released (Tewksbury and Stengel, 2006). Furthermore, other more indirect benefits of education such as increased awareness (Morris, 1962), moral reasoning (Duguid, 1998), emotional maturity and better social skills (Ripley, 1993) and greater control and confidence over their lives (Mezirow, 2000) are likely to support their search for employment and their ability to sustain employment. Savolainen (2009) suggests that more should be done in order to increase the employment prospects of the person. This is in line with human rights approaches that call for community and social institutions to work to create more favourable conditions for the reintegration of ex-prisoners such as the creation of employment incentives and opportunities.

Prison education for employment

There was a deliberate decision on the part of the researcher not to mention employment in the questions that were posed to those being interviewed so as to avoid suggestion. However, employment emerged as a strong theme in response to questions about the reasons for participating in education and plans for release. Many of those who were participating in prison education were doing so with a view to gaining employment on release. There were several perspectives here, and a strong differential was evident in the accounts of those participating in prison education and those who were not. Many of those who participated in prison education were either very optimistic about their chances of securing employment or were very aware of the challenges they would face in getting a job and had planned for this. By contrast, those prisoners who were not participating in education were very pessimistic. They felt they would not secure employment and did not offer alternative plans to compensate for this in the same manner as the educational participants did; in fact, many of the non-participants indicated that they would probably return to criminality in order to make money.

Prisoners participating in prison education felt that by increasing their skills and education, they would improve their chances of finding employment, since many tended to only have some secondary education, with few or no formal qualifications. However, a small number of prisoners had left school early in order to pursue a career as a tradesman, and these participants felt that they could use the opportunity for prison education to update skills and develop professionally. Many of the prisoners, the majority of whom were participants and only two of whom were non-participants, said they planned to look for a job, with several stating that education would help in this task either by using the skills they had acquired through education or by showing that they had used their time in prison constructively. This was in the hope of demonstrating to prospective employers that they were willing to work hard and that they were making an effort to change their life. Prisoners also mentioned how education had provided them with greater confidence to speak to others and felt they could now represent themselves well, which would be advantageous in job interviews and in a variety of employment settings. Other participants felt prison education would give them options which they might not have otherwise had. Brian, a Shelton Abbey participant, for example, felt that he would have more and better employment options on release for having participated in education:

BRIAN: (I)f I just sat out there and didn't do (education), I wouldn't have gotten all these certs and I wouldn't be looking at going back to school or college to have a profession later on . . . I'd be just looking to get a bit of painting work here or driving work there, so it's given me options.

(Shelton Abbey, participant)

The ex-prisoners were extremely resolute in endorsing the rehabilitative nature of education. Most of them said that without education they would not have moved away from crime. The following quotation from Anthony, an ex-prisoner, sums up the essence of many of the comments made by the other ex-prisoners in relation to both the rehabilitative nature of prison education overall and the impact that it had on the key structural elements such as employment. It is significant that these statements came from the ex-prisoners, as they were arguably in the best position to judge education's impact on desistance, having participated during their sentences and now working towards desistance in the community.

ANTHONY: Honestly, I think it's the only way . . . education for me was the only way I could change. It was something that gave me something to live for and that changed my prospect of employment and just improved my whole lifestyle. Other than that, education gives people the opportunities. If they don't get education in prison, what do they do? In education I'm including practical skills or some sort of vocational training too that will help with jobs.

(Ex-prisoner)

Stigma and prejudice as a barrier to employment

Perhaps the greatest obstacle that prisoners face in the labour market after they are released from prison is stigma and prejudice. Several prisoners, particularly the non-participants, were extremely pessimistic about their chances of securing employment on release. This was being fuelled by a wider anxiety about the way that society would treat them, and this was a prevalent theme among both participants and non-participants. Many of those interviewed mentioned that they did not know how society, particularly employers, would perceive them or treat them for being in prison. Prejudice and stigma appeared to be concerns of many of the prisoners. Several felt that participating in education could ultimately be pointless if they were unable to get a job because of their past. Gary, an ex-prisoner, stated the following:

GARY: I know that even if I have the degree I probably still won't get a job, because they'll keep looking at my CV and he can't be trusted, it's holding me back and it's always there . . . because I know the barriers, I'm losing motivation.

(Ex-prisoner)

Another of the ex-prisoners stated that while the benefits of education were extensive, he still found himself unable to apply for certain jobs, as his past offending remained a barrier:

PATRICK: (Education) is liberating in that it will open doors on a self-confidence or on a society basis. But it still doesn't create a level playing field in Ireland anyway. Education can help there in that you can begin to be seen for something else . . . but I find myself getting a bit bitter in that I'm so highly qualified but yet I can't apply for a lot of jobs, and there's a lot that I'm qualified for that I'd never get because of my conviction.

(Ex-prisoner)

Something that was notable in the accounts of those participating in prison education was a strong recognition of the challenges that would be faced on release. This was not a theme reflected among the non-participants. Participants believed that education would help them in relation to employment, yet most were hesitant, using phrases such as education would "possibly" help them to get a job. Recognising the impact of prejudice again, they appeared to be aware of the limitation their criminal record and the recession would have on their efforts to find employment. Encouragingly, however, they also seemed to have planned for this and had alternative paths into employment such as self-employment. Perhaps it is a case that those who participate in prison education are more aware of the realities they will face on release and that education is allowing prisoners to "see over the prison wall", forming an awareness of what is to come and what they need to do in order to overcome the challenges. This is evidenced in the advanced planning they are doing to overcome the obstacles to employment.

Friends, family and previous employers or connections offered the best chances of employment and often eased the pressure on prisoners knowing they had a job on release. Some prisoners, one participant and one non-participant were relying on family members with their own businesses to employ them after they were released. Others participants stated that they had the option of returning to their old job when they were released from prison. A few participants stated that they would have little trouble in getting work, as they had friends or previous connections with businesses that would employ them on release.

MICHAEL: Yeah, my friend has his own business so I'll go back to work for him. I was a sign fabricator before I came to prison so I'll go back there . . . I'd like to work in a hotel or something but I probably wouldn't get a job there anyway.

(Mountjoy, participant)

Such sources of employment represent a good deal of hope and alleviate stress for prisoners, as they feel they will at least have a source of income when they are released and if they are studying relevant subjects that their education will not go to waste.

Another option mentioned by a small number of participants was starting their own business. Mark spoke about his plan to get a van to do odd jobs, rather than take his chances in the employment market.

> MARK: Its only my first time in prison so I don't know what to expect when I get out so. Like jobs are very hard to come by now, so I don't know the chance of me getting one so I may do something on me own, like get a van or something like that.
>
> (Mountjoy, participant)

Education appears to promote agency, which helped ex-prisoners to regain control of their lives and helped in undoing some of the damage caused the labelling and stigma that goes with a conviction and prison sentence.

> ANTHONY: It's hard to even go for a job because most people want to know your history and work history at least. So in that sense I don't have control over a lot, but I'm improving it by educating myself.
>
> (Ex-prisoner)

The importance of money and financial stability

As outlined in Chapter 5 in relation to the issue of self-responsibility, when asked about the main reasons behind their offending there were two dominant responses. Showing a strong degree of self-awareness and responsibility for their actions, prison education participants took responsibility for their actions, claiming their offending was a result of their own greed and desire for money. Non-participants tended to shift the blame elsewhere – they could not survive financially on their state social welfare payments, for example. However, most pertinent to the current discussion is that the commonality among most responses was that money was a highly influential factor. Access to money to support their lifestyle was a key factor in the rationale behind offending for most prisoners, and this would potentially cause them to reoffend when released. An example can be seen in Willy's quote here. Some of those interviewed said they had bills to pay, which could not be done if they did not commit crime. Several of the non-participants mentioned how financially lucrative crime is compared to working a regular job, showing again the financial motivation for committing crime and the weighing of the risk of the financial gain against the sanction of prison. This analysis of the risks and benefits is illustrated by David, a non-participant, who mentioned that he did not mind the thought of returning to prison. Since he didn't feel there was much on the outside for him, the financial payoff of crime was worth the risk. Wayne, a Mountjoy non-participant, also stated that he offended for financial gain because he wanted the luxuries in life and he could quickly make the money to provide this.

WILLY: I want to mend me ways, but I was used to a certain lifestyle. And that's one of the hardest things to get over. So never say never. . . . Like I wouldn't be able to live on €200 a week.

(Shelton Abbey, participant)

WAYNE: Like I wanted to get out and have a nice lifestyle. It was that if you made money quickly you could have so much stuff. Holidays and all that . . . I can work one hour and in the space of that get ten grand. Whereas nine to five I'd only get a few quid. Like money is the fact of it. It's just financial like.

(Mountjoy, non-participant)

DAVID: There's job opportunities there for me, I'm a qualified fixer glazer from years ago . . . yer man that does that is a friend of the family so he'd take me back anytime but I don't see the point of it, working 40 hours a week for €500 or €600. Like I'd make double that in 20 minutes . . . I don't care about coming back; I've a lot of mates in here . . . . what's out there for me miss?

(Mountjoy, non-participant)

These quotes show several things. First, that low social bonds can severely lessen the chance that a prisoner will make any significant effort to remain in the community after release. They also show the lucrative nature of crime by comparison to legitimate employment in terms of providing financial gain. However, this also demonstrates the need for any employment gained to be adequate in providing a decent standard of living, in line with Pezzin's (1995) recommendations; otherwise the lure of a high-paying criminal career will simply win out – that is, until the person acquires other social bonds that they deem more valuable than money to anchor the person in society and render criminal acts and the threat of imprisonment too low a payoff. Finally, it also shows that money is the most important thing – the economic benefits of offending are significant and when this is contrasted with the accounts of those who are participating in education, it shows that until there is a realisation that other things are more important than money or that there are other ways to earn money, they will likely continue to offend.

Pezzin (1995) asserts that legitimate employment needs to pay enough to provide a good standard of living in order for it to be successful in keeping the offender from reoffending. These concerns are shared by prisoners who indicate the importance of having stable, well-paid employment in the journey towards desistance. While employment is not the sole factor in desistance, it is certainly important. For most who resort to criminality, money is the catalyst.

Together with other structural bonds, employment must become a significant enough bond to deter future offending.

Discussing prison education, employment, finances and desistance

To summarise here, financial stability is important and in order to achieve this many of the participants plan on seeking employment or self-employment. Prison education provides the skills and confidence to purse these goals of legitimate employment, with most participants hoping that education will leave them more qualified but will also give them the confidence to represent themselves well at job interviews and show that they used their time in prison constructively. Furthermore, those who were participating in education were already contemplating the stigma they would face and were planning ways to overcome this, which was not reflected in the accounts of the non-participants. Education also appeared to promote a sense of awareness that there are many options for employment and indeed there are other factors that bond a person to the community, such as family, that money simply cannot buy. There was evidence in the accounts of participants, outlined in Chapter 5, of a greater sense of self-awareness and being able to see the things that were truly important and valuable in life. Perhaps those who are participating in education may be more inclined to exercise their awareness by doing the maths and realise that while a regular working week may pay less than a week of criminal activity, when the months and years in prison are removed, ultimately the legitimate income will usually yield the greater amount of money over the years.

An overall limitation here is the inability to draw accurate conclusions due to the qualitative nature of the study design and lack of opportunity for follow-up. It is impossible to know whether these prisoners were successful in securing employment on release. Furthermore, most of the ex-prisoners had either gone on to further education or were pursing alternatives to employment, and therefore actually securing employment as a theme was severely lacking in their accounts. For that reason, it is impossible to adequately judge the impact of prison education in the creation of social bonds through employment. All that can be asserted is that many of the prisoners are optimistic about the role that education will play in their search for employment. Furthermore, based on previous research, those participating in education appear to be improving their chances of securing employment on release.

Prison education: supporting the early stages of reintegration

Strong family relationships, stable employment and pro-social peers are viewed as being the key structural aspects relevant to the desistance process, particularly due to their significant capacity to create strong social bonds and social capital.

Most of the men interviewed, whether participating in prison education or not, were very aware of the importance of these factors to their success after release. Before leaving prison, a person will probably be given some pearls of wisdom such as to get a job or settle down. However, perhaps this message is misguided. While these elements are critical to the structures that support and maintain desistance, there is a reality that these are essentially carts before the horse. When prisoners emerge from prison, their heads are often occupied with the "big" things they must or should do – must get a job, be on good terms with family, settle down and have children, forget about my old friends and get new ones. Yet two basic realities exist. First, each of these structural factors are the outcome of a process, achieved over time with consistent effort and persistence. Second, there are very basic struggles that must be overcome before these high-value social bonds can even prioritised, much less achieved, by the person.

When prisoners are released, there are usually a very basic set of vital needs and services that must be put in place before they can begin to address the greater structural aspects in life (Martynowicz and Quigley, 2010). Gaining access to accommodation, financial supports, social services, medication and/or addiction support can be urgent, difficult and overwhelming. Some prisoners will have been in the privileged position of being able to undertake temporary release or had access to inreach services that facilitated them in putting these basics in place. However, most prisoners arrive at the prison gate with only a bag of belongings and a bus fare and often with little warning that this would be the day they would leave prison. The way in which they navigate these days and weeks ahead, putting in place the basic structures of their lives, will greatly dictate how likely they are to progress to the stage of being able to secure employment, work on family relationships and integrate into new social circles. Many prisoners are likely to have become institutionalised to some extent by the prison experience, which will further compound the sense of shock and trauma at needing to put all of these things in place in a very short space of time. Paperwork, red tape and formalities are significant barriers to reentry. Yet these very basic things will be the very foundation upon which further efforts at desistance will be built. Where these foundations are weak or uncertain, a person will be more likely to struggle to secure the high-value social bonds such as employment that will ultimately root them in a new conventional, non-criminal lifestyle and identity.

This transitional stage that an offender finds themselves in is not so well researched in the desistance literature. The structural theories generally explore factors that characterise secondary and ongoing desistance. However, they ignore overall life stability to an extent. Where a person has family or supportive pro-social friends who are willing to lend support in the early stages after release, that is of course a significant advantage. Yet based on the characteristics of the typical offender, these are likely to be the exception rather than the rule. Prison education would be of little benefit to desistance if it did not support the person throughout their journey, from the day of release. Therefore, it is also important to look at how education can support the early post-release phase of the journey, where the foundations for both day-to-day stability and the bigger structural changes are being put in place. For instance, Anthony described how he was "constantly filling out things, but education helped with that".

Reintegration and resettlement are difficult processes. Surviving this transitional stage will require a combination of two things – the mobilisation of the person's own inner resources and for the person to get the necessary resources in place as quickly as possible. The following section will look at several of the key barriers that must be overcome in the initial post-release phase and the potential role of education in supporting this part of the journey towards desistance.

From the data collected in the current study, it appears that education can act as a strong support in these efforts. While the impact of education is outlined under the relevant headings later, here Noel sums up both the struggles and the factors he believes are important in the early post-release phase:

> NOEL: It's hard to pin down one thing. I would say there has to be a lot of internal stability, that the person must feel grounded and there are various factors that help that and if you have friends around you that are trying to push you one way, when you know that's not the way you want to go, that's not going to be a help. If you have a family that don't want you there in their home because of what you done, that's going to push you towards those things again. Work? Unless you have some sort of routine initially, you're not going to go out with nothing and you may have learned a few skills, like I had done a little bit of gym instructing and I found out it's not that easy just to walk into a gym and get a job out of that. So definitely having something every day, having goals to work towards is very important whether they are creative goals or educational goals.
>
> (Ex-prisoner)

Accommodation

Supportive friends and family members play a significant role in the successful reintegration of the ex-prisoner (Visher and Travis, 2003; Weaver, 2016), particularly when it comes to assistance with accommodation (et al., 2004). It is usually the family, intimate partner or friends of the person who will provide accommodation upon release, but homelessness is a significant barrier nonetheless (LaVigne et al., 2004; Visher et al., 2004). Many ex-prisoners have limited choices and often end up staying in hostels or shelters, which are usually rife with drug and alcohol abusers as well as others who have also just been released from prison (Martynowicz and Quigley, 2010). This type of environment is likely to perpetuate offending, making reintegration and desistance more difficult (Shinkfield and Graffam, 2009). Where accommodation is unsafe and unstable, it makes medication adherence and continuation of care for mental or physical problems extremely difficult (Hammett et al., 2001; Seymour and Costello, 2005).

It appeared from the narratives of prisoners that education in prison had gone some way to helping with accommodation stresses from several perspectives. For example, prisoners who were participating in prison education spoke about how education had helped in repairing relationships with their family and this meant they had a home to return to when they were released.

STEPHEN: I'll be goin' back to me missus when I get out. When I came in here like, I don't think there was anything left, but I was a mess. She told me to sort meself out or she wasn't waiting around on me and me bags would be in me mother's (house). So I done that. She's proud of what I do in here, getting education, and that's helped sort me head so it's only for that that I'll be goin' back home when I get out.

(Mountjoy, participant)

This shows how the breakdown of relationships can leave a person without a home and vulnerable to homelessness and how in this case education helped in mending the bridges between this couple, which will act as a support in the early stage of reintegration.

Others noted how education helped facilitate planning and action prior to release to secure accommodation. For instance, Sean saw the benefits of engaging with education and integrated sentence management as this rendered him eligible for day release in advance of his official release date with a view to finding accommodation and engaging with other services that would act as supports on his release.

SEAN: Cos I was doing the education and ISM I was able to get TR to go out lately and sort a room to stay and where I'd go after I got out. I got a place in Pathways to go to keep up my studying and a lad who was there knew of another lad with a room who was clean for years so it was a good place. You have to be careful like, so I'm getting out shortly and that's all sorted now.

(Mountjoy, participant)

Those who were not participating in prison education were far more unsure of how things would go when they were released. There was little evidence of planning and much seemed to be left to luck. The sad reality is that many of those interviewed felt they would be back in prison before too long anyway so were not too worried about post-release plans. This attitude is shown here in Richie's statement about returning to prison.

RICHIE: Ye, big time . . . I've a lot of mates in here . . . (e)veryone looks forward to getting out, but the thing is when you're in here everyone does be screaming to get out and then when you get out like what's out there, there's nothing really out there. More charge sheets.

(Mountjoy, non-participant)

Addiction

Martynowicz and Quigley (2010) report that 80% of Irish prisoners struggle with drug and/or alcohol addictions. Approximately 80% of the prison population in the United States has been identified as having a drug or alcohol problem of some degree, with 74% of prisoners due for release reporting having a high drug/alcohol dependency (Shinkfield and Graffam, 2009). The barriers faced by offenders on release from prison make it difficult for them to remain in control of their addiction (O'Donnell, 2002). The prison setting, while chaotic to an extent, is based on strict routine which can be very beneficial when tackling and managing addiction. In that chaotic and transitionary period after release, such routine is likely impossible to emulate. Issues such as access to methadone and other treatments can be difficult to put in place immediately after release (Martynowicz and Quigley, 2010). The reality is that many of the prisoners interviewed claimed drugs and alcohol dependencies among the reason for ending up in prison. One can imagine that in prison, drug use will go in either one of two directions for many: increase or decrease. A number of those who were participating in prison education felt that education had helped with their issues with drugs. Both Vincent's and Barry's quotes reflect these ways in which education can help with those who want to overcome addition in prison:

VINCENT: Yeah I have got control over what way my life goes. I can choose to go back to "Smack Cul de sac", I call it that cos its dead end, or live a life on "Quality Street". Like it's up to me I make them decisions at the end of the day, and for years I was a victim and blamed everyone else so today I'm more about taking responsibility for where my life goes.

(Shelton Abbey, participant)

BARRY: If you're down there, you just end up getting dragged back into the same shit again. Up here you're away from the same people and situation(s) that drag you back into your old ways. I'm not getting clean to go back to that.

(Mountjoy, participant)

Education can help in two ways, it seems. First, through its cognitive benefits it can create self-control and focus and help to strengthen the mind to process any issues it may have. The second way is by creating physical distance between themselves and the situations that would usually leave them susceptible to drug use such as time in the prison yard.

Institutionalisation and prison harm

While the prison sentence is no longer physically brutal, the hurt is no less severe for being mental pain. In his seminal work, "The Society of Captives" Sykes (1958) explored the pains of imprisonment that those under a sentence of imprisonment are exposed to. These are (1) loss of liberty; (2) desirable goods and services; (3) heterosexual relationships; (4) autonomy; and (5) security. On the face of it, each of these "harms" are physical in nature: physical confinement, lack of physical goods and services, lack of physical intimacy and concerns for physical safety. However, the true harm with each of these elements is caused at the mental level. In terms of the loss of liberty, this results in a lack of contact with family and friends and therefore means a deprivation of their emotional support at a time of great stress and anxiety. There is also the removal from society and sense of death as a citizen, rejection, loneliness and boredom to overcome (Liebling and Maruna, 2005). When this is added to the other deprivations that are suffered, such as deprivation of possessions, intimacy, decision making, control over various aspects of their life and safety, the weight of imprisonment is significant. All of this can have a severely detrimental impact on the mind of the person. Crewe (2011) revisited these harms and added several new pains of imprisonment that are features of the new form of prison governance such as uncertainty, a sense of second guessing how every action will be construed, being removed from the central source of power and a false responsibility, again each of which are mental in effect (Crewe, 2011). Irwin and Owen (2005) refer to the considerable harm of imprisonment and suggest that this harm causes considerable difficulty to the offender when reintegrating. They propose that the longer a person is in prison the more they begin to lose the skills required to function in the outside world (Irwin and Owen, 2005). Further harm comes in the form of anxiety, depression, uncertainty, powerlessness, trauma, fear and violence, which are all part of the harms inherent with the prison sentence (Liebling and Maruna, 2005). The lasting effects of these forms of mental harm and institutionalisation render reintegration evermore problematic as the offender has to overcome the mental impact of their prison sentence, in addition to the various other barriers to reintegration. This was also reflected in Chapter 3, with Warner (2007) outlining the need to support efforts to minimise the harm that is caused by the prison sentence. In many ways, this relates to the ability of the prisoner to cope with their sentence and to have a degree of mental resilience to the harms inherent with the sentence. The more that can be done to lessen the impact of these features of the sentence, the easier the process of reintegration and efforts at desistance will be. In the previous chapter and earlier in this chapter, the use of the school to create distance between the person and either the prison environment or other people and situations within the prison emerged as a strong theme. While this was with a view to avoiding boredom, managing addictions and breaking ties with criminal peers, for example, spending time away from the prison environment in the relaxing space and energy of the school was often as much of a benefit to the person as the actual classes themselves. Furthermore, there were several quotes in Chapter 5 that outlined the sense of agentic growth experienced by those participating in prison education such as confidence, self-awareness, self-control and self-efficacy, for example, all of which can be seen as counterbalances to the harms referred to by Sykes and Crewe earlier. Developing attributes such as these can act as counterbalances to the harms caused by the prison sentence, acting in a protectionist way to minimise the harm to the person and their mind.

During the interviews, prisoners were not actually asked about what they foresaw as being the greatest challenges on release. Overcoming institutionalisation was mentioned by a few participants as being a likely challenge on release. Two participants said that they feared how the world will have advanced and how things will have been upgraded. Another participant felt that in prison all of his needs are met but on release he will have to manage all these things by himself again. While this is a worry for Vincent, it is positive that he is thinking ahead, recognising the challenges and planning to do what he can to overcome them in advance:

VINCENT: I've being asking myself am I a bit institutionalised now, where there's a fear factor in getting released. I'm having all me needs met, roof over my head. But as of the past few weeks, I am thinking a bit more about it and my plan is to try do a personal development course and things like that that will help me with reintegration.

(Shelton Abbey, participant)

This institutionalisation can be repugnant to the idea of prison as a deterrent. Prisoners can get comfortable in the prison setting, and the bonds they have in prison can be stronger than anything that can root them to mainstream community. One of the non-participants, Richie, stated that he would be back to prison as there was nothing for him on the outside, and with many of his friends in prison he did not mind coming back.

RICHIE: Big time. I've a lot of mates in here . . . (e)veryone looks forward to getting out, but the thing is when you're in here everyone does be screaming to get out and then when you get out like what's out there, there's nothing really out there. More charge sheets.

(Mountjoy, non-participant)

This demonstrates the way in which prisoners can get comfortable in prison; their needs are met and they have bonds to others in the prison too. It is a sad reflection of the fact that prison is sometimes a more attractive option for people than life in the community, where they have much weaker bonds and significantly lower capital. It reflects the dangers of both low social bonds in the community and the operation of prison-based social capital within the prison. With fewer ties in the community, the offender has little reason to fear a return to prison. It also highlights the importance of prison education in keeping the person from being in the "prison" all of the time – creating a space where they can distance themselves from the detrimental aspects of the prison, maintain a degree of independence and agency and prevent their immersion in the culture of the prison that fosters that sense of institutionalisation even further. This is emphasised further in the next section on social bonds.

Summarising the role of prison education in structural and social bonds

The final section of this chapter will simply draw together the foregoing information to demonstrate and summarise again the impact that education can have on the formation, maintenance and destruction of social bonds and the structural elements important for desistance.

The impact of prison education on the formation of social bonds and in supporting the desistance process can be both direct and indirect. The narratives of those who were participating in prison education and therefore still in prison and those ex-prisoners who were at varying stages of reintegration provided many insights into the ways in which education can help in this multifactorial journey. The ex-prisoners were the most resolute in their opinions on the valuable nature of education. Most of them said that without education they would not have moved away from crime. The following quotes from Anthony and Gary, two ex-prisoners, really indicate the impact of education on the formation of social bonds and in the desistance process.

ANTHONY: Honestly, I think it's the only way . . . education for me was the only way I could change. It was something that gave me something to live for and that changed my prospect of employment and just improved my whole lifestyle. Other than that, education gives people the opportunities. If they don't get education in prison, what do they do? In education I'm including practical skills or some sort of vocational training too. I think it's essential because if it's not there I've seen it so much, especially the two years I was in the Midlands, people just rot . . . and go out the same way, probably worse than they came in because they're more exposed to drugs and even more angry than when they came in because they haven't actually done anything with themselves, so unless they actually do something with themselves while they're in jail they'll probably reoffend. So I think education in prison is key.

(Ex-prisoner)

GARY: I honestly think it's the biggest reason why I'm not in trouble again. I'm focusing and I'm getting my goals and it's keeping me on the right road.

> I have a vision for myself . . . plus education has opened my mind up to so many different things . . . I'm learning about the world.
>
> (Ex-prisoner)

Reading into these statements, they show the way in which education can support the formation of social bonds on release such as improved lifestyle, increased opportunities, better employment prospects, transformed outlook, help in achieving goals and fostering ambition. These two statements alone show the power of education in prisons. Education is not claimed as a panacea; rather it is just one of a range of measures that can support the efforts of the individual and that may ultimately culminate in desistance.

While the influence of prison education on the formation of pro-social bonds is readily ascertainable throughout this chapter, perhaps the most notable point is the nature of the relationship. Rather than having a direct relationship to the formation of social bonds, prison education's influence is indirect. The formation of social bonds is supported by the various cognitive changes such as increased confidence, self-awareness, self-control, self-efficacy, empathy, a changed outlook and being more open-minded and self-reflective. These cognitive changes, which based on the accounts of participants are attributable to prison education, facilitate the creation of a range of pro-social bonds, building the structures upon which the efforts to desist are grounded. These supports are instrumental at each stage of the penal experience, from coping with the prison sentence, through the early stages of release and integration, right through to secondary desistance. Again, this represents a strong endorsement of the potential of prison education, and the manner in which prison education is connected to the desistance process is becoming clearer. It also shows the education of itself is not increasing employability or creating bonds or social capital. Rather, it is the underlying changes that are fostering the ability to achieve these outcomes. This reinforces the need to ensure that the focus of education is not narrowed to simply a mechanism of rehabilitation and employment. While a person may benefit from a work-based or skills-based programme in prison, they will not see the same level of personal change that will arise from engaging with a broad curriculum aimed at the whole person. The findings presented in this chapter and Chapter 5 support the calls to ensure a holistic approach to education in prison in order to provide the maximum benefits for the person. Where such transformation and personal development occurs, the results are usually witnessed on a societal level too, with a person building strong pro-social relationships in their life and often moving towards a more conformist lifestyle,

Finally, Healy (2010) notes that when a person is released from prison, their main objective is getting the various structural elements in place. They will only focus on more self-actualising goals after this has been achieved. While it appears that education plays a role in securing the structural factors and social bonds required to ground the offender in society and aid their desistance, the accumulation of these bonds can be slow since they are self-perpetuating in nature and will therefore not materialise immediately on release. To that end, the sense of agency, self-belief, confidence and control that prisoners said they gained from prison education will be important in supporting the offender immediately after release as they struggle to put their foundational structures and relationships in place. Based on the accumulation of the earlier findings and discussions, it appears that prison education can assist the ex-prisoner in putting the necessary structural factors and social bonds in place and also can also enhance the accumulation of the various cognitive factors required to support that process in the early stages. To that end, prison education may be acting as a form of pre-desistance, by facilitating early changes that can contribute towards greater stability through the turbulence of primary desistance.

Conclusion

This chapter has covered a significant amount, exploring how prison education can contribute to both structure and support in the lives of prisoners and ex-prisoners in the early and later stages of desistance. These findings have built upon the material explored in Chapter 5 by showing the very practical ways in which the cognitive benefits of participating in prison education can manifest themselves during reintegration and the later stages of desistance. These cognitive changes form the foundations to support and stabilise the person in the early stages after release, while repairing and enriching key relationships, all of which can later contribute to stronger social bonds and greater levels of social capital that will hopefully ground the person in the community. The idea of social relationships, social bonds and social capital are explored in more detail in the upcoming chapter.

References

Abell, L. (2018) Exploring the Transition to Parenthood as a Pathway to Desistance. *Journal of Developmental and Life Course Criminology* 4, pp. 395–426. doi:10.1007/s40865-018-0089-6.

Baldry, E., McDonnell, D., Maplestone, P. and Peeters, M. (2003) *Ex-Prisoners and Accommodation: What Bearing Do Different Forms of Housing Have on Social Reintegration for Ex-Prisoners?* Melbourne: Australian Housing and Urban Research Institute.

Baskin, D.R. and Sommers, I.B. (1998) *Casualties of Community Disorder: Women's Careers in Violent Crime*. Boulder: Westview Press. doi:10.1177/0093854813485412.

Bersani, B.E. and Doherty, E.E. (2013) When the Ties That Bind Unwind: Examining the Enduring and Situational Processes of Change behind the Marriage Effect. *Criminology* 51, pp. 399–433. doi:10.1111/1745-9125.12008.

Bersani, B.E. and Doherty, E.E. (2018) Desistance from Offending in the Twenty-First Century. *Annual Review of Criminology* 1, pp. 311–334. doi:10.1146/annurev-criminol-032317-092112.

Biggam, F.H. and Power, K.G. (1997) Social Support and Psychological Distress in a Group of Incarcerated Young Offenders. *International Journal of Offender Therapy and Comparative Criminology* 41(3), pp. 213–230. doi:10.1177/0306624X97413002.

Boonstoppel, S. (2019) 'It's Not about Me No More': Fatherhood and Mechanisms of Desistance among at-Risk Men. *Journal of Developmental and Life Course Criminology* 5, pp. 235–265. Doi:10.1007/s40865-019-00120-9.

Central Statistics Office (2019) *Marriages 2018: Press Statement Marriages 2018*. Cork: Central Statistics Office. Viewed 23rd July at www.cso.ie/en/releasesandpublications/er/mar/marriages2018/.

Colvin, M. (2000) *Crime and Coercion: An Integrated Theory of Chronic Criminality*. New York: Palgrave MacMillan.

Craig, J.M., Diamond, B. and Piquero, A.R. (2014) Marriage as an Intervention in the Lives of Criminal Offenders. In Humphrey, J. and Cordella, P. (eds) *Effective Interventions in the Lives of Criminal Offenders*. New York: Springer Science and Business Media.

Crewe, B. (2011) Depth, Weight, Tightness: Revisiting the Pains of Imprisonment. *Punishment & Society* 13(5), pp. 509–529. doi:10.1177/1462474511422172.

Cusson, M. and Pinsonneault, P. (1986) The Decision to Give Up Crime. In Clarke, R. and Cornish, D. (eds) *The Reasoning Criminal*. New York: Springer-Verlag.

Duguid, S. (1998) Policy, Praxis and Rehabilitation: Prison Education in Canada 1945–1995. In Forster, W. (ed) *Education behind Bars: International Comparisons*. Leicester: National Institute of Adult Continuing Education.

Edin, K., Nelson, T.J. and Paranal, R. (2004) Fatherhood and Incarceration as Potential Turning Points in the Criminal Careers of Unskilled Men. In Pattillo, M. Weiman, D. and Western, B. (eds) *Imprisoning America: The Social Effects of Mass Incarceration*. New York: Russel Sage Foundation.

Elliott, D.S. and Menard, S. (1996) Delinquent Friends and Delinquent Behaviour: Temporal and Developmental Patterns. In Hawkins, D.J. (ed) *Delinquency and Crime: Current Theories*. Cambridge: Cambridge University Press.

Farrington, D.P. and West, D.J. (1995) Effects of Marriage, Separation, and Children on Offending by Adult Males. In Smith Blau, Z. and Hagan, J. (eds) *Current Perspectives on Aging and the Life Cycle: Vol. 4: Delinquency and Disrepute in the Life Course*. Greenwich: JAI Press.

Giordano, P.C., Cernkovich, S.A. and Holland, D.D. (2003) Changes in Friendship Relations over the Life Course: Implications for Desistance from Crime. *Criminology* 41(2), pp. 293–328. doi:10.1111/j.1745-9125.2003.tb00989.x.

Giordano, P.C., Cernkovich, S.A. and Rudolph, J. (2002) Gender, Crime and Desistance: Towards a Theory of Cognitive Transformation. *American Journal of Sociology* 107(4), pp. 990–1064. doi:10.1086/343191.

Glueck, S. and Glueck, E.T. (1940) *Juvenile Delinquents Grown Up*. New York: Commonwealth Fund.

Glueck, S. and Glueck, E.T. (1950) *Unravelling Juvenile Delinquency*. New York: Commonwealth Fund.

Glueck, S. and Glueck, E.T. (1968) *Delinquents and Nondelinquents in Perspective*. Cambridge, MA: Harvard University Press.

Glueck, S. and Glueck, E.T. (1974) *Of Delinquency and Crime: A Panorama of Years of Search and Research*. Springfield, IL: Charles C Thomas.

Gottfredson, M. and Hirschi, T. (1990) *A General Theory of Crime*. Stanford, CA: Stanford University Press.

Graham, J. and Bowling, B. (1995) *Young People and Crime: Home Office Research Study No. 145*. London: Home Office.

Hammett, T., Roberts, C. and Kennedy, S. (2001) Health-Related Issues in Prisoner Re-Entry. *Crime & Delinquency* 47(3), pp. 390–409.

Healy, D. (2010) *The Dynamics of Desistance: Charting Pathways through Change*. Cullompton: Willan Publishing.

Home Office (2002) *Breaking the Circle: A Report of the Review of the Rehabilitation of Offenders Act*. London: Home Office, July.

Horney, J., Osgood, W.D. and Marshall, I.H. (1995) Criminal Careers in the Short-Term: Intra-Individual Variability in Crime and Its Relation to Local Life Circumstance. *American Sociological Review* 60(5), pp. 655–673.

Irwin, J. and Owen, B. (2005) Harm and the Contemporary Prison. In Liebling, A. and Maruna, S. (eds) *The Effects of Imprisonment*. Cullompton: Willan Publishing.

Kendler, K.S., Lönn, S.L., Sundquist, J. and Sundquist, K. (2017) The Role of Marriage in Criminal Recidivism: A Longitudinal and Co-Relative Analysis. *Epidemiology and Psychiatric Sciences* 26(6), pp. 655–663. doi:10.1017/s2045796016000640.

Kerr, D.C.R., Capaldi, D.M., Owen, L.D., Wiesner, M. and Pears, K.C. (2011) Changes in at-Risk American Men's Crime and Substance Use Trajectories Following Fatherhood. *Journal of Marriage and Family* 73, pp. 1101–1116.

King, S. (2013) Assisted Desistance and Experiences of Probation Supervision. *Probation Journal* 60(2), pp. 136–151. doi:10.1177/0264550513478320.

Knight, B.J., Osborn, S.G. and West, D.J. (1977) Early Marriage and Criminal Tendency in Males. *British Journal of Criminology* 17, pp. 348–360.

Knight, B.J. and West, D.J. (1975) Temporary and Continuing Delinquents. *British Journal of Criminology* 15, pp. 43–50.

Knoester, C. and Eggebeen, D.J. (2006) The Effects of the Transition to Parenthood and Subsequent Children on Men's Well-Being and Social Participation. *Journal of Family Issues* 27, pp. 1532–1560.

Knoester, C., Petts, R.J. and Eggebeen, D.J. (2007) Commitments to Fathering and the Well-Being and Social Participation of New, Disadvantaged Fathers. *Journal of Marriage and Family* 69(4), pp. 991–1004. doi:10.1111/j.1741-3737.2007.00426.x.

Laub, J.H., Nagin, D.S. and Sampson R.J. (1998) Trajectories of Change in Criminal Offending: Good Marriages and the Desistance Process. *American Sociological Review* 63(2), pp. 225–238.

Laub, J.H. and Sampson, R.J. (1993) Turning Points in the Life Course: Why Change Matters to the Study of Crime. *Criminology* 31(3), pp. 301–332.

Laub, J.H. and Sampson, R.J. (2001) Understanding Desistance from Crime. *Crime and Justice* 28, pp. 1–69.

LaVigne, N.G., Visher, C. and Castro, J. (2004) *Chicago Prisoners' Experiences Returning Home*. Washington, DC: Urban Institute Justice Policy Center.

Law Reform Commission (2007) *Report on Spent Convictions*. LRC 84. Dublin, July.

LeBel, T., Burnett, R., Maruna, S. and Bushway, S. (2008) The 'Chicken and Egg' of Subjective and Social Factors in Desistance from Crime. *European Journal of Criminology* 5(2), pp. 131–159.

Liebling, A. and Maruna, S. (2005) Introduction: The Effects of Imprisonment Revisited. In Liebling, A. and Maruna, S. (eds) *The Effects of Imprisonment*. Cullompton: Willan Publishing.

Lipsey, M. (1995) What Do We Learn from 400 Studies on the Effectiveness of Treatment with Juvenile Delinquents? In McGuire, J. (ed) *What Works: Reducing Re-Offending: Guidelines from Research and Practice*. Chichester: Wile.

Louks, N., Lyner, O. and Sullivan, T. (1998) The Employment of People with Criminal Records in the EU. *European Journal on Criminal Policy and Research* 6, pp. 195–210.

MacKinnon, J. and Wells, P. (2001) Criminal Records and Employment: A Case for Legislative Change. *New Zealand Universities Law Reviews* 19, pp. 287–308.

Martynowicz, A. and Quigley, M. (2010) *'It's Like Stepping on a Landmine': Reintegration of Prisoners in Ireland*. Dublin: Irish Penal Reform Trust.

Maruna, S. (1997) Going Straight: Desistance from Crime and Life Narratives of Reform. In Lieblich, A. and Josselson, R. (eds) *The Narrative Study of Lives*. New York: Sage.

Maruna, S. (2001) *Making Good: How Ex-Convicts Reform and Rebuild Their Lives*. Washington: American Psychological Association. doi:10.1037/10430-000.

Maruna, S. and Roy, K. (2007) Amputation or Reconstruction: Notes on the Concept of 'Knifing Off' and Desistance from Crime. *Journal of Contemporary Criminal Justice* 23(1), pp. 104–124.

Meisenhelder, T. (1977) An Exploratory Study of Exiting from Criminal Careers. *Criminology* 15, pp. 319–334.

Mezirow, J. (2000) Learning to Think Like an Adult: Core Concepts of Transformation Theory. In Mezirow, J. (ed) *Learning as Transformation: Critical Perspectives on a Theory in Progress*. San Francisco: Jossey-Bass.

Mischkowitz, R. (1994) Desistance from a Delinquent Way of Life? In Weitekamp, E.G.M. and Kerner, H.J. (eds) *Cross-National Longitudinal Research on Human Development and Criminal Behaviour*. Dordrecht: Kluwer Academic.

Moore, J. (1996) Bearing the Burden: How Incarceration Weakens Inner-City Communities. In The Urban Institute (ed) *The Unintended Consequences of Incarceration*. Washington, DC: Urban Institute Justice Policy Center.

Morgan, M. and Kett, M. (2003) *The Prison Adult Literacy Survey: Results and Implications*. Dublin: Irish Prison Service.

Morgan, P.S. and Waite, L. (1987) *Parenthood and the Attitudes of Young Adults*. Santa Monica, CA: RAND Corporation.

Morris, C.W. (1962) *Mind, Self and Society: From the Standpoint of Social Behaviourist*. Chicago: University Press of Chicago.

National Economic and Social Forum (2001) *The Reintegration of Prisoners: Forum Report No. 22*. Dublin: National Economic and Social Forum.

Nugent, B. and Schinkel, M. (2016) The Pains of Desistance. *Criminology & Criminal Justice* 16(5), pp. 568–584. doi:10.1177/1748895816634812.

O'Donnell, I. (2002) The Reintegration of Prisoners. *Administration* 50(2), pp. 80–97.

O'Mahony, P. (1997) *Mountjoy Prisoners: A Sociological and Criminological Profile*. Dublin: Stationary Office.

Osgood, D.W. and Lee, H. (1993) Leisure Activities, Age, and Adult Roles across the Lifespan. *Loisir et Société/Society and Leisure* 16(1), pp. 181–207. doi:10.1080/07053436.1993.10715448.

Pezzin, L.E. (1995) Earning Prospects, Matching Effects, and the Decision to Terminate a Criminal Career. *Journal of Quantitative Criminology* 11, pp. 29–50.

Porporino, F.J. and Robinson, D. (1992) *Can Educating Adult Offenders Counteract Recidivism?* Ontario: Correctional Services of Canada.

Ripley, P. (1993) *Prison Educations Role in Challenging Offending Behaviour*. Mendip Papers, MP 047, ED 379405. Bristol: Staff College.

Sampson, R.J. and Laub, J. (1993) *Crime in the Making: Pathways and Turning Points through Life*. Cambridge, MA: Harvard University Press.

Sampson, R.J. and Laub, J. (2003) Desistance from Crime over the Life Course. In Mortimer, J.T. and Shanahan, M. (eds) *Handbook of the Life Course*. New York: Kluwer Academic/Plenum.

Sampson, R.J., Laub, J. and Wimer, C. (2006) Does Marriage Reduce Crime? A Counterfactual Approach to Within-Individual Causal Effects. *Criminology* 44, pp. 465–508. doi:10.1111/j.1745-9125.2006.00055.x.

Savolainen, J. (2009) Work, Family and Criminal Desistance: Adult Social Bonds in the Nordic Welfare State. *British Journal of Criminology* 49, pp. 285–304. doi:10.1093/bjc/azn084.

Schuller, T., Brassett-Grundy, A., Green, A., Hammond, C. and Preston, J. (2002) *Learning, Continuity and Change in Adult Life*. Wider Benefits of Learning Research Report No. 3. London: Centre for Research on the Wider Benefits of Learning.

Seymour, M. and Costello, L. (2005) *A Study of the Number, Profile and Progression Routes of Homeless Persons before the Court and in Custody*. Dublin: Centre for Social and Educational Research.

Shapland, J. and Bottoms, A. (2011) Reflections on Social Values, Offending and Desistance among Young Adult Recidivists. *Punishment and Society* 13(3), pp. 256–282.

Sherlock, J. (2007) Employing Ex-Offenders. *Running Your Business* 13(9), p. 36.

Shinkfield, A. and Graffam, J. (2009) The Relationship Between Emotional State and Success in Community Reintegration for Ex-Prisoners. *International Journal of Offender Therapy and Comparative Criminology* 54, pp. 346–360. doi:10.1177/0306624X09331443.

Shover, N. (1996) *Great Pretenders: Pursuits and Careers of Persistent Thieves*. Boulder: Westview Press.

Skardhamar, T. and Savolainen, J. (2012) *Does Employment Contribute to Desistance? Offending Trajectories of Crime-Prone Men Around the Time of Job Entry: Discussion Papers 716*. Oslo: Statistics Norway Research Department.

Skardhamar, T., Savolainen, J., Aase, K.M. and Lyngstad, T.H. (2015) Does Marriage Reduce Crime? *Crime and Justice* 44, pp. 385–446. doi:10.1086/681557.

Sutherland, E.H. (1947) *Criminology*. 4th ed. Philadelphia: Lippincott.

Sykes, G.M. (1958) *The Society of Captives*. Princeton: Princeton University Press.

Tewksbury, R. and Stengel, K.M. (2006) Assessing Correctional Education Programs: The Students' Perspective. *Journal of Correctional Education* 57(1), pp. 13–25.

Trasler, G.B. (1980) *'Aspects of Causality, Culture, and Crime', Fourth International Seminar at the International Centre of Sociological, Penal and Penitentiary Research and Studies*. Messina, Italy.

Vaughan, B. (2007) The Internal Narrative of Desistance. *British Journal of Criminology* 47(3), pp. 390–404.

Visher, C.A., La Vigne, N. and Travis, J. (2004) *Returning Home: Understanding the Challenges of Prisoner Reentry: Maryland Pilot Study: Findings from Baltimore*. Washington, DC: Urban Institute Justice Policy Center.

Visher, C.A. and Travis, J. (2003) Transitions from Prison to Community: Understanding Individual Pathways. *Annual Review of Sociology* 29, pp. 89–113. doi:10.1146/annurev.soc.29.010202.095931.

Visher, C.A. and Travis, J. (2011) Life on the Outside: Returning Home after Incarceration. *The Prison Journal* 91(3), pp. 102–119. doi:10.1177/0032885511415228.

Walters, G.D. (1995) The Psychological Inventory of Criminal Thinking Styles: Part I: Reliability and Preliminary Validity. *Criminal Justice and Behaviour* 22(3), pp. 307–325. doi:10.1177/0093854895022003008.

Warner, K. (2007) Against the Narrowing of Perspectives: How Do We See Learning, Prisons and Prisoners? *Journal of Correctional Education* 58(2), pp. 170–183.

Warr, M. (1993) Age, Peers and Delinquency. *Criminology* 31, pp. 17–40.

Warr, M. (1998) Life-Course Transitions and Desistance from Crime. *Criminology* 36(2), pp. 183–216.

Warr, M. (2002) *Companions in Crime*. Cambridge: Cambridge University Press.

Weaver, B. (2016) *Offending and Desistance: The Importance of Social Relations*. Abingdon: Routledge.

Wright, J. and Cullen, F. (2004) Employment, Peers and Life-Course Transitions. *Justice Quarterly* 21(1), pp. 183–205.

Chapter 7

Social capital, prison education and desistance

A key requirement for desistance is access to pro-social structures and relationships. The previous chapters have highlighted the importance of access to opportunities and supports in reintegration and desistance success. A key objective of this book is to explore the possibility of links among prison education, desistance and social capital. While previous studies have looked at the relationships among mainstream education, human capital and social capital, there is no past literature or research addressing the relationship between education in the prison setting and levels of social capital. Therefore, in order to begin addressing this gap in the literature and to explore the relationships that might exist between social capital and prison education and in turn how this might impact desistance, an objective of the current study was to attempt to examine these concepts and their interactions. This chapter will begin with an overview of the concept of social capital, including its definition and relevant theories. From there, the chapter will begin to examine the links between social capital and desistance and social capital and education in order to build a picture of the framework into which this element of the research fits. Furthermore, the prison setting could be described as an anti-capital setting, where it is impossible to accumulate or exercise social capital. Given that the prison itself can be viewed as a unique community, with its own form of culture, rules and norms, the idea of a form of prison-based social capital as a concept is also examined later in the chapter. This will culminate in a discussion of the findings of the current study and the potential implications for theory and practice.

Overview of social capital

Social capital is a relatively recent concept and encompasses social support, social networks and social cohesion (Lafferty et al., 2015). While every person has their own stock of social capital, it is not concerned solely with the individual, but it is a concept that embodies the relations and social ties that exist among people in families, social groups, communities or wider society (Grootaert and Van Bastelaer, 2001). Reflecting its rooting in relationships and interactions, it is perhaps best described as social connections between people

(Bourdieu, 1986). It is an extremely broad sociological and economic concept whose definition is made difficult, partly due to the fact that the concept itself is still somewhat in its infancy and also because it applies to various aspects of the social world. Another difficulty in defining social capital is the lack of theoretical consensus on the structures and processes of which it is composed. Within criminology and the desistance framework in particular, social capital is often referred to as the social connections and social ties between people (Coleman, 1988). While a more desistance-focused view of social capital will be examined later, for now, the general concept of social capital will be outlined to give a brief introduction to the topic. Putnam (2000: 19) credits the following quote from a state school supervisor in the United States in 1916 as being the first account of social capital:

> those tangible substances that count for most in the daily lives of people: namely good will, fellowship, sympathy, and social intercourse among the individuals and families that make up a social unit. . . . The individual is useless socially if he is left to himself. . . . If he comes into contact with a neighbour, and they with other neighbours, there will be an accumulation of social capital, which may immediately satisfy his social needs and which may bear a social potentiality sufficient to the substantial improvement of living conditions in the whole community. The community as a whole will benefit by the cooperation of all its parts, while the individual will find in his associations the advantages of the help, the sympathy, and the fellowship of his neighbours.

This conceptualisation of social capital comprised all the crucial elements that any subsequent interpretations of the phrase encompassed (Putnam, 2000), highlighting both the individual and community aspects it entails. While this first mention of social capital attracted little or no attention at the time, in recent decades there has been a surge in interest in the concept (Putnam, 2000). In relation to the study of social capital, several prominent theorists and theories have emerged, each fielding a particular definition and view of social capital. The following is a brief outline of their key contributions to social capital theories.

Social networks, relationships and bonds are a feature of social capital in most mainstream conceptualisations. Bourdieu (1977: 503) defined social capital simply as the "capital of social relationships which will provide, if necessary, useful supports". Expanding on this definition, he stated that social capital was

> the actual or potential resources which are linked to possession of a durable network of more or less institutionalised relationships of mutual acquaintance and recognition . . . which provides each of its members with the backing of collectively owned capital.
>
> (Bourdieu, 1986: 286)

Social connections are therefore a key feature of Bourdieu's theory. Coleman (1988) also focuses on social ties in conceptualising social capital and believed that social capital makes possible the achievement of certain goals that would not be possible if it did not exist. An example of this could be connections with people who might help another in getting a new job through their networks and connections. Social capital is a central factor in creating ties that bind a person in society to social institutions and conformity. Bonds self-perpetuate; the more bonds and connections a person has, the more they can create. Coleman's concept of social capital comprised three elements: levels of trust, information channels and norms and sanctions promoting common good over self-interest. He believed that social capital and human capital are complimentary (Coleman, 1994); the greater a person's level of education and skills, the greater their stock of social capital. Social capital is usually a by-product of other activities, and its creation is generally unintentional (Coleman, 1994). Putnam's (1996) theory focuses on civil engagement and in a similar way to Coleman he proposed that social capital comprises social networks, norms and trust. It facilitates effective collective action to pursue shared objectives. This definition illustrates the three key components of social capital – networks, norms and trust. Interpersonal networks and social bonds between people are created, facilitating the development of a set of social and community norms by which people live. Within these networks and through observing norms, a trust develops between the members of the networks and the wider community and "lubricates social life" (Putnam, 2000: 21). Social capital is a wider concept than just the immediate ties that bind people in networks and community. Social capital involves a level of social trust (Fukuyama, 1995). Forrest and Kearns (2001) argue that social capital involves empowerment, participation, association, support and reciprocity, collective norms and values, trust, safety and belonging. This broader conceptualisation becomes very relevant when discussing social capital and prison education later in this chapter. Empowerment in this context means that community members have a voice, are involved in processes that affect them and can take action to initiate change. Participation refers to being involved in social and community activities. Association means cooperating with others, resulting in the formation of formal and informal groups to further collective interests and joint purposes. Collective norms and values refer to the similar rules and values that the community shares and adheres to. Trust is the collective trust among coresidents, residents and local organisations. Safety is the feeling of security resulting in low levels of restriction of public space due to fear. Belonging describes the way in which people feel connected to each other and their home area and feel that they belong to the place and its people. Collectively, these definitions of social capital centre on the existence of a set of cohesive and reciprocal social ties that create the resources that can be used to help both the individual and society achieve their goals.

While social capital exists at the community level, it is individuals who make the decision to invest in social capital. Therefore, all definitions and efforts to promote social capital should begin at the individual level (Glaeser, 2001). For the individual, social capital can be seen as the resources available to achieve one's goals (Farrall, 2004). Social capital is an asset required for action (Heitfield, 2003). It allows individuals to use resources they would not have access to if they were acting alone such as social connections, social supports, relationships, reciprocity and having people to call on if needed (Lafferty et al., 2015), all of which are important for those attempting to reintegrate after a prison sentence. Many former prisoners rely on social connections such as family and friends for the identification of job opportunities, for example (Lafferty et al., 2015). They may also need emotional and financial support after they are released. Social capital, in the form of relationships and bonds to the people who can provide these resources, can be the difference between success and failure for the ex-prisoner. According to Hattery and Smith (2010), there are two important aspects of social capital, namely social networks and resources. Social networks comprise the people with whom we are sufficiently familiar that would enable us to ask for advice or assistance (Hattery and Smith, 2010). Most individuals will usually have both strong and weak social relationships. From the perspective of accessing opportunities, it is suggested that plentiful weak social ties are better than a small number of strong ties. This is because the people with whom we have strong ties are often very similar to us and thus give us access to similar connections to those we already have. By having lots of weaker ties, it gives access to a much more diverse array of social ties that are likely to be far different to our own (Hattery and Smith, 2010). For access to work opportunities, lots of weaker but more diverse ties are preferable for creating the necessary connections. However, for the provision of reintegrative support such as finance and accommodation, stronger ties, though less numerous, will be more important. This shows the necessity for a good array of networks and connections.

Not all social capital is positive, and not all social networks and social capital are contained within the mainstream culture (Hattery and Smith, 2010). There are many networks in the illegitimate economy in which social capital forms. Putnam (2000) warns that while social capital appears to be a positive concept for both the individual and the community, these ties and networks can also facilitate the formation of gangs and perpetuate crime. Bourdieu (1977) identifies social capital as one of the cultural mechanisms by which society maintains persons within their social classes, with most of the collectively owned capital, such as physical, cultural, social and human capital, belonging to the higher social classes. This class division causes marginalisation and societal strain that facilitates the development of a more anti-social form of social capital. As networks are formed within society, it can have the effect of excluding those who have weaker ties. Those who are marginalised and have weaker social ties create bonds with other low-bonded peers. A culture and ethos develops between these low-bonded peers that facilitates anti-social actions. These less legitimate social networks, such as gangs, provide rich sources of social capital for many of the less franchised in society and can provide significant returns on the investment in these anti-social ties such as income generation, housing, safety and even promotion (Hattery and Smith, 2010). Putnam (1996) described social capital as networks, norms and trust that enable participants to act together to pursue shared objectives. Pro-social capital involves consequences such as support, trust, cooperation and institutional and community effectiveness (Putnam, 2000). Sources of pro-social capital are political and civic participation, religious participation and employment. Where the norms of a group are anti-social, the collective action in pursuance of the shared objective will also be anti-social in nature (Putnam, 2000). The consequences of anti-social capital include sectarianism and corruption (Putnam, 2000). The idea of anti-social capital is important to the conceptual framework of this research. While it will be explored in greater detail later, Draine and Wolff (2009) contend that as social capital is depleted by the harmful experience of imprisonment, it is replaced by a type of anti-social capital, which will be referred to "prison-based social capital" that comprises the connections, norms and behaviours that characterise the prison community and is deeply harmful to reintegration and desistance. Furthermore, any prisoner who is reintegrating into society and relies on these groups characterised by anti-social capital for support and bonds will find it difficult to make any meaningful attempt to go straight. The income they can make among peers, by drug dealing for instance, is lucrative compared to what they might expect from social welfare or any entry-level job they may be lucky enough to acquire on release.

Social capital and desistance

The various factors that have a role in the desistance process were outlined in previous chapters. Marriage, stable employment, pro-social peer relations and strong personal attributes have been shown to have an impact on the process of desistance. Social capital is increasingly seen as having an important role in a person's ability to desist from crime. For instance, McNeill and Whyte (2007: 183) claim that "without access to social capital, it may be very difficult indeed to embark upon and sustain a pathway towards desistance". McNeill (2006) argues that interventions that aim to support desistance should focus on building human and social capital. These interventions should also to aim to promote respect, agency and reflexivity and exploit strengths, while addressing needs and risk in the offender. It could be argued that prison education, as an intervention, may meet these aims by building not only human capital but social capital too, by increasing agency and by maximising the strengths of the person and allowing them to see their own strengths for themselves. However, before an extensive discussion relating to prison education and its role in building social capital is undertaken, this section will examine the relationship between social capital and desistance as outlined in the desistance literature to date.

Several definitions of social capital mentioned its role in meeting "objectives" or "goals". Coleman (1988) stated that social capital makes possible the achievement of certain ends, which would otherwise not be possible. The question is, therefore, where the objective or goal is desistance, what role does social capital play in supporting the journey towards that end? Social capital is a growing area of interest in criminology with increasing empirical evidence demonstrating the relationship between social capital and criminality. It is similar to the concept of social bonds outlined in Chapter 6 given the reliance of social capital on ties and connections in one's social world. The general principle is that the greater a person's stock of social capital (job, relationships, networks, etc.), the more likely it is that they will desist from criminal offending (Laub and Sampson, 1993). The lower their stock of social capital, the more likely they will continue offend (Farrall, 2004).

A person's capacity to change is enhanced by social investment or social capital (Laub and Sampson, 1993). Social capital is created when a person's interpersonal relationships and relationships with social institutions change in a way that facilitates action or life change (Laub and Sampson, 1993). One of the most important factors in change is the concept of social capital, especially in institutional relationships (Laub and Sampson, 1993). Lack of social capital is one of the primary features of weak social bonds. The fewer social bonds a person has, the lower their stakes in conformity and the higher the chances that they will offend (Meisenhelder, 1977). Moreover, having low social capital and social ties will mean a person has access to fewer resources to draw upon when released from prison when attempting to put in place pro-desistance structures (Farrall, 2004). The more social ties a person has access to, in turn giving access to opportunities and support, the less likely they will be to commit crime (Farrall, 2004) and the more likely they will thereby accumulate more social capital as time goes on (Laub and Sampson, 1993). The idea of social capital and social bonds are quite closely linked, with one perpetuating the other. In a "chicken and egg" style consideration, Farrall (2004) questions which perpetuates the other. Do social bonds emerge out of increasing social capital or is social capital a by-product of strong social bonds? It would appear that it is a reciprocal relationship, with one supporting and perpetuating the other (Farrall, 2004).

It seems that many of the elements explored under the heading of social bonds are relevant to the makeup of social capital. Social networks with family, workmates, law-abiding peers or perhaps with people in elevated positions of authority within society and the interpersonal interactions that underlie those networks are inherent in the concept of social capital. In this way, social capital has an impact on the desistance process. This pro-desistance effect arises from a person becoming more embedded in society as they acquire more social capital. With increased capital and ties to conformity, the opportunity cost of crime begins to shift as offenders start having more to lose by offending, thus having an impact on desistance (Farrall, 2004).

Farrall (2004) explored the concept of social capital and its relationship to desistance. The data used for the study came from a project that aimed to understand the processes that occurred during probation which promoted either desistance or persistence. The probationers involved were divided into five groups on the basis of the nature of their previous offending and other personal characteristics, and interviews were conducted with each of them (Farrall, 2004). In relation to facilitating desistance, the most significant factor was paid employment. Most probationers reported that they relied on social ties and resources in the form of family and friends who had their own businesses or had contacts with other employers to secure work for them (Farrall, 2004). Employment led to a decrease in unstructured time, an income, an opportunity to leave home and gain independence, a greater civic identity and increased self-esteem. Furthermore, employment leads to a decrease in time spent with their peer group and an opportunity to meet a future partner or spouse. It also presents an opportunity to set and achieve goals such as promotion at work (Farrall, 2004). This demonstrates the way in which social capital operates. The network of bonds (family and friends) provides the offender with employment and opportunities, demonstrating trust. The offender will likely honour that trust by working hard and integrating into the networks within the workplace, acquiring other social bonds. Of course, if the offender has no intention of going straight, the job will be of little benefit and will have the opposite effect, as they will weaken their bonds by dishonouring the trust of the employer, friend or family member. Employment usually represents a positive change, and the probationers all spoke of how it increased their confidence and gave them more to lose if they returned to offending again (Farrall, 2004). Furthermore, employment leads to a diversification of social networks and is often a source of bridging capital, which creates "bridges" to wider social resources. McNeill (2006) stated that the creation of social networks and links with those outside of one's immediate network improves the odds of desistance as it gives the offender the opportunity to access wider social resources.

Meisenhelder (1977) found that good family relationships are also important in the process of desistance. Families are a strong source of social capital (Farrall, 2004), tending to structure time and therefore provide stability and act as a support network. Horney et al. (1995) also found that the nature of the marital relationship is such that it interferes with the leisure time of a person and results in much less time being spent with peers. In the case of offenders, many of whom associate with delinquent peers who increase their chance of offending, the increase of social capital and pro-social relationships could result in a fracturing of these delinquent peer relations. Farrall (2004) suggests making probation more desistance-focused. In doing so, the primary aim ought to be to improve familial relations and help the probationer gain stable employment. It is these changes in the life course that can build social capital and facilitate a legitimate, law-abiding existence for those aiming to desist from crime (Farrall, 2004).

Social capital is pertinent to the very structures of an offenders life which are considered barriers to reentry. Thus, allowing prisoners access to social capital on release from prison lowers these barriers significantly and promotes desistance (Hattery and Smith, 2010). However, when prisoners leave prison, they will often only have a small circle of social contacts remaining, mostly made up of close family if those ties have not been severed by their previous offending. This leads to a double disadvantage for the person – first, their place in the social hierarchy will have been damaged by imprisonment and, second, their network of supports and social contacts may be diminished (Hattery and Smith, 2010). This limits social capital and can pose challenges to reintegration. Those prisoners who do not have strong positive social support in the community on release are at increased risk of recidivism (Jang and Canada, 2014). In overcoming the barriers to reentry and lowering recidivism rates, criminal justice systems need to work to develop and invest in programmes that will create sources of and open doors to social capital on release (Hattery and Smith, 2010).

While there is a growing body of research that supports the significant role that social capital can play in the desistance process, it must be questioned whether it is possible to leave prison with much social capital left. The lifestyle and background of the typical offender is not conducive to having high stocks of social capital to begin with. Their offending, prosecution and imprisonment will likely have reduced their social capital to an even greater extent. Such low levels of social capital will leave the person vulnerable to reoffending on release. Therefore, since social capital appears to perpetuate itself, the more pro-social capital a person can maintain or build during their prison sentence, the better placed they will be for success on release. However, given the damaging impact of imprisonment, the maintenance or building of social capital during incarceration would surely be difficult. In fact, it could be said that because of the nature of prison itself being completely at odds with life in wider society, it could not support or generate mainstream social capital. Draine and Wolff (2009) stated that the social capital of prisoners is affected by the instability created by incarceration. It is proposed that prison education is a way of remedying this, yet the question as to how prison education achieves this remains. Glaeser (2001) criticises the lack of theory and empirical work on the causes of social capital, stating that if there is a desire to change or promote social capital within particular communities, groups or settings there must be a model for the formation of social capital, norms and networks. This poses a difficulty in examining how pro-social capital can be promoted through the prison sentence. Essentially, there is a need to piece together a conceptual framework from various disciplines in order to propose a solution. In light of this critique and the focus on prison education, the upcoming section will explore the relationships between education and social capital in order to consider the consequent role of prison education in the creation of social capital and in the desistance process.

Education and social capital

Education and human capital have significant roles in the creation of social capital (Schuller et al., 2002). Both education and human capital are closely linked. Education often refers to mainstream schooling and is often labour market-focused, whereas human capital is the knowledge, skills and capabilities that a person possesses that allow them to function in all aspects of social life. Human capital is therefore quite reflective of the broad, whole-person developmental view of education. According to the OECD (2001), the key skills and personal attributes relevant to human capital include communication skills, literacy and numeracy, intrapersonal skills and social skills. By developing these areas of skill and competence, people become more confident, enjoy increased self-esteem and begin to identify more strongly with themselves. This in turn facilitates them in participating more readily in society either in the workplace or the community setting (OECD, 2001). These categories of human capital are reflective of the broad approach to education, encompassing more than just the traditional notion of education but also reflecting the aspects of learning that enhance the person and enrich their life. This is illustrated by Weiss (1995: 151), who states that

> education does not have to be justified solely on the basis of its effect on labour productivity. . . . Students are not taught civics, or art, or music solely in order to improve their labour productivity, but rather to enrich their lives and make them better citizens.

The impact of education on social capital

Education is one of the most significant predictors of social capital (Putnam, 1995, 2000; Brehm and Rahn, 1997; Helliwell and Putnam, 2007; Huang et al., 2009). Social capital and human capital are both widely regarded as being associated with social status. In such a meritocratic world, education is seen to be about sorting people into their appropriate place in society (Nie et al., 1996). As well as increasing skills, knowledge and civic participation, education is concerned with the distribution of opportunities for gainful participation (Nie et al., 1996). Therefore, where either human capital and/or social capital are lacking, it will have a strong impact on social exclusion and societal equity (Helliwell and Putnam, 2007). The better educated a person is, the more able they are to compete for opportunities and a place of influence in society, thus increasing their own social capital levels (Nie et al., 1996). The number of years in formal education is the single strongest determinant of many aspects of social capital (Glaeser, 2001). Education is not simply the acquisition of knowledge or human capital. It will also involve learning social skills such as behaviour in social settings, cooperative skills and positive interaction with peers (Fuller and Clarke, 1994, Glaeser, 2001). Furthermore, engagement with sports, groups and societies throughout school and college, including membership of fraternities and sororities, all serve as methods of social skill development and network creation that can be drawn upon later in life (Fuller and Clarke, 1994; Glaeser, 2001). This may also mean that those who leave school at an early age may miss out on vital sources of social capital, as opposed to just human capital, compared to those who remain in education.

Higher levels of education are associated with higher levels of social trust (Helliwell and Putnam, 2007). People with higher levels of social trust are more likely to engage with others and participate in community life, finding this more enjoyable if there is a sense of trust and tolerance among people, thus enhancing social capital. Schuller et al. (2002) maintain that the impact of education on social capital is diverse. Conceptualising social capital as civic skills and engagement, social networks and social values, Schuller et al. (2002) found that education has a role in building each of these elements. Learning has a direct and indirect impact on civic skills and engagement, occurring by way of skill and knowledge acquisition (Schuller et al., 2002). As people learn more about society, they are more willing to participate, by voting for instance. Indirectly, as a person's confidence in their own knowledge and competencies increases, it allows them to feel capable of social and civic participation (Schuller et al., 2002).

Family and social ties, both of which are an important aspect of social capital, are also enhanced by education. Swanson et al. (2012) found that those with the highest levels of education perceived their social support from family and friends to be higher. The converse was true of those who had not finished high school (Swanson et al., 2012). Social ties can also be established with potential mentors through education programmes that can subsequently provide access to opportunities and build social capital (Lafferty et al., 2016). Schuller et al. (2002) propose that education's impact on the enhancement of family and social ties is achieved in four ways, namely by extending social networks, enriching relationships, repairing broken ties and dismantling anti-social networks (Schuller et al., 2002). Networks can be extended through education as people begin to meet like-minded people and can also be an important source of bridging social capital as people are introduced to more senior authorities and potential employers within their area of learning (Schuller et al., 2002). In terms of enriching and even repairing social networks, Schuller et al. (2002) note that increasing levels of respect and self-confidence have an impact on relationships with partners and wider family due to things like improved communication, interaction and relations, thus enhancing social capital. Education can also have the effect of dismantling certain relationships. This may be relevant to the current study, where education may result in dismantling relationships with anti-social peer groups. Schuller et al. (2002) note that self-esteem and confidence can allow people greater insight into their relationships and identify the negative aspects of certain relationships. A deficit in social time can also result in severed bonds as a person spends more time in education and less time with friends. Furthermore, participating in education can also alter a person's personality, outlook and characteristics and as interests change, this has an impact on the people they bond with. Each of these points were reflected in Chapter 6 in the narratives of the ex-prisoners when they spoke about how prison education had caused a distance and drifting away from friends as their own interests changed and they no longer had as much time for friends due to college and study. While Schuller et al. (2002) see this as somewhat of a disadvantage of education, in the context of prison education and the impact of anti-social peer bonds on offending, severing ties between an offender and peers may be a distinct advantage of education and social capital in the desistance process.

In line with Mezirow (2000), Schuller et al. (2002) found that education promotes an "open-mindedness" in relation to the world and of other people. Some of those men who participated in Schuller et al.'s (2002) study reported that they tended to look at people and things differently after becoming more educated. This is echoed in the interviews of those in the current study who reported that they developed a new outlook on life and insight into themselves, which is a reflection of the level of open-mindedness that can develop through education. Certain subject areas were seen to enhance particular values; history and sociology, for example, had an impact on empathy. Finally, some of those interviewed reported that through education, they found new, more appropriate ways to interact with people and this contributed to strengthening social ties, social networks and social capital (Schuller et al., 2002).

Impact of social capital on educational outcomes

Coleman (1988) was primarily responsible for introducing the concept of social capital to educational research, emphasising the importance of surrounding young people with adults who are embedded in their community and have strong social networks. This is because social capital is seen to have a significant impact on educational outcomes. Those from communities or families characterised by lower levels of social capital are likely to be more at risk of early school leaving and being marginalised learners, thus limiting the life opportunities of the person (Coleman, 1988). There is a relationship between levels of initial and continuing education and levels of social participation and trust which illustrates a virtuous and reciprocal cycle between both human and social capital (OECD, 2001). This may go some way to explaining why so many of the prisoners described their previous experience with education in quite negative tones. They did not connect with this structure, they did not trust or respect teachers and they felt their teachers did not respect or trust them. There was little in the way of positive reciprocity that could foster social capital, and their own human capital suffered as a result. Those with low levels of education, skills and ability are at much higher risk of social exclusion by way of unemployment and lower earning expectations (OECD, 2001). Education, social background and access to social capital may act together to influence life chances (OECD, 2001). Therefore, education and the acquisition of skills play an important role in the formation of social capital and thus have a potentially strong influence on the desistance process. This point will be raised again in the upcoming section where the potential theoretical links among prison education, social capital and the desistance process are discussed.

Social capital, prison education and desistance

The previous section asserted that education, by increasing skills and enhancing a person's inner resources, can increase and assist in opening many doors to the accumulation of social capital through a greater capacity to participate in both personal and social relationships. It is hypothesised that it is primarily by these means that prison education can have some influence in the process of desistance.

Research suggests that criminal behaviour is closely associated with the restriction of life chances caused by a lack of education in early life. For example, truants (Social Exclusion Unit, 1997) and those who are expelled from school (Graham and Bowling, 1995) are more likely to experience unemployment, social exclusion and criminality. Amin and Thrift (2002) stated that the developmental and social aspects of education and learning are "the most important enabler of individual and collective freedom".

The impact of education on the criminal life course is material from even a young age. At-risk children often circumvented criminal trajectories if certain factors were present, shielding them from the difficulties posed by being from marginalised socioeconomic groups (Rutter, 1990). One of the main factors was education and those children who enjoyed and attended school often tended to plan more readily for better futures and had better outcomes in later life such as in stable marriages and employment (Rutter, 1990). Several education-centred factors have an impact on youth offending. Detachment from education, either by non-attendance or expulsion, low educational attainment and a negative experience of school such as bullying or anti-social behaviour were all associated with offending (McMahon et al., 2006). However, the actual causal relationships in these processes were unclear (McMahon et al., 2006).

Offenders from socially disadvantaged backgrounds tend to have lower levels of education than the general population (O'Mahony, 1997). Low levels of experience and skills are major obstacles on release from prison (Glaser, 1969). This is further compounded by men in prison having unrealistic expectations of occupational advancement following release given their low levels of work experience and skills (Glaser, 1969), not to mention the social obstacles they will face, such as stigma. The provision of and participation in prison education could potentially address these issues. Education has the capacity to improve the skill levels of prisoners. However, based on the findings discussed in previous chapters, it is suggested that education would also provide them with a more realistic outlook on the situation they are facing on release and equip them with the skills to cope with the obstacles they face. This was shown in two ways through the interviews with the prisoners in the current study. First, those who were participating in prison education were very aware and quite realistic about their likelihood of securing employment upon release. They were planning for it to be difficult and were quite mindful of the stigma and obstacles they would face. They also seemed to be much more balanced and had better coping mechanisms than those who were not participating. Second, the data from the ex-prisoners suggested that the increase in skills from education undertaken in prison had helped to secure either employment or further educational opportunities after they were released.

Academics involved in desistance research have called for an approach which builds both human and social capital (Farrall, 2004; McNeill, 2006). Human capital is the knowledge, skill and motivation to change. But this is of little benefit if the offender does not have the opportunity to exercise these assets, which is facilitated by social capital (McNeill, 2006). Building human capital is of little benefit without social capital; the offender must be able to access opportunities to make use of their new capabilities (Farrall, 2002). It might be contended that prison education, while increasing an offender's human capital in the form of skills, qualifications and motivation, is also building the very resources that facilitate social capital since skills and qualifications render the person more employable. Employment in turn is a strong source of social capital (Coleman, 1994). However, social capital operates on a reciprocal basis, and the person must be given the opportunity to participate in society. Where this opportunity is not available, the human capital and any social capital they have built become meaningless. Prejudice and stigma from the members of society can therefore be significant obstacles to the growth of social capital after release from prison.

Prison education can provide the confidence and self-belief (Ubah and Robinson, 2003) to allow offenders to access opportunities when they do come along or perhaps to create their own opportunities. There is also a view that the intervention is not the most important factor in desistance; rather it is an accumulation of chance occurrences, external events and factors personal to the offender (McNeill et al., 2005). However, it might be said that prison education, while it is not being presented as the only factor influencing change, may impact the person's ability to recognise, "hook" onto (Giordano et al., 2002) and maximise the potential of chance opportunities and external events. For example, social psychological development theory suggests that prison education fosters new behavioural patterns and develops cognitive processes (Ubah and Robinson, 2003). Giordano et al. (2002) focus on the role of cognitive changes in the desistance process, whereby the actors' openness to change increases their receptiveness to opportunities which can in turn influence identity change and the creation of a self that no longer sees crime as an option. This again demonstrates the links that can exist between prison education theory and the desistance literature.

Finally, it is suggested that prison education maintains pre–prison sentence levels of social capital by shielding the prisoner from its deterioration. By maintaining social capital, the prisoner is less likely to build harmful prison-based social capital, which is proposed as hindering reintegration (Draine and Wolff, 2009). The existence and effect of this type of prison-based social capital will be examined in the next section.

Prison education and social capital: examining the findings

Chapter 2 outlined the decision to include a survey in the research design in order to examine the social capital levels among prisoners and to a lesser extent examine for the awareness among prisoners of a prison-based social capital. While it is possible to observe the indicators of social capital qualitatively, such as in Farrall's (2004) study, the standard method of measuring social capital is through quantitative surveys. Interviews and surveys were carried out simultaneously, and the survey data was subsequently analysed using SPSS, a statistical analysis software package. Various statistical tests were carried out in order to test the relationships between the variables. Most of the results relate to social capital or prison-based social capital. Since the preliminary data for each man, collected at the start of each interview, was also inputted into SPSS, it was possible to look at additional connections relating to social capital levels. Several other relationships of interest emerged that supported the explanation of the social capital findings. The account of the results will begin with those relating to social capital only, followed by an overview of prison-based social capital and the findings relating to that concept later in the chapter.

Social capital, while a notoriously difficult concept to define, embodies the relations and social ties that exist among people in families, social groups, community and wider society. The difficulty in defining social capital was outlined in Chapter 2, and this study took a broad approach to its examination in line with the SCQB (Ruston and Akinrodoye, 2002). This involved measuring social capital under five indictors or "themes" adapted to take account of the prison context. These themes were (1) participation, social engagement and commitment; (2) control and self-efficacy; (3) perceptions of community and structures; (4) social interaction, social networks and social supports; and (5) trust, reciprocity and social cohesion, reflecting the composite elements of social capital in the broad sense. Following the surveys, the interviews were scored and the results inputted into SPSS for analysis. The following is an outline of the results from these surveys and statistical tests.

Participation in education and social capital

Social capital is proposed as having a strong role to play in the desistance process (Laub and Sampson, 1994; Farrall, 2004; Hattery and Smith, 2010).

Throughout the preceding chapters, it was pointed out many times that there is a significant degree of overlap between the various cognitive and structural benefits of prison education and the elements important to the creation of social capital. Therefore, it is questioned whether prison education can assist with desistance through the creation or maintenance of social capital among those incarcerated. In order to test this hypothesis, to determine whether those who participated in prison education had higher levels of social capital than those who did not, tests were carried out on the data gathered during the interviews and surveys with each person. At the outset, it should be noted in terms of the results reported later that they are not based on intervention. The social capital levels of prisoners when they originally began their sentence is unknown, and as such this is a limiting factor in the report of the results and the links among prison education, social capital and prison-based social capital. Therefore, at each point the results are reported and discussed as suppositions as opposed to causal facts.

In order to determine whether there was a difference in the social capital levels of prisoners who either participated or did not participate in prison education, an independent samples t-test was carried out in order to compare the total social capital scores for both participants and non-participants. The t-test showed that there was a significant difference in the total social capital scores for participants ($M = 119.50$, $SD = 16.147$) and non-participants ($M = 58.57$, $SD = 4.91$; $t = 12.12$, $p = .000$). The magnitude of differences in the means (mean difference = 60.929, CI: 71.140 to 50.717) was very large (eta squared = .811). This shows that participants have higher levels of social capital than non-participants. Since this was not an intervention-based study, it is not possible to tell whether the participants had higher levels of social capital coming to prison and have simply maintained it or whether they have increased their level of social capital through participation in prison education. However, some other tests were carried out on the data gathered that sheds further light on this, the results of which are discussed later.

A similar question here, the answer to which further reinforces the findings of the previous test, is whether or not increased levels of engagement in prison education had an impact on social capital levels. In order to examine this, the participants were ranked in terms of their self-estimated levels of participation over the previous three months. Those participating for an average of 14 to 20 hours per week were considered to participate at a high levels, those participating for between 7 and 13 hours per week were considered moderate participators and those with fewer than 7 hours per week were considered low-level participators. The relationship between the levels of participation in prison education and social capital among prisoners was examined using Pearson product moment correlation coefficient. There was a strong positive correlation between the two variables ($r = .88$, $n = 41$, $p < .000$), with higher levels of engagement in prison education associated with higher levels of social capital. This shows that those who spent more time in prison education each week tend to have higher levels of social capital than those who are spending less time participating in education each week. This again gives a strong indication that prison education is contributing to either the creation or maintenance of social capital levels among prisoners. Furthermore, this also appears to show that the effects of prison education on social capital are cumulative and as such the more a prisoner engages with education, the greater the benefits.

In order to further test the idea of the prison sentence depleting social capital levels, two tests correlating time spent in prison with social capital levels were carried out. The prison is a harmful environment, and it has been reiterated throughput this study that the prison sentence has a detrimental impact on the person. This harm often leaves the offender in a worse position leaving prison than before they began their sentence (Sykes, 1958; Liebling and Maruna, 2005; Irwin and Owen, 2005; Warner, 2007; Crewe, 2011). Faced with the barriers to reintegration, the offender is often in a poor position to overcome these hurdles and desist from crime. Draine and Wolff (2009) argued that each prison sentence increasingly depletes the offender's social capital levels. This renders them increasingly susceptible to reoffending. In order to investigate this, an independent samples t-test was carried out to compare levels of social capital between prisoners who were on their first conviction and those who were in prison for a second or subsequent time to investigate whether there was a significant difference between the two groups. The t-test showed that there was a significant difference in the total social capital levels for those who were imprisoned for the first time ($M = 112.09$, $SD = 32.39$) and those who were on second or subsequent imprisonments ($M = 90.00$, $SD = 35.73$; $t(39) = 2.07$, $p = .045$), with higher numbers of previous offences associated with lower levels of social capital and vice versa. Therefore, offenders with a greater number of convictions had lower levels of social capital. This would tend to support Draine and Wolff's (2009) hypothesis that the prison sentence strips away a prisoner's social capital level and appears to show that with each prison sentence the social capital levels of a prisoner are depleted, thus making reintegration and desistance more problematic and reoffending more likely.

Recognising that someone who has spent one very long prison sentence in prison may have served far more time than someone who has had several short sentences, the same test was repeated to examine the relationship between the total accumulated time spent in prison by a prisoner and their level of social capital. Using a Pearson product moment correlation coefficient, it was found that here was a negative correlation between the two variables ($r = .397$, $n = 37$, $p < .015$), with greater amounts of time served in prison associated with lower levels of social capital. This showed that social capital levels were lower for those who have spent the longest amount of time in prison. Again, this appears to reinforce the earlier findings and Draine and Wolffe's theory relating to the depletion of social capital throughout time in prison. These results also demonstrate the harmful impact of the prison sentence on the person and more specifically on social capital levels. This will be discussed again later.

Overall, the survey results showed that prisoners who were participating in prison education had higher levels of social capital than those who did not participate, and this level of social capital was higher among those who participated more frequently or more consistently. Given the strength of the correlation that exists between the two variables, the data suggests that participation in prison education can do either one or both of the following things: (1) support the creation of social capital or (2) maintain or protect against the depletion of social capital levels during the prison sentence. The primary assumption when looking at the strength of the correlation between the variables across the two tests is that social capital is being created through the benefits that come from participating in education. However, this may be an overly simplistic explanation, and there is a need to recognise context in this. The prison is the complete antithesis to any environment that one would expect could foster social capital (Heitfield, 2003). Even if prison education were completely optimal, the extent to which it could operate to build social capital could be questioned, especially since the person is not actually in society – where social capital exists and is perpetuated. The alternative explanation is that prison education guards against the depletion of social capital over time. The latter two aforementioned tests showed that social capital levels were lower for those who have spent the longest amount of time in prison. Perhaps it is a case that their social capital levels have been depleted over time through their subjection to the harmful prison environment. It is likely that a combination of two things account for these results. First, the prison experience has a negative effect on social capital, resulting in greater depletion of capital stocks over time. Second, those who have less social capital are at greater risk of reoffending, and then they return to prison where social capital is depleted further, in a continuous harmful cycle.

Therefore, it is most likely that greater social capital levels among participants result primarily from the insulating effect of prison education against the mental harms of the prison and time spent in the prison school, both of which guard against the depletion of social capital levels. This assumption is in line with the proposal that one of the most significant effects of and rationales for the provision of prison education relates to its role in minimising the harmful impacts of imprisonment (Council of Europe, 1990; Warner, 2007). Again, this cannot be concluded definitively in the absence of data to show the social capital levels of prisoners prior to commencing prison education. It also demonstrates the strong links between participation in prison education and higher levels of social capital.

The interview data explored in the previous two chapters is also valuable in determining why there was such a difference between the social capital levels of participants and non-participants across all categories including civic participation, control and self-efficacy, and interaction with social networks. Prison education participants scored higher across all of these areas by comparison to those who were not participating in prison education. Since these accounts were explored in detail in Chapters 5 and 6, a brief synopsis will be given here. Both participants and ex-prisoners made many comments about the benefits and impact of prison education on their lives. Within the prison, they reported that their time in the school felt like time away from the prison environment, a time when they could enjoy some mental distance from the negative aspects of prison life. By being in the prison school, they could avoid situations and people that they felt were hostile or negative. The school represented a positive place that they could go and feel relaxed. Darren likened it to "an oasis of civility". Prison education therefore allowed both a physical and mental distance between the person and the prison. This is further evidence of the fact that part of the effectiveness of prison education in maintaining or increasing social capital is a result of the insulating effect of prison education. Moreover, both participants and ex-prisoners also spoke of various personal benefits relating to cognitive change such as changed perspectives and outlook, greater self-awareness, self-control, self-belief and empathy confidence. They were more likely to think ahead and plan for the challenges of release. In relation to release, the prisoners hoped to continue to build strong relationships with family, particularly their children, get jobs or start businesses and many were adamant that they would be more in control of their lives and not make the same mistakes. The ex-prisoners gave retrospective accounts of similar benefits, stating that it helped them to stay focused in the early stages of release; had given them the tools to repair relationships, get jobs or places in college; and created distance with their old peer groups. When looking at the indicators of social capital earlier such as control and self-efficacy, interaction with social networks and civic participation, it is clear that prison education can have an impact on these areas in terms of these benefits. Prison education promotes a greater interaction with society through the open-mindedness, employment, relationships and knowledge it creates, thus enhancing social capital levels across all of these core areas. These findings reinforce the survey data by showing the ways in which prison education can contribute to social capital creation and maintenance in the prison.

Prison capital

Social capital is a concept that is based on the strength of social networks and social trust. However, prison is a place that by its nature is based on mistrust and frayed networks. Therefore, it would seem that the generation or maintenance of social capital in prison would be impossible. There are, however, examples to the contrary, with Lafferty et al. (2016) finding that several features of social capital transfer to the prison environment and contribute to a person's overall stock of social capital. For example, Behan (2012) found that many prisoners had exercised their civic duty to vote while in prison, some of whom were voting for the first time. Civic engagement is a key feature of social capital (Putnam, 2000); thus Behan's (2012) study shows a desire among prisoners to participate socially and have a connection with society. Draine and Wolff (2009) stated that the social capital of prisoners tends to be depleted by the instability created by a sentence of imprisonment. Lafferty et al. (2016) found various aspects of prison life that were anti–social capital in nature, such as the experience of not being seen as a person by staff, needing to "mask" vulnerabilities for self-protection and having an end date on friendships and networks. On release, those who were employed will be likely to face unemployment on release; ties with family, friends and society will likely have been frayed or severed; and the mental impact of imprisonment will itself have, in all probability, depleted the prisoners' own stock of inner resources. However, this does not always have to be the scenario. Wolff and Draine (2004) depicted social capital as a store of ties and resources that could be used to assist the return to the community. They stated that the store could be drained or filled during incarceration, depending on the person's experiences while in prison. Wolff and Draine (2004) pointed to treatments such as cognitive behavioural therapy to help maintain or increase a person's social capital in prison by promoting positive change, self-esteem and well-being, among other things. This study explores the extent to which participation in prison education can produce similar effects and fill the stores of social capital which might otherwise be drained by the prison experience, and the findings of this aspect of the study were explored earlier.

The idea that community-based social capital is difficult to maintain in prison raises the question as to what replaces community-based social capital as it depletes. Draine and Wolff (2009) warn that depreciation in community-based social capital may be replaced by a type of prison-based social capital which relies more on anti-social connections and ties in prison such as connections with gangs. Several factors can be identified as being conducive or related to the creation of a prison-based social capital. They are (1) the size of the prison population, (2) means through which inmates can repeatedly interact, (3) inmate diversity, (4) number of correctional officers, (5) programme participation and (6) correspondence with family (Heitfield, 2003). The following sections will look at the evidence supporting the existence of this type of prison-based social capital.

Studies have shown the existence of value systems and norms among prisoners. Prisons are highly organised systems, despite the fact that the norms, values and rules within them are much different to mainstream society (Heitfield, 2003). Lindberg (2005) suggests that a specific culture exists in prison, with specific values, norms and forms of interaction, and when prisoners arrive in prison, they must learn and adapt to this culture. There are specific codes of conduct and rules that should be observed in prison, much like in society (Crewe, 2006). These values and rules specify things such as prisoners not associating with officers or other members of the regime, prisoners holding anti-authority views, and prisoners being loyal to fellow inmates by not "grassing each other up", for example, and displaying emotional and physical fortitude (Crewe, 2006). Prisoners were reportedly vehement about adherence to the prison codes and rules of conduct which developed among prisoners (Sykes and Messinger, 1960). Within this culture and its set of norms, as with any social system, there are core participants, followers and isolates who do not actively participate (Ackers et al., 1977). There is also a unique power dynamic between prison staff and prisoners (Owen, 1988). The delicate interactions and respect between the two tend to contribute to social order in the prison (Owen, 1988). This is much like society where, for the most part, the general public respect the authority of the police, knowing that their role is to maintain order and ensure the protection and well-being of the community. The main difference between the police and the prison staff is that prisoners are completely reliant on the prison staff for all of their needs. Food and shelter are both provided by the prison service, and the lives of the prisoners are entirely regulated by the staff. Therefore, the more common ground and amicable relations between the two, the easier the sentence will be for the offender (Lindberg, 2005). However, such micromanagement of prisoners can lead to an institutionalised mindset that would render reintegration much more difficult.

Another aspect of prison life that mirrors community life and could be therefore seen as supporting a type of social capital is the mix of informal groups within the prison setting. Upon arriving in prison, many prisoners actively try to find a peer group and integrate into its culture so as not to be marginalised and excluded (Lindberg, 2005). These groups exhibit loyalty, organisation, solidarity, attachments and competition (Clemmer, 1958). This mix of groups creates an internal structure that is often characterised by both personal and group conflicts, power struggles and hierarchies (Owen, 1988). Within groups, inmates may have their own way of communicating, a form of profanity and slang, which reinforces the relationships among them (Useem and Reisig, 1999). Lindberg (2005) refers to the prison slang, or "argot", as being a source of power for inmates that gives them the currency to interact in the prison setting. However, Lindberg (2005) notes that the problem with this is that carrying this argot into society after release can be stigmatising and detrimental when one is looking for employment, for instance, in a similar way to institutionalisation. There is an expectation on prisoners from the time they arrive in prison that they will integrate into and form allegiances to a particular group of peers and will take on the norms and values of this group (Crewe, 2006). These anti-social ties result in the prisoner becoming entrenched in prison-based social capital quite quickly and makes it much more difficult for them to break away and take a more individual approach to their sentence and "do their own time" (Crewe, 2006). To overcome this, some prisons segregate those prisoners who are undertaking some form of correctional work or treatment with a view to rehabilitation, ensuring that they are not influenced by the negative values of others, limiting the chances of successful change (Lindberg, 2005).

Within social groups, there is a sense of hierarchy and status among members and the prison setting is no different. This is dependent on their participation in the social system and the perceptions others have of them (Lindberg, 2005).

In everyday society, most people's status is dictated by socioeconomic background and education, for example. In the prison setting, status comes from their crimes and their current and/or past sentences. For instance, those who are serving sentences for drug offences or for killing an abusive male partner attract status, while those serving sentences for child neglect or abuse tend to have low status (Lindberg, 2005). Those who are at the top of the hierarchy dictate informal codes and prison culture. Lindberg (2005) referred to these as "Queens" in her study of a women's prison in Sweden. It could be said therefore that the Queen is the one possessing the most prison-based social capital. She is at the top of the class structure within prison and, like society, it is those who are in the upper classes that possess most social capital and exert the most power.

Prison capital and prison education: examining the findings

Arguably some of the most interesting findings arose from the decision to include a small element in the survey to determine whether there was a recognition among prisoners of a type of prison-based social capital. The prison itself can be seen as a form of closed society, having its own structure, and therefore possibly attracts its own form of social capital, as outlined earlier. Draine and Wolff (2009) propose that the harmful prison experience depletes prisoners' stores of social capital. As social capital is depleted, it is replaced by a more detrimental form of social capital based on anti-social ties, negativity and prison-acquired bonds and norms, which they refer to as prison-based social capital (Draine and Wolff, 2009). This, they acknowledge, is purely speculation, and such a process has not been confirmed through empirical research (Draine and Wolff, 2009). Heitfield (2003) also refers to this idea of a unique form of social capital in prison. This supposition arose from the notion that in an environment such as prison, based on the deprivation of liberty and characterised by anti-socialism and mistrust, there was little hope that social capital in its regular form could exist. However, prison is an environment and "community" in itself and therefore a type of prison capital could be seen to develop.

Based on this, several questions were included in the survey in order to determine whether prisoners recognised a type of prison-based social capital. While the initial purpose of these questions was only to examine whether or not prisoners identified certain characteristics of prison life which could be said to be indicators of a prison-based social capital, such as a hierarchical structure among inmates or a desire to gain status within such a hierarchy, when the analysis of this part of the survey was performed, it showed some interesting correlations. While it was initially expected that prisoners would identify rather strongly with the indictors of prison-based social capital and to a large extent that was what was found, the recognition of these indictors and characteristics was not as universal as expected. Instead what was found were several interesting relationships between other variables such as social capital and participation in education, all of which will be outlined later.

Interaction between prison-based social capital and mainstream social capital

Draine and Wolff (2009) predict that as a person's stores of social capital are depleted by the prison experience, they are replaced by an anti-social form of social capital, based on prison norms. This is referred to here as prison-based social capital. In order to examine whether such a relationship exists, the correlation between levels of social capital among prisoners and their prison-based social capital scores was investigated using Pearson product moment correlation coefficient. There was a strong negative correlation between these two variables ($r = .81$, $n = 41$, $p<.000$), with high levels of social capital associated with significantly lower levels of prison-based social capital. This showed that those prisoners who had higher levels of social capital tended to have a correspondingly low level of prison-based social capital. A second test was carried out, drawing again on Draine and Wolff's (2009) assertion that prison depletes social capital which is in turn replaced by a prison-based social capital. It was questioned whether those who had spent more time incarcerated over their lifetime had higher levels of awareness of prison-based social capital. The relationship between the accumulated total time of previous prison sentences and prison-based social capital among prisoners was examined using Spearman rank order correlation coefficient. There was a significant positive correlation between the two variables ($r = .339$, $n = 37$, $p < .040$), with greater amounts of time served in prison associated with higher levels of awareness of prison-based social capital.

Based on the strength of the relationships discussed earlier, these findings appear to confirm the proposition by Draine and Wolff (2009), showing that where a prisoner has strong social capital, he seems to identify less with the system of prison-based social capital. They are not as aware of the system of unwritten rules, behaviours and structures as those prisoners who have lower levels of social capital and can perhaps be seen to be avoiding the prison mindset. It appears that prisoners will have opposing levels of one or the other. Where they are rich in one form of social capital, they will be low in the other and vice versa. This is reassuring since it appears that those who maintain or grow their levels of social capital are less likely to have become immersed in the prison culture and its associated norms, mindset and behaviours to the same extent as prisoners who have low levels of social capital and correspondingly high levels of prison capital. The findings also demonstrate that those who have spent more time in prison are more aware of prison-based social capital, norms and behaviours. This would seem to make some sense. As a person spends more time in the prison environment, their social capital is being continually depleted due to the various harms of imprisonment. It therefore stands to reason, based on Draine and Wolff's theory, that this "space" in their capital reserves is filled with the prison capital. As they spend more time in prison, they are drawn further into prison life, with social ties in the prison rather than in the community and taking on the mindset of prison as a normalised society.

In terms of reintegration, the greater the length of a sentence or the greater a number of sentences a person serves, the higher the barrier of shedding this growing stock of prison capital will become. The concept of institutionalisation is also relevant here, particularly in light of Lindberg's (2005) assertion that those who are immersed into the prison mindset and the prison community with its rules, structures and "argot" find it more difficult to reintegrate into the community when they are released. Thus, by maintaining social capital levels among prisoners, it will leave less space for the accumulation of a more negative prison capital to become pervasive. In terms of desistance, those who are less institutionalised and less saturated with prison capital will find the process of leaving prison and establishing a new, crime-free life somewhat easier than those who return to the community with high stocks of prison capital. It reinforces the need to find ways of minimising the harm that is being caused to prisoners by the prison experience. Efforts to maintain social capital, such as through prison education, could be significant in achieving this. There is a crucial need to minimise the time that a person spends in the prison, either through decreased use of the prison as a mainstay sanction with a move to more community-based punishment or by using mechanisms such as prison education to reduce the prisoner's exposure to the prison environment while they serve their sentence. In this way, the prisoner is protected from unnecessary exposure to prison capital and is in a better position to maintain or increase their own social capital levels, giving desistance a greater chance of being successful.

Prison education and prison-based social capital

One of the primary purposes of prison education is to minimise the harmful impact of the prison sentence on the person (Council of Europe, 1990; Warner, 2007). The accumulation of prison-based social capital, characterised by immersion in the prison mindset, norms and culture, is one such harmful impact of incarceration. In order to ascertain whether prison education could affect the accumulation of this harmful prison-based social capital, the relationship between participation in prison education and a prisoner's recognition of the characteristics/indictors of prison-based social capital was examined using a Pearson product moment correlation coefficient. This showed a significant negative correlation between the two variables ($r = .700$, $n = 41$, $p < .000$), with participation in prison education associated with lower levels of awareness of a prison-based social capital. Furthermore, in order to determine whether the level at which the prisoner was participating in education was also significant to their awareness of prison-based social capital, based on the breakdown of high, moderate and low levels of participation outlined earlier, a Pearson product movement correlation coefficient was carried out. There was a significant negative correlation between the two variables ($r = .687$, $n = 41$, $p < .000$), with increased levels of participation in prison education associated with lower scores on the prison-based social capital element of the survey.

These combined findings show that (1) those prisoners who participate in prison education generally have lower levels of awareness of prison-based social capital than non-participants and (2) those who are participating in prison education more frequently have a lower level of awareness of prison-based social capital. An important aspect of this finding is that it appears to show that participation in education has a role to play in shielding prisoners from an awareness of prison-based social capital and, it is speculated, from the harmful mindset of the prison. It appears that the more a prisoner engages with education and consequently the less time they have available to spend in the mainstream prison, the less immersed they become in the prison culture and norms. Furthermore, it is proposed that while they are in the mainstream prison, they are "insulated" by the positive and constructive mindset created through education. This prevents them from accumulating the prison currency and mindset when outside of the prison school. Lindberg (2005), in investigating prison culture, found that those who take on the currency or mindset of the prison setting can carry this mindset back into society, and this can significantly hinder their reintegration, acting as another barrier to reintegration. Prison education, it is proposed, reduces this barrier to reintegration by minimising the chances of accumulating the prison capital and the various other prison harms in the first place and thereby influences desistance. Furthermore, Crewe (2006) notes that the use of different schemes and incentives that focus prisoners on a particular goal such as reduced sentences, temporary release or transfer to different prisons with better conditions (such as open prisons) can also cause a disruption in prison bonds and culture. These incentives keep the prisoner focused on their own sentence and less likely to become involved with groups in prison that would jeopardise that. Prisoners who are participating in education would appear to have plenty of their own goals and achievements to keep them occupied. Furthermore, they also have less time to socialise with the general prison population, especially if they attend the school every day. In this way, prison education may be disrupting the opportunity for prison-based solidarity and culture to establish itself among participants, thus reducing the opportunity for the accumulation of prison-based social capital.

Conclusion

The aim of this chapter was to build upon the literature and findings of the previous four chapters relating to prison education and desistance. These chapters showed the potential benefits of prison education such as changed outlooks, creation of opportunities and improved family relationships. They also explored desistance theory and showed the ways in which prison education can contribute to agency, hope, cognitive changes and creating, repairing and enriching pro-social bonds. Each of these are relevant to the current chapter, they are important aspects of building social capital, which is also an important contributor to the desistance process. This chapter began by drawing upon various pieces of literature relating separately to social capital, education and desistance in order to create a theoretical picture of how prison education could contribute to desistance in the form of increased levels of social capital or through maintenance of social capital levels. To a large extent, this relationship had been drawn out in previous chapters, particularly Chapter 6, where the findings showed the way in which education can influence the creation of stronger social ties and relationships, which are key components of social capital. This chapter then went on to explore the findings of the survey that was designed to examine various aspects of the relationship among prison education, social capital and prison-based social capital. In brief, the surveys showed that those who were participating in prison education had higher levels of social capital than those who were not participating in prison education. Those prisoners who were spending more time each week in education also had higher levels of social capital, showing that it is not just participation that is important but the amount of time spent in education. The prisoners who were participating in education also had lower levels of awareness of prison-based social capital than the non-participants and, again, those who were participating in prison education for more time each week had lower levels of prison capital awareness than those spending less time in the school or not participating at all. All of this appears to show that education is important in maintaining social capital levels and shielding participants from the harmful impact of the prison. This goes back to the first of the findings outlined in Chapter 4 that prisoners are using education as means of escape from the harmful prison environment. It appears that their approach is working and they are being insulated from the potential harm that can be caused by imprisonment.

The next chapter will discuss the totality of the findings of this study, drawing together the findings from each aspect of the study to form a cohesive discussion of how the concepts interlink and the mechanisms through which prison education operates to promote desistance and negate the harmful impacts of the prison sentence.

References

Ackers, R., Hayner, N. and Gruninger, W. (1977) Prisonization in Five Countries: Type of Prison and Inmate Characteristics. *Criminology* 4(4), pp. 527–554.

Amin, A. and Thrift, N. (2002) *Cities: Reimagining the Urban*. Cambridge: Polity Press.

Behan, C. (2012) 'Still Entitled to Our Say': Prisoners' Perspectives on Politics. *Howard Journal of Criminal Justice* 51(10), pp. 16–36. doi:10.1111/j.1468-2311.2011.00676.x.

Bourdieu, P. (1977) *Outline of a Theory of Practice*. Cambridge: Cambridge University Press.

Bourdieu, P. (1986) The Forms of Capital. In Richardson, J. (ed) *Handbook of Theory and Research for the Sociology of Education*. Westport, CT: Greenwood Publishing.

Brehm, J. and Rahn, W. (1997) Individual-Level Evidence for the Causes and Consequences of Social Capital. *American Journal of Political Science* 41(3), pp. 999–1023. doi:10.2307/2111684.

Clemmer, D. (1958) *The Prison Community*. New York: Holt, Rinehart and Winston.

Coleman, J.S. (1988) Social Capital in the Creation of Human Capital. *American Journal of Sociology* 94, pp. S95–S120.

Coleman, J.S. (1994) *Foundations of Social Theory*. Cambridge, MA: Belknap Press.

Council of Europe (1990) *Education in Prison: Recommendation No. R (89) 12*. 13th October 1989. Strasbourg: Council of Europe.

Crewe, B. (2006) Codes and Conventions: The Terms and Conditions of Contemporary Inmate Values. In Liebling, A. and Maruna, S. (eds) *The Effects of Imprisonment*. Cullompton: Willan Publishing.

Crewe, B. (2011) Depth, Weight, Tightness: Revisiting the Pains of Imprisonment. *Punishment & Society* 13(5), pp. 509–529. doi:10.1177/1462474511422172.

Draine, J. and Wolff, N. (2009) *Social Capital and Reentry to the Community from Prison*. New Brunswick: Centre for Behavioural Health Services and Criminal Justice Research.

Farrall, S. (2002) *Rethinking What Works with Offenders*. Cullompton, Devon: Willan Press.

Farrall, S. (2004) Social Capital and Offender Reintegration: Making Probation Desistance Focused. In Maruna, S. and Immarigeon, R. (eds) *After Crime and Punishment: Pathways to Offender Reintegration*. Devon: Willan Publishing.

Forrest, R. and Kearns, A. (2001) Social Cohesion, Social Capital and the Neighborhood. *Urban Studies* 38(12), pp. 2125–2143.

Fukuyama, F. (1995) *Trust: The Social Virtues and the Creation of Prosperity*. New York: The Free Press.

Fuller, B. and Clarke, P. (1994) Raising School Effects While Ignoring Culture? Local Conditions and the Influence of Classroom Tools, Rules and Pedagogy. *Review of Educational Research* 64(1), pp. 119–157.

Giordano, P., Cernkovich, S. and Rudolph, J. (2002) Gender, Crime and Desistance: Towards a Theory of Cognitive Transformation. *American Journal of Sociology* 107(4), pp. 990–1064. doi:10.1086/343191.

Glaeser, E.L. (2001) The Formation of Social Capital. *Canadian Journal of Policy Research* 2(1), pp. 34–40.

Glaser, D. (1969) *The Effectiveness of a Prison and Parole System*. Indianapolis: Bobbs-Merril.

Graham, J. and Bowling, B. (1995) *Young People and Crime: Home Office Research Study No. 145*. London: Home Office.

Grootaert, C. and Van Bastelaer, T. (2001) *Understanding and Measuring Social Capital: A Synthesis of Findings and Recommendations from the Social Capital Initiative*. Washington, DC: The World Bank.

Hattery, A. and Smith, E. (2010) *Prisoner Reentry and Social Capital: The Long Road to Reintegration*. Lanham, ML: Lexington Books.

Heitfield, H. (2003) Prison Violence and Social Capital: An Analysis of Adult State Correctional Facilities. *The Public Purpose: An Interdisciplinary Journal, American University Graduate School of Public Affairs* 1(1), pp. 43–68.

Helliwell, J.F. and Putnam, R.D. (2007) Education and Social Capital. *Eastern Economic Journal, Eastern Economic Association* 33(1), pp. 1–19.

Horney, J., Osgood, W.D. and Marshall, I.H. (1995) Criminal Careers in the Short-Term: Intra-Individual Variability in Crime and Its Relation to Local Life Circumstance. *American Sociological Review* 60(5), pp. 655–673.

Huang, J., Maassen van den Brink, H. and Groot, W. (2009) A Meta-Analysis of the Effect of Education on Social Capital. *Economics of Education Review* 28(4), pp. 454–464.

Irwin, J. and Owen, B. (2005) Harm and the Contemporary Prison. In Liebling, A. and Maruna, S. (eds) *The Effects of Imprisonment*. Cullompton: Willan Publishing.

Jang, E. and Canada, K.E. (2014) New Directions for the Study of Incarcerated Older Adults: Using Social Capital Theory. *Journal of Gerontological Social Work* 57(8), pp. 858–871. doi:10.1080/01634372.2014.900841.

Lafferty, L., Chambers, G.M., Guthrie, J. and Butler, T. (2015) Indicators of Social Capital in Prison: A Systematic Review. *Health Justice* 3(7). doi:10.1186/s40352-015-0020-8.

Lafferty, L., Treloar, C., Butler, T., Guthrie, J. and Chambers, G.M (2016) Unlocking Dimensions of Social Capital in the Prison Setting. *Health Justice* 4(9). doi:10.1186/s40352-016-0040-z.

Laub, J.H. and Sampson, R.J. (1993) Turning Points in the Life Course: Why Change Matters to the Study of Crime. *Criminology* 31(3), pp. 301–332.

Laub, J.H. and Sampson, R.J. (1994) Unemployment, Marital Discord, and Deviant Behaviour: The Long-Term Correlates of Childhood Misbehaviour. In Hirschi, T. and Gottfredson, M.R. (eds) *The Generality of Deviance*. Abingdon: Routledge.

Liebling, A. and Maruna, S. (2005) Introduction: The Effects of Imprisonment Revisited. In Liebling, A. and Maruna, S. (eds) *The Effects of Imprisonment*. Cullompton: Willan Publishing. doi:10.1111/j.1468-2311.2007.00467.

Lindberg, O. (2005) Prison Cultures and Social Representations: The Case of Hinseberg, a Women's Prison in Sweden. *International Journal of Prisoner Health* 1(2–4), pp. 143–161.

McMahon, G., Parsons, C., Godfrey, R., Flanagan, K., Renshaw, J., Bielby, K., Adams, M. and Sapsed, E. (2006) *Barriers to Engagement in Education, Training and Employment: Research Report*. London: Youth Justice Board for England and Wales.

McNeill, F. (2006) A Desistance Paradigm for Offender Management. *Criminology and Criminal Justice* 6, pp. 39–62.

McNeill, F. and Whyte, B. (2007) *Reducing Reoffending: Social Work and Community Justice in Scotland*. Cullompton: Willan Publishing.

McNeill, F., Batchelor, S., Burnett, R. and Knox, J. (2005) *21st Century Social Work, Reducing Reoffending: Key Practice Skills*, Scottish Executive, Edinburgh.

Meisenhelder, T. (1977) An Exploratory Study of Exiting from Criminal Careers. *Criminology* 15, pp. 319–334.

Mezirow, J. (2000) Learning to Think Like an Adult: Core Concepts of Transformation Theory. In Mezirow, J. (ed) *Learning as Transformation: Critical Perspectives on a Theory in Progress*. San Francisco: Jossey-Bass.

Nie, N.H., Junn, J. and Stehlik-Barry, K. (1996) *Education and Democratic Citizenship in America*. Chicago: University of Chicago Press.

OECD (2001) *The Well-Being of Nations: The Role of Human and Social Capital*. Paris: Organisation for Economic Co-operation and Development.

O'Mahony, P. (1997) *Mountjoy Prisoners: A Sociological and Criminological Profile*. Dublin: Stationary Office.

Owen, B.A. (1988) *The Reproduction of Social Control: A Study of Prison Workers at San Quentin*. New York: Praeger Publishers.

Putnam, R.D. (1995) Bowling Alone: America's Declining Social Capital. *Journal of Democracy* 61, pp. 65–78.

Putnam, R.D. (1996) Who Killed Civic America. *Prospect*, March, pp. 66–72.

Putnam, R.D. (2000) *Bowling Alone: The Collapse and Revival of American Community*. New York: Simon and Schuster Paperbacks.

Ruston, D. and Akinrodoye, L. (2002) *Social Capital Question Bank: Questions from Social Capital Surveys Included in the Social Capital Survey Matrix*. London: Office for National Statistics.

Rutter, M., Quinton, D. and Hill, J. (1990) Longitudinal Data in the Study of Causal Processes: Some Uses and Some Pitfalls. In Rutter, M. (ed) *Studies of Psychological Risk: The Power of Longitudinal Data*. Cambridge: Cambridge University Press.

Schuller, T., Brassett-Grundy, A., Green, A., Hammond, C. and Preston, J. (2002) *Learning, Continuity and Change in Adult Life*. Wider Benefits of Learning Research Report No. 3. London: Centre for Research on the Wider Benefits of Learning.

Social Exclusion Unit (1997) *Social Exclusion Unit: Purpose, Work Priorities and Working Methods*. London: The Stationary Office.

Swanson, C., Lee, C., Sansone, F.A. and Tatum, K.M. (2012) Prisoners' Perceptions of Father-Child Relationships and Social Support. *American Journal of Criminal Justice* 37, pp. 338–355. doi:10.1007/s12103-011-9132-4.

Sykes, G.M. (1958) *The Society of Captives*. Princeton: Princeton University Press.

Sykes, G.M. and Messinger, S. (1960) The Inmate Social System. In Cloward, R. (ed) *Theoretical Studies in Social Organisation of the Prison*. New York: Social Science Council.

Ubah, C.B.A. and Robinson, R.L. (2003) A Grounded Look at the Debate over Prison-Based Education: Optimistic Theory versus Pessimistic Worldview. *The Prison Journal* 83, pp. 115–129. doi:10.1177/0032885503083002001.

Useem, B. and Reisig, M.D. (1999) Collective Action in Prisons: Protests, Disturbances, and Riots. *Criminology* 37 p. 736.

Warner, K. (2007) Against the Narrowing of Perspectives: How Do We See Learning, Prisons and Prisoners? *Journal of Correctional Education* 58(2), pp. 170–183.

Weiss, A. (1995) Human Capital vs. Signalling Explanations of Wages. *Journal of Economic Perspectives* 9(4), pp. 133–154.

Wolff, N. and Draine, J. (2004) The Dynamics of Social Capital of Prisoners and Community Reentry: Ties That Bind? *Journal of Correctional Healthcare* 10, pp. 457–490. doi:10.1177/107834580301000310.

Chapter 8

Changing perspectives on prison education and desistance

This chapter draws together the preceding chapters. It briefly reiterates the key findings, along with undertaking a discussion of the implications and relevance of these outcomes to the prison education and desistance frameworks. Chapter 1 outlined the overarching research aim underpinning the current study, namely an exploration of the effects of prison education in the context of the desistance framework. Chapter 2 provided an overview of the key research methods used in the study, including the measures taken to access the samples of prisoners and ex-prisoners and overcoming the issues associated with undertaking research in the prison environment. Chapters 3 and 4 related entirely to prison education. Chapter 3 explored the prison education literature, including the various rationales for the provision of prison education and examining the various approaches to and philosophies of prison education. Chapter 4 was the first chapter to present empirical findings and focused primarily on the motivations and barriers to participation in education. Chapters 5 and 6 explored the research findings that related to desistance. Chapter 5 was based on the narrative theories of desistance, giving an overview of the relevant literature and subsequently relating the findings of the current research to that literature in order to examine the links between the two. A similar approach was taken in Chapter 6, with a focus on the structural theories of desistance. Chapter 7 undertook an exploration of social capital, with an overview of the literature relating to social capital, education and desistance in order to build a picture of how prison education might have a role in the creation of social capital. Chapter 7 also looked at the idea of prison capital. The results of the social capital surveys were then presented and the implications discussed. Each chapter has acted as a potentially stand-alone chapter and has therefore included discussion of the findings relating to each particular topic. This chapter will now look at the totality of the findings in order to draw these points together to reach conclusions, recommendations and point to further avenues of future research to move this contribution made by this research forward.

The broad aim of the research that forms the foundation of this book was to explore prisoners' experiences of prison education in Ireland and, based on those experiences, to draw links between the accounts of prisoners and the desistance literature with a view to understanding more about how prison education can support a person's reintegration and desistance from crime. Given the potential of prison education and a growing interest in understanding its various benefits, it remains an under-researched discipline. Due to the lack of academic research, particularly outside of the "what works" paradigm, the research that underpins this book generally reflects an exploratory approach to investigating prisoners' experiences. The research was designed to bridge various gaps that existed in the literature, to move away from the focus on recidivism rates as a measure of the impact of education and towards a more person-centred exploration of the value of education.

Recidivism, it is evident in the literature, is the default measure of the effects of prison education. Recent decades have seen an increasing demand for evidence-based approaches in research, originally emerging in the hard sciences but eventually infiltrating all disciplines including the social sciences. The penal world has not escaped this, and there has been a growing practice of prison education research focusing on "what works" in order to inform programme development, funding and budgetary allocations and practices. Yet this approach is not representative of the philosophies or approaches of most educators. There is a distinct dichotomy in the purposes of prison education, referred to as the prosaic and isoteric views by Hawley (2011). On the one hand, there are the prosaics, usually policy makers and prison service management, who view education as a means of reducing recidivism through increased skills and employment readiness. Conversely, those practitioners who are responsible for the provision of education and many academics view education in the isoteric sense, as having more holistic purposes. They value prison education for its potential as a means of providing education to those who might wish to access it, to update their skills or to gain an education that they did not get when younger. Whatever the motivation, this perspective on education's purpose lies in the belief that education is provided for the sake of education and for the personal development of the person, with no other purpose beyond that. If other benefits accrue, that is simply a bonus. The "what works" approach to measuring prison education overlooks much of this perspective. This leads to an underlying conflict since those who fund prison education research and prison education programmes are most often prosaics, whose conceptualisation of prison education is as a means of addressing reoffending. Therefore, practitioners must work in an environment that often does not value or support their approach and philosophy in the classroom. Researchers must also ask what are seen to be the most economically valuable questions in the eyes of their funders, leading to an over-representation of quantitative studies examining how prison education has reduced offending. These studies tend to show that prison education has a positive effect on reoffending. However, what is not clear from these studies is how prison education achieves this. Although they show that prison education reduces recidivism rates, they cannot tell us how or why this is. Such an approach also ignores the various other benefits that could be gained through education and reduced the value of prison education to the single variable of reoffending. They also ignore the role of human agency in the process – prison education and subsequent employment are the only possible explanations. The philosophy of adult education and that of most educators and practitioners in the area, to provide education as a means of developing the whole person, is lost. There are many qualitative studies capturing various "personal" benefits of prison education, such as increased confidence or self-esteem. However, these studies are generally carried out on programmes of education that are akin to treatment, such as cognitive thinking courses or parenting skills modules. Therefore, they are looking for the improvement in a particular attribute, rather than an overall degree of personal development. Moreover, these studies do not appear to connect these results to any significant framework that would offer a theoretical perspective on how prison education reduces recidivism or promotes desistance. The "what works" movement has given much. It has shown that prison education works to reduce recidivism (Hull et al., 2000; Steurer et al., 2001: Social Exclusion Unit, 2002; Petersilia, 2003; Lochner and Moretti, 2004; Chavez and Dawe, 2007; Anders and Noblitt, 2011; Nally et al., 2012; IPSOS, 2018). It is now time to advance our knowledge and look at the interventions that work, such as prison education, and ask "why and how it works". Only by asking these questions can the value of prison education be understood. In fact, it is only by asking these questions that prison education can be taken from its narrow place in the penal world and be incorporated into the mainstream criminological literature as a potentially important factor in supporting the desistance process.

In light of these issues, the aim of the current study was to contextualise the findings within the broader criminological framework. Given the view of desistance as a process, rather than a singular event, it examines a wide range of factors that support the changes that underlie the move away from crime. On that basis, it appeared to be the most appropriate fit with the philosophies of education and more aligned to the broad nature and benefits of prison education than the narrow focus of the "what works" approach. Recidivism and desistance are different sides of the same coin; the idea of desistance as a process fitted well with the exploratory concept of the research, which aimed to look at the processes through which prison education influenced the lives of prisoners. Therefore, while maintaining the exploratory approach to examining prison education, a significant element of the research was to explore the links between prison education and desistance, focusing in particular on the role that prison education can play in the creation of pro-social bonds and the creation or maintenance of social capital, both of which are interrelated concepts. Exploring prison education through such a lens offers an alternative perspective on how prison education might be related to desistance as well as providing an opportunity to examine the relationship between prison education and reduced recidivism, consequently explaining the intervening process in the reduction of recidivism rates. By understanding this process, it provides the opportunity to further explore the ways in which prison education can be optimised to have the maximum impact on the lives of those who undertake it.

Drawing together the main points

Motivations to participate in prison education

Building on the findings of Costelloe (2003), the current study found that prisoners are participating in prison education for a variety of reasons. For some, it was a means of escaping the boredom of prison and certain aspects of prison life. For others, it was a means of furthering their education, of reaching certain goals on release such as repairing relationships or getting a job, or of following up on an interest or hobby. What is primarily important here is that prisoners, for whatever reasons, are participating in prison education and are therefore open to the benefits it has to offer.

In terms of saliency to desistance, several important points arose in relation to the motivations to participate in prison education. There were two *prima facie* motivations that link directly to the desistance literature, with the remaining motivations linking to desistance in a less direct way. In terms of the direct links, first, several prisoners were participating with a view to repairing family relationships, perhaps having been given an ultimatum by a partner or in order to improve relationships with their children. Other prisoners were participating with a view to creating opportunities or getting a job when released. Both family and employment are strong sources of pro-social bonds (Meisenhelder, 1977; Sampson and Laub, 1993; Shover, 1996), demonstrating that prison education can contribute to achieving these goals and support desistance.

Motivations to participate can be categorised into push and pull factors (Forster, 1990; Costelloe, 2003), with those factors "pushing" prisoners towards education being seen to be less favourable since "pull" factors result in greater levels of educational engagement, longevity and success (Costelloe, 2003). The most likely reason for participation in education was to escape some aspect of prison life. Factors that "push" prisoners to education are generally seen to be less worthy motivations for participating in education. Yet escape motives can also reflect a strong orientation towards personal change, as was evident in the current research. Of those who said they were participating in prison education as a means of escape, this often related to escaping people and situations that had the capacity to be criminogenic. When these escape motives are examined further, they reveal a desire to create distance with members of their peer group, situations where there may be temptation to use drugs, or simply the same stories and posturing that go on in the prison yard or landings. Prison society is characterised by negativity and mistrust and is built upon anti-social norms and bonds. The impact that life in such an environment has on the person is outlined by Warner (2007), who speaks of the negative impact that the prison sentence can have on the person and the role of education in minimising this harm. It is also highlighted by the Council of Europe (1989), which recommends prison policy makers, administrators and practitioners do all possible to minimise the harmful impact of prison on the person. By using the school as a form of escape from detrimental people and situations, participants are showing a desire to distance themselves from this negative mindset and to break ties with anti-social peers, and it may show that they have had enough of the criminal life. Therefore, these escape factors can represent an orientation towards desistance.

This study supports previous findings that motivations can also change from push to pull factors as a person progresses in education (Forster; 1990; Costelloe, 2003). While many of those participating originally used prison education as a means of escape, they subsequently said they participated out of enjoyment. This enjoyment often stemmed from the wider benefits, such as greater confidence, an opened mind, working towards post-release or personal goals or realising they were capable of doing well in education. Therefore, it appears that the reasons for participation can change towards a more goal-orientated motivation, demonstrating the ability of education to act as a "hook:" in terms of education, retaining the prisoners in education on the one hand and changing their outlook, goals and plans on the other. It also reflects a degree of optimism on the part of participants that education can help them achieve their goals. Such cognitive changes are also reflected in the desistance research as being important indicators of pro-social identity change (Maruna, 2001), showing yet another indication of how evolving motivations can support desistance.

Barriers to participation in prison education

The current research explored the barriers to participation in prison education and showed that situational and dispositional factors are the most common. These barriers were manifest in the form of low motivation, a negative previous experience of education, adherence to routines, addiction and embarrassment surrounding low literacy levels. This gave rise to the consideration of wider issues, particularly in relation to low motivation. Many prisoners lacked the motivation to participate in prison education, as they felt it could not help them in the face of stigma and prejudice in society. They recognise the reality that opportunities for ex-offenders are scarce and they will face many obstacles on release. They view these obstacles as insurmountable, believing in the face of adversity that nothing can help them succeed. Such negative beliefs are characteristic of the condemnation script highlighted in the work of Maruna (2001) as being prevalent among the narratives of persisters. It generally represents a view that nothing will help so there is little point in trying. This lack of self-belief and confidence related to their own future prospects but also appeared to relate to their chances of being successful with education; both most likely stem from their previous experiences, particularly with mainstream education. Although a negative experience of mainstream education was not mentioned by any of those interviewed, it was observed in their answers to questions about their previous education. While a past negative experience of mainstream education is a significant barrier to participation in education (Darkenwald and Merriam, 1982), it can also leave people with low self-esteem, feeling "less than", and have a limiting impact on future progression and opportunities (Flynn et al., 2011) which can therefore contribute to criminality. Furthermore, this may be further compounded by negative attitudes and beliefs in their family or community around the importance of education. Thus, the person does not believe that education can hold any benefit for them, since it was only ever a negative experience. The problem with dispositional barriers is that because they are internalised, they are significantly more difficult to overcome through action or policies aimed at improving participation rates. This poses a problem in encouraging prisoners to undertake prison education. Confounding this even further is the problem of overcoming such negative attitudes in an environment that is inherently negative in itself. These are issues of considerable importance and will be returned to later in this chapter.

Literacy also appeared to be an issue, with many participants saying that this is why many prisoners are not participating in education. However, despite the number of non-participants interviewed, none reported this as a reason they were not participating in education. While it might be the case that none of these men actually had literacy issues, given the reported prevalence of these issues (Morgan and Kett, 2003) it is unlikely. This can represent several things. There remains a great deal of shame in having issues with literacy, and it is still a hidden problem that deters people from seeking help. This can also represent the masculinity and bravado that must prevail in the prison setting, where no weakness or vulnerability is shown as a person wants to keep their place in the prison hierarchy, which is likely part of the harms of imprisonment referred to in the literature (Sykes, 1958; Warner, 2007; Crewe, 2011). It can also reflect a lack of awareness or insight on the part of non-participants as to the reasons they do not participate. It may be that they are blaming external sources such as timetables, waiting lists or not having interesting subjects. The real reason may be more personal and the prisoner may not even realise that. Such levels of insight, awareness and reflection are very relevant to the agentic benefits of education and to cognitive changes associated with desistance. The ability to be introspective and take responsibility is associated with lower levels of criminal thinking (Walters, 1995), which is important to desistance. Such issues may therefore be prevalent across and hindering many aspects of the person's life, not simply the decision to participate in prison education but also their ability to desist from crime or to even want an alternative life to the life of crime.

Prison education and desistance

As outlined earlier, an objective of the study was to explore the links between prison education and the desistance process in order to offer a unique empirical view of the process through which prison education reduces reoffending, as evidenced in the literature. While there are many theories of desistance, it was evident from the overlaps in the respective bodies of literature that the benefits of prison education are connected to the structural aspects of desistance such as social bonds theory and the concept of social capital. The initial expectation was that education would support the development of structural aspects of the person's life such as creating skills for employment and, perhaps on that basis, have a role in creating social capital. However, despite the focus being on the role of prison education in the formation of pro-social bonds and social capital, one of the strongest themes to emerge from the findings was the strength of the reported level of cognitive change among the participants, which in turn demonstrated the process and interactions that underlie the influence of prison education on social bonds, social capital and desistance.

Cognitive change, agency and prison education

The accounts of the participants were characterised by positivity, and participants referred to the various ways in which prison education had benefited them on a cognitive and personal level, including increased confidence, awareness and control. Agency is seen to play a significant role in the process of desistance (Maruna, 2001; Healy, 2010; King, 2013). In very simplistic terms, it relates to a person's ability to be their own agent by having the inner resources to be effective in their life. It involves a wide variety of attributes and characteristics such as self-awareness, self-control, self-efficacy, self-belief, a sense of empowerment and an open mind. All of these attributes were outlined in the prison education literature in Chapter 3 as being reported benefits of undertaking mainstream adult education. The participants in the current study reported these same attributes as being among the benefits of participating in prison education. An increased sense of self-awareness was one of the most often mentioned effects. The men reported being more aware of the mistakes they had made and the hurt they had caused and had greater clarity on the things that matter in their life. As a result, many wished to make amends for the hurt they had caused others. They also reported increased belief in their own abilities. This self-belief referred to their belief in their own abilities to set goals and achieve them, stating that for the first time they believed they could achieve the things they put their mind to.

It appeared that many of these men had come from backgrounds where they were often unsuccessful in school and perhaps were not very successful in holding onto or progressing within employment. Furthermore, typically being from the lowest social classes, there may have been a prevailing message of being seen as "less than" by society. The feeling of being successful in education appeared to give the men renewed hope and confidence in their ability to be successful in other goals that, much like education, they may have previously seen as being outside of their reach. Therefore, those who were participating in education were far more likely than those who were not participating in education to state they would not reoffend, believing they could overcome the challenges that face them on release. This also showed an element of hope that was outlined in Chapter 5 as being important to people's chances of desistance (Burnett, 1994; Farrall and Calverley, 2006), showing further ways in which prison education can contribute to desistance.

Mezirow (2000) refers to the power of education to transform the way that a person sees the world. In many ways, the prison is such a negative space that it is more likely that perspectives are narrowed than opened. However, participants referred to the role that education had in opening their minds to new ways of looking at situations, in reassessing priorities and in considering other ways of life after release. Warner (2007) refers to the capacity of prison education in minimising the harms of imprisonment, an aim that is also enshrined in the Council of Europe Report (1990); it appears that these aims are being achieved. Such cognitive changes are highly relevant to desistance. Moreover, those participating in education were strong in realising their own contribution to their current situation, tending to accept responsibility for their actions and also now taking responsibility and planning for life after release. This was not the case with the non-participants, who tended to blame others and had not planned beyond the end of their sentence, except to assume they would return to offending. This showed little evidence of taking responsibility for either their past or their future. These points tend to show the power of prison education to contribute to a variety of pro-desistance personal changes. In terms of desistance, many theories refer to the power of cognitive changes in the desistance process (Graham and Bowling, 1995; Maruna, 2001; Giordano et al., 2002). There was strong evidence of various cognitive changes in the accounts of participants, in addition to those outlined earlier, which participants attribute to their participation in prison education. All of these points demonstrate the significant ways in which prison education can foster cognitive change in the person, which can in turn support the desistance process. These points will be returned to later in this chapter in order to draw together the proposed role of prison education in supporting desistance.

Social bonds and prison education

While cognitive changes emerged as a significant theme, the objectives of the study related to the structural theories of desistance and in particular social bonds theory. It is argued that social bonds have a significant impact on the desistance process (Shover and Thompson, 1992), with social bonds and ties to conformity inhibiting an offender from committing crime (Meisenhelder, 1977). The greatest sources of social bonds are seen to be relationships, most often viewed in terms of the importance of the marital bond and employment. Several of the participants were undertaking education with a view to finding employment after release. They saw education as contributing to their chances of employment directly, by providing the requisite skills and education, and indirectly, by highlighting that their time spent in prison was at least used constructively. All of those interviewed were aware of the degree of stigma and prejudice they would face upon release, particularly in relation to employment. The difference between the participants and non-participants was their attitude towards this obstacle to employment. The participants were taking action to try mitigate the harsh judgements they may face, while those not participating remained in their hopeless state, stating that nothing could help them. This was representative of the difference between those who were and were not participating in prison education. Those who were participating were looking ahead, planning and preempting hurdles and visualising redemption, while the non-participants remained in their condemned state, in line with Maruna's (2001) characterisation of persisters and desisters.

Pro-social relationships were also a feature of the findings relating to the structural theories of desistance. However, while the focus of the literature in this area is on the importance of marital bond, to the desistance process, this did not arise as a significant feature of the current research. Instead children and parenthood were a strong theme. Many participants were participating in education in order to enrich and repair relationships with their children when they were released from prison. Participation in education had given them the self-awareness to realise the hurt they had caused, and they wished to make amends for being absent from the lives of their children. Education was also part of facilitating the work on these relationships. Participants mentioned how they were now able to engage with their children about what they were learning in school and understood what their children were going through. They also looked forward to now being able to support their children and help with their homework when they were released. The ex-prisoners also gave accounts of how education had built the resilience required to help them build a relationship with their children over time, realising it was an ongoing process. Being a good father appeared to be a strong motivation for desistance among many of the participants and ex-prisoners. In general, there was a notable lack of evidence of statements relating to pro-social relationships in the accounts of non-participants, except for Kevin, who was planning on outsourcing responsibility for his desistance to his girlfriend, noting how he was going to settle down with his girlfriend and "try get a baby with her" believing that you "want a missus that if I say I'm going off to do this and that she'll start fighting with me". The plans of the participants therefore appeared far more robust.

Civic and societal participation has a significant element in building social bonds and social capital. Participants referred to how education had made them feel they could engage actively with society now, including voting, since they now felt sufficiently confident in their own increased levels of knowledge and self-worth to do so.

On a less positive note, the anti-social nature of peer relations was evident throughout the accounts of those interviewed. Non-participants spoke about how their offending often resulted from a desire to impress friends or simply going along with the plans of the group. This showed that an anti-social or delinquent peer group is highly influential in criminality, and it also demonstrates readiness on the part of non-participants to place the blame on external sources, rather than acknowledge their own role in the decision-making process. This latter point relates to higher levels of criminal thinking and is indicative of lower chances of desistance (Walters, 1995). In relation to the influence of prison education on peer relations, there were two aspects to education's impact. First, participants said they had reassessed their priorities and were aware of how putting friends first had resulted in bad outcomes. The resolved to put their children and family before friends in the future. The ex-prisoners gave accounts of how prison education had simply resulted in a "drifting" away from old friends. Having participated in education, they no longer had similar interests or priorities to their old friends and as a result they had simply spent far less time with them until the relationships effectively dissolved. This demonstrates the role that prison education can play in building pro-social relationships and dismantling those relationships that may be problematic in going straight.

Prison education, cognitive change and social bond formation

It is clear from the foregoing sections and chapters that prison education can play a role in building pro-social bonds. This is a very positive outcome, especially for those who see prison education solely as a mechanism of rehabilitation. However, prison education does not in itself create employment opportunities or fix broken relationships. The contribution of prison education is indirect and structural changes such as pro-social relationships and employment are most often facilitated by the cognitive changes that result from participation in prison education. Therefore, it is proposed that the value of education does not lie in its ability to directly influence social bond formation. Instead, one of its strongest contributions is in the cognitive changes that it fosters that support the formation of these social bonds. These cognitive changes form the foundation for most of the structural elements explored in Chapter 6 and outlined earlier. The accounts of participants were rife with examples of this. When speaking about the benefits of education, the most often mentioned benefits were some form of cognitive change such as greater confidence, awareness, self-belief or new perspectives. The ex-prisoners also gave similar accounts. Where structural factors were mentioned, such as children or options for study or employment after release, the emphasis was always on the cognitive changes that formed the foundation upon which to build the relationship or achieve the goal. Participants and ex-prisoners often spoke about relationships, for example. Each time, they pointed out how prison education had made them more aware of how their actions had impacted their families. They hoped to repair the relationships and were using education as part of this effort. They felt capable of being more empathetic, more patient and more resilient to knock-backs, which would undoubtedly be important in rebuilding relationships with children and family. Ex-prisoners also spoke about the indirect role that education played in dismantling anti-social peer relationships. As a result of cognitive changes such as a new outlooks, interests and perspectives, those who had been released from prison simply did not have enough in common with old friends to sustain the relationships. Again this shows the way in which the cognitive changes, facilitated through prison education, underlie the formation of the various pro-desistance structures and pro-social bonds. This shows the importance of adhering to a broad, holistic adult education approach in prison education. The cognitive changes outlined earlier result from a wide conceptualisation of education. While more narrow offerings of training or treatment programmes might yield some results in terms of employability or improved behaviours, relying on such an approach would neglect the person, their personal development and the various advantages they could accrue through participating in a broad curriculum as envisaged by the Council of Europe (1990). It is these broad cognitive and personal developments that support their move towards change. Without this strong foundation, any results from more narrow programmes might essentially be built on a house of cards.

Prison education, social capital and prison-based social capital

The preceding conclusions are reinforced by the findings in relation to social capital. This study found that those who were participating in prison education had significantly higher levels of social capital than those who were not participating in prison education. Those who spent more time participating in prison education tended to have higher levels of social capital. The survey also showed that those who had spent more time in prison or served more sentences had lower levels of social capital than those who had served less time.

Furthermore, Draine and Wolff (2009) suggest that the harmful prison experience depletes stores of social capital and replaces it with an alternative form of prison-based social capital, which was considered to be anti-social in nature. This relationship was confirmed in the current study, with those who had high levels of community-based social capital having low levels of awareness of prison-based social capital and vice versa. It also seemed from the survey data that those who were participating in prison education had a much lower awareness of prison-based social capital than those who were not participating. Similar to the findings in relation to social capital, those who had spent more time in prison had higher levels of awareness of prison-based norms than those who had served less time.

These results appear to show several things. First, prison is a harmful environment that results in the cumulative depletion of social capital levels over time. Second, prison education has a role in either increasing social capital levels or protecting against its depletion. Prison capital is cumulative and is greater for those who have spent more time in prison. Finally, prison education has a role in avoiding the negative aspects of the prison sentence that result in a greater awareness or immersion into the prison norms and mindset. Since this was not an intervention-based study, there is a limited ability to conclusively state the exact nature of the relationship between prison education and social capital. However, based on the totality of the social capital survey results, the information relating to the recognition of prison capital norms and the data obtained from the interviews, it appears that prison education is maintaining and contributing to social capital in several ways. The prison is a deeply negative and harmful setting (Warner, 2007; Costelloe and Warner, 2014). An aim of prison education is to minimise the harmful aspects of the prison sentence. It appears that prison education can achieve this by removing the person from the prison setting for several hours each day or each week. This time away from the physical prison creates a mental barrier between the person and the prison environment that shields them from the harmful aspects of the prison. Furthermore, those who were participating in prison education reported a range of cognitive changes such as a more positive outlook, a changed perspective, greater levels of confidence, self-awareness and hope. Such cognitive strengths are in keeping with the aims of education to minimise the harms of imprisonment, but in doing so are also likely to prevent against the depletion of social capital. Conversely, these factors are also likely to prevent against the accumulation of prison capital. Pro-social relationships are also strong contributors to social capital levels. The participants reported doing a lot of work in order to repair relationships with their children. Even while still in prison, they said that education was helping them to engage better with their children, and this will contribute to social capital levels. Participants also said they were more likely to engage with politics by voting after release since they now had greater confidence in their knowledge about society. Moreover, they also appeared to have higher levels of social trust than non-participants. It might be speculated that this resulted from the impact of education on self-awareness and self-responsibility. Non-participants did not tend to trust the court system or the Gardaí, with some *ad hoc* comments during the surveys about attempts to "stitch" them up. However, participants seemed far more accepting of the responsibility for their own situation and did not seem to have such levels of hostility towards social institutions. The willingness to plan for release, to attempt to reestablish relationships and to strive to achieve goals such as employment or study after release is an indication of the desire and capacity to mobilise greater levels of social capital after the prison sentence. All of these foregoing points show the various ways in which participation in education can contribute to social capital levels and protect against the harms of imprisonment.

Recommendations

Lowering the barriers to prison education

While there has been little previous research on the barriers to participating in prison education, there is little question that the findings outlined in Chapter 4 will not come as much surprise to practitioners. Most are well aware of the motivations of their learners and the reasons that many decide not to access education. However, these findings may prove valuable in some way in informing future attempts to reform curricula, make adjustments to the school environment or optimise recruitment of participants. It is important to look at ways to lower the barriers to participation in order to make prison education as accessible as possible. In making these recommendations, the logical starting point must be the barriers to participation. This research showed that a bad previous experience of mainstream education was a barrier to participation. It is important that potential learners realise the differing approach to education in the prison school, with a view to showing them that adult education can provide them with a more positive encounter with education. This might be achieved by word of mouth, by asking participants to share their experience with others where they are comfortable doing so or perhaps by holding an open class outside of the school, in the mainstream prison, on topics of interest to prisoners, which might ignite their interest. Furthermore, ensuring access across the full year would optimise the chances of attracting students who arrive during holiday times and who might otherwise fall into an alternative routine. In a similar way, ensuring sufficient capacity in subjects that are popular and that may act as "hooks" for further education is important. Literacy is a well-known, yet hidden problem among the prison population. Extending the use of peer mentoring programmes to target literacy issues would prove beneficial for both the person who is using the service and the mentor who gains tremendous pride and confidence from their role. Finally, increasing the amount of time available to access the school from only recreational time to regular school hours might be an important factor in encouraging prisoners to participate. It would also be beneficial to those who are studying for exams or qualifications, as prisoners mentioned they often did not feel prepared due to the limited time they had in the school. Having so much out-of-cell time might also act as an incentive for some to try education. Furthermore, given the findings relating to social capital, any extra time spent away from the prison environment is likely to be beneficial to the person in minimising the harms of imprisonment.

Maintain a broad adult education approach

The broad adult education approach to prison education is recommended widely based on its ability to enhance the development of the whole person. With an increasing punitiveness infiltrating penal thinking and policy in many states, there has been a consequent narrowing of perspectives on how prison education should be conceptualised and valued (Warner, 2007). This narrowing fuels the drive to make prison education more focused on reducing reoffending and results in treatment-based approaches manifested as education. These programmes are often shown to have empirical benefits, and there is no denying that any form of education is preferable to none. However, the benefits, much like the programme, will be narrow in scope. The current research was carried out with participants of education based on the broad, adult education approach. The results showed broad and significant benefits for the person. The recommended aim of prison education is to provide education to enhance the whole person, and it appears that prison education in Ireland is achieving this based on the accounts of the participants, particularly when compared to the accounts of the non-participants. While a focus of this research is to create links with the desistance literature, it is encouraging to see that the implications of participation in education are so valuable to the person. The broad and rich benefits truly appear to be important to the participants in enriching their lives. This is the true value of education. Regardless of the desistance-related outcomes for these men, their lives will have been enhanced in many ways for having participated in education. It is firmly believed that this could not be achieved through education that is narrow in scope, and therefore maintaining this broad approach to education is to be recommended.

The "what works" movement and desire for increasingly evidence-based decision making has played a role in narrowing the perspectives in relation to prison education. This narrowing is a result of a general infiltration of a more punitive ethos throughout the penal system. However, where there is a desire for evidence-based decision making, there must also be research informing the policies and decisions. The current questions being asked by policy makers and researchers predominantly relate to what will work to reduce reoffending. While funding and other considerations often tie the hands of researchers, there is a need to fight back against this research agenda. By maintaining a broad focus in the research, the results and decisions relating to prison education will subsequently be made on the basis of broader and more comprehensive outcomes that are based on a greater view of the overall picture, rather than a small snapshot of it. The reality is that in many states the provision of prison education is becoming increasingly based on the evidence presented; if the broad approach is to be maintained in the prison classrooms, it must pervade at every aspect of the system that guides its provision.

Investigate pre- and early-stage desistance

The critique was made early in this book that the prison education research to date has been overly narrow and does not reflect the essence of education's value. Yet, there is also a similar critique to be made in relation to the often narrow approach taken by the desistance research. Desistance relates to a process of moving away from criminality and represents the long-term abstinence from crime (Maruna, 2001) or "the moment when a criminal career ends" (Farrall and Bowling, 1999: 258). While it is understandable that the focus of the desistance research is on the later stages of the process, where one has shown their intention to live a crime-free life, rather than focusing on those who are only just released and whose journey may go either way, it tends to overlook the early stages of desistance to a large extent. This is not to say that there is no research; it is simply far more scarce than the research relating to secondary desistance. If it were possible to draw an analogy between a person working towards desistance and an athlete preparing for a race, investigating only secondary desistance seems akin to focusing on what will optimise speed in the last few miles of a marathon. If that athlete was not successful, he would look at how he trains, how he might optimise preparation for the race and what approaches he could take in the early miles, the middle and the end. Desistance, much like a marathon, is a process, albeit with higher stakes. The rationale used in the desistance literature to justify the focus on secondary desistance is that we can learn more from those who have been successful than from those who have reverted from criminality. This is flawed. There is much to learn from those who are at all stages of the journey, those who have succeeded and those who have failed, and the role of various factors and interventions at each stage and outcome. This research shows how prison education can support the desistance process at each stage. The accounts of the participants show how education can start as a mechanism to overcome boredom but support subsequent results in pro-desistance cognitive changes. The ex-prisoners were resolute in the way in which prison education gave support to their journeys in the early stages after release. The findings of the current research also showed the way in which prison education can have a role to play in overcoming the barriers to reintegration in the early post-release phase, such as promoting better planning and reducing feelings of institutionalisation. During the prison sentence, education could in many ways be classified as a form of pre-desistance. It creates the foundations upon which formal stages of desistance can be laid after release. Such factors and interventions can have a significant impact on desistance and as such should be researched as important aspects of the desistance framework.

The "whole-prison" approach to education

Many sources refer to the need for the whole-person approach to prison education (Council of Europe, 1990; Munoz, 2009; Warner, 2018). However, perhaps there is also necessary to take a "whole-prison" approach to education. There is a need to move away from the idea of prison education as being something that only takes place in the prison school. So long as education is situated only in the prison school there will be a tendency among many stakeholders to conceptualise this education in the narrow, utilitarian sense. Education, in its broadest sense, includes social, cultural, physical, moral and spiritual education.

Those in prison are often lacking in skills across all of these areas, which has most likely contributed to their criminality. The attitude that education is only provided to those who choose it and consists of traditional-style schooling is a narrow view that is the antithesis of what is necessary to ensure prisons are not the harmful, negative environments that those pushing increasingly punitive agendas would hope. If education is taken in its broad sense so as to include holistic social and personal education that is aimed at enhancing the whole person, there is perhaps a role in ensuring that all of those who work with prisoners throughout the prison take on the role of teacher as opposed to officers. There is a reality that many of those who are in prison do not have the skills to care adequately for themselves, to take personal control and responsibility for their life or to engage in community or social life at even very basic levels. While education helps address these issues, there is an extremely large cohort who does not participate and who has similar needs. These men need to be met where they are, both physically and mentally. If they will not physically attend school, there is a need to provide education in all interactions throughout each day of the prison sentence. This education also needs to be aimed at developing the whole person to as great an extent as possible. This might include pro-social modelling of social skills and expectations of self-responsibility, respect, empathy and dignity. There is no reason that the development of these attributes must be the preserve of the work undertaken in the school. It may be aspirational, yet the application of the principles and ethos of adult education that prevail within the school, that makes it an "oasis" in the words of Darren, to life on the prison landings could turn routine daily contacts with officers into consistent opportunities for learning for those who consider their situation so hopeless that finding their way to the prison school is unlikely to happen. The holistic, whole-person, whole-prison approach is key.

Further research

As outlined throughout the thesis, there is considerable lack of empirical research in Ireland in relation to prison education. For that reason, there are countless avenues of further research that could be explored. However, bearing in mind the findings and conclusions of the current research, the recommendations for further research will be limited to those which related to the issues raised by this study.

Intervention-based social capital survey

The measurement of social capital levels among participants and non-participants in prison education was a unique feature of the research. While the current study measured social capital, it was not an intervention-based approach, making it impossible to definitively conclude that it was prison education that was influencing the higher levels of social capital in participants. In order to address this gap and this uncertainty, further research that measures social capital before prisoners begin education and after a certain period in education would give a more definitive picture of how prison education influences social capital levels.

Study to explore the concept of prison-based social capital

In a similar way, the issue of prison-based social capital was raised. This concept, much like social capital, could potentially have a strong contribution to make to the desistance and reintegration literature. However, far more research needs to be carried out into the concept in general and the influence that prison education can have on its accumulation. Again, this would involve measuring prison-based social capital and social capital as the prisoner arrives in prison and prior to any interventions such as education. Such research would be a significant undertaking but could potentially illuminate an area of literature which might have a considerable bearing on a prisoner's likelihood of desistance.

Longitudinal study of impact of prison-based social capital on desistance

Lindberg (2005) proposed that prisoners who take on the prison mindset and "argot", which is similar to the concept of prison-based social capital used in the current study, find it much more difficult to reintegrate into society. A recommended avenue of further research is to continue to measure social capital and prison-based social capital levels after release and at specific intervals post-release to explore the influence that release has on both types of social capital and also the influence that both of these forms of social capital have on release.

Post-release, longitudinal social bonds study

During the discussion of the findings it was mentioned, in relation to social bonds, that many of the statements made by prisoners were statements of intent or aspiration. Since a follow-up after release was outside of the scope of the current study, it is impossible to know how prison education influenced the creation of social bonds or how it impacted the desistance process as a whole. A longitudinal study would be helpful in addressing this.

Exploration of prison education as a form of pre-desistance

The reality is the most prisoners will eventually be released from prison. The early phase after release will often determine whether or not a person will return to criminality or desist. Therefore, this is a crucial phase. The ex-prisoners spoke about the ways in which education supported them during this time as they attempted to put in place the various structures that would allow them to resume, or in some cases assume for the first time, their roles as people and citizens in society. Yet this phase is largely overlooked in the desistance and prison education literature. It is recommended that further research be carried out to examine the ways in which prison education can impact this crucial phase of the desistance process.

These represent the main recommendations for further research. There are countless others, and further research is important to address the overall lack of literature in the area of prison education in particular. However, studies such as this add to that literature and through taking an exploratory approach to prison education, this research has bridged some of the gaps that exist, but it has highlighted many more. Given the significant influence that prison education has been shown to offer in the lives of prisoners, further research should be prioritised towards understanding how to maximise the benefits and influence of prison education in the lives of prisoners.

References

Anders, A.D. and Noblitt, G.W. (2011) Understanding Effective Higher Education Programmes in Prisons: Considerations from the Incarcerated Individuals Program in North Carolina. *Journal of Correctional Education* 62(2), pp. 7–23.

Burnett, R. (1994) Recidivism and Imprisonment. *Home Office Research Bulletin* 36, pp. 19–22. London: Home Office.

Chavez, R. and Dawe, S. (2007) International Research and Trends in Education and Training Provision in Correctional Settings. In Dawe, S. (ed) *Vocational Education and Training for Adult Prisoners and Offenders in Australia.* Adelaide: National Centre for Vocational Education Research.

Costelloe, A. (2003) *Third Level Education in Irish Prisons: Who Participates and Why?* Unpublished Doctoral thesis, Milton Keynes: Open University.

Costelloe, A. and Warner, K. (2014) Prison Education across Europe: Policy, Practice, Politics. *London Review of Education* 12(2), pp. 175–183. doi:10.18546/LRE.12.2.03.

Council of Europe (1990) *Education in Prison: Recommendation No. R (89) 12.* 13th October 1989. Strasbourg: Council of Europe.

Crewe, B. (2011) Depth, Weight, Tightness: Revisiting the Pains of Imprisonment. *Punishment & Society* 13(5), pp. 509–529. doi:10.1177/1462474511422172.

Darkenwald, G.G. and Merriam, S.B. (1982) *Adult Education: Foundations of Practice.* New York: Harper & Row.

Draine, J. and Wolff, N. (2009) *Social Capital and Reentry to the Community from Prison.* New Brunswick: Centre for Behavioural Health Services and Criminal Justice Research.

Farrall, S. and Bowling, B. (1999) Structuration, Human Development and Desistance from Crime. *British Journal of Criminology* 39, pp. 253–268.

Farrall, S. and Calverley, A. (2006) *Understanding Desistance from Crime: Theoretical Directions in Resettlement and Rehabilitation.* Maidenhead: Open University Press.

Flynn, S., Brown, J., Johnson, A. and Rodger, S. (2011) Barriers to Education for the Marginalized Adult Learner. *Alberta Journal of Educational Research* 57(1), pp. 43–58.

Forster, W. (1990) The Higher Education of Prisoners. In Duguid, S. (ed) *Yearbook of Correctional Education 1990.* Burnaby: Institute for the Humanities, Simon Fraser University.

Giordano, P., Cernkovich, S. and Rudolph, J. (2002) Gender, Crime and Desistance: Towards a Theory of Cognitive Transformation. *American Journal of Sociology* 107(4), pp. 990–1064.

Graham, J. and Bowling, B. (1995) *Young People and Crime: Home Office Research Study No. 145*. Home Office: London.

Hawley, J. (2011) *Prison Education and Training in Europe: A Review and Commentary of Existing Literature, Analysis and Evaluation*. Birmingham: GHK.

Healy, D. (2010) Betwixt and between: The Role of Psychosocial Factors in the Early Stages of Desistance. *Journal of Research in Crime and Delinquency* 47(4), pp. 419–438. doi:10.1177/0022427810375574.

Hull, K.A., Forrester, S., Brown, J., Jobe, D. and McCullen, C. (2000) Analysis of Recidivism Rates for Participants of the Academic/Vocational/Transition Education Programmes Offered by the Virginia Department of Correctional Education. *Journal of Correctional Education* 52(2), pp. 256–262.

IPSOS (2018) *Evaluation of Prisoner Learning: Initial Impacts and Delivery*. London: Ipsos MORI Social Research Institute.

King, S. (2013) Assisted Desistance and Experiences of Probation Supervision. *Probation Journal* 60(2), pp. 136–151. doi:10.1177/0264550513478320.

Lindberg, O. (2005) Prison Cultures and Social Representations: The Case of Hinseberg, A Women's Prison in Sweden. *International Journal of Prisoner Health*, June–December 2005, 1(2–4), pp. 143–161.

Lochner, L. and Moretti, E. (2004) The Effect of Education on Crime: Evidence from Prison Inmates, Arrests, and Self Reports. *The American Economic Review* 94, pp. 155–189.

Maruna, S. (2001) *Making Good: How Ex-Convicts Reform and Rebuild Their Lives*. Washington: American Psychological Association. doi:10.1037/10430-000.

Meisenhelder, T. (1977) An Exploratory Study of Exiting from Criminal Careers. *Criminology* 15, pp. 319–334.

Mezirow, J. (2000) Learning to Think Like an Adult: Core Concepts of Transformation Theory. In Mezirow, J. (ed) *Learning as Transformation: Critical Perspectives on a Theory in Progress*. San Francisco: Jossey-Bass.

Morgan, M. and Kett, M. (2003) *The Prison Adult Literacy Survey: Results and Implications*. Dublin: Irish Prison Service.

Munoz, V. (2009) *The Right to Education of Persons in Detention*, A/HRC/11/8, 2nd April 2009, New York: Human Rights Council.

Nally, J., Lockwood, S., Knutson, K. and Ho, T. (2012) An Evaluation of the Effect of Correctional Education Programmes on Post-Release Recidivism and Employment: An Empirical Study in Indiana. *The Journal of Correctional Education* 63(1), pp. 69–88.

Petersilia, J. (2003) *When Prisoners Come Home: Parole and Prisoner Reentry*. New York: Oxford University Press.

Sampson, R.J. and Laub, J. (1993) *Crime in the Making: Pathways and Turning Points through Life*. Cambridge, MA: Harvard University Press.

Shover, N. (1996) *Great Pretenders: Pursuits and Careers of Persistent Thieves*. Boulder: Westview Press.

Shover, N. and Thompson, C.Y. (1992) Age, Differential Expectations, and Crime Desistance. *Criminology* 30, pp. 89–104. doi:10.1111/j.1745-9125.1992.tb01094.

Social Exclusion Unit (2002) *Reducing Re-Offending by Ex-Prisoners*. London: HMG Cabinet Office.

Steurer, S.J., Smith, L. and Tracy, A. (2001) *Three State Recidivism Study*. Washington: United States Department of Education.

Sykes, G.M. (1958) *The Society of Captives*. Princeton: Princeton University Press.

Walters, G.D. (1995) The Psychological Inventory of Criminal Thinking Styles: Part I: Reliability and Preliminary Validity. *Criminal Justice and Behavior* 22(3), pp. 307–325. doi: 10.1177/0093854895022003008.

Warner, K. (2007) Against the Narrowing of Perspectives: How Do We See Learning, Prisons and Prisoners? *Journal of Correctional Education* 58(2), pp. 170–183.

Warner, K. (2018) Every Possible Learning Opportunity: The Capacity of Education in Prison to Challenge Dehumanisation and Liberate 'the Whole Person'. *Advancing Corrections, Journal of the International Corrections and Prisons Association* 6, pp. 32–45.

Appendix I
Interview guide

Choose prompts as necessary to pick up on points or explore other avenues.

Participants

Reasons for becoming involved in prison education at first.
Reasons for continuing to do it.
Is it worthwhile? Prompt reason.
Further prompt if necessary: Does it help in any other ways?

Non-participants

Why do you not participate? Did you ever participate and, if so, why did you leave?
If early school leaver, what were the reasons?

Ex-prisoners

Why did you become involved in prison education at first?
Was it worthwhile and reasons for answer?
Do you think it has impacted your family life? (Wait for family prompt.)
Do you think you will return to prison?
Tell me about what happened after you were released. Challenges/experiences
How do you think education is impacting your life since release?

Everyone

Did you enjoy school? What was your experience of it? Prompt a bit here if necessary
How do they experience the prison school, and how does it compare? (Participants)
Reasons for ending up in prison?
Feelings about your crime now?
Do you think education is rehabilitative? Is anything rehabilitative?

Plan for release?
What level of control do you think you will have over what will happen to you after release?
How do you think education will impact after release
Do you think you will return to prison?
Would the answer be different if you did not participate in education?

Index

Printed in Dunstable, United Kingdom

65300448R00145